Islamophobia and Lebanon

Islamophobia and Lebanon

*Visibly Muslim Women and
Global Coloniality*

Ali Kassem

I.B. TAURIS
LONDON • NEW YORK • OXFORD • NEW DELHI • SYDNEY

I.B. TAURIS
Bloomsbury Publishing Plc
50 Bedford Square, London, WC1B 3DP, UK
1385 Broadway, New York, NY 10018, USA
29 Earlsfort Terrace, Dublin 2, Ireland

BLOOMSBURY, I.B. TAURIS and the I.B. Tauris logo are trademarks of
Bloomsbury Publishing Plc

First published in Great Britain 2023
Paperback edition first published 2024

Copyright © Ali Kassem, 2023

Ali Kassem has asserted his right under the Copyright, Designs and Patents Act, 1988, to be identified as Author of this work.

For legal purposes the Acknowledgments on pp. viii-ix constitute an extension of this copyright page.

Series design by Adriana Brioso
Cover image © Fotokon/Shutterstock

All rights reserved. No part of this publication may be reproduced or transmitted in any form or by any means, electronic or mechanical, including photocopying, recording, or any information storage or retrieval system, without prior permission in writing from the publishers.

Bloomsbury Publishing Plc does not have any control over, or responsibility for, any third-party websites referred to or in this book. All internet addresses given in this book were correct at the time of going to press. The author and publisher regret any inconvenience caused if addresses have changed or sites have ceased to exist, but can accept no responsibility for any such changes.

A catalogue record for this book is available from the British Library.

A catalog record for this book is available from the Library of Congress.

ISBN: HB: 978-0-7556-4798-9
PB: 978-0-7556-4802-3
ePDF: 978-0-7556-4799-6
eBook: 978-0-7556-4800-9

Typeset by Newgen KnowledgeWorks Pvt. Ltd., Chennai, India

To find out more about our authors and books visit www.bloomsbury.com and sign up for our newsletters.

To all those wounded by Eurocentric Modernity.

Contents

Acknowledgments	viii
Prologue	x
1 Introduction: Thinking Islamophobia Elsewhere and Otherwise	1
2 Historicization and Framing: Lebanon and Muslim Dress	17
3 Racialization at the Intersection of the Local and the Global: From an Expulsion from Citizenry to Dehumanization	33
4 Domestic, Public, Work, and State Spheres: Lived Anti-Muslim Racism and Its Workings	51
5 A Kaleidoscopic Spectrum of Muslim Dress and the Reproduction of Anti-Muslim Racism	85
6 From *Difaʿ* to Delinking: Anti-Muslim Racism and the Reproduction of Modernity/Coloniality	111
Conclusion	145
Notes	159
Bibliography	167
Index	199

Acknowledgments

This book is anything but my work. It is, first and foremost, that of participants and it is to them that it is dedicated. Their time, their effort, their support, their shared experiences, their generosity, and their pertinent insights and analyses that made everything so much easier were only some of the boundless ways they made all of this possible. It is to them that I owe the deepest gratitude and debt. I must here, additionally, extend my thanks to all those who facilitated and aided fieldwork; it would not have been possible without you.

Second, this book is the work of Dr. Aneira June Edmunds, Prof. Kimberley Brayson, and Prof. Nuno Ferreira who provided this project with vital contributions from various positions. I will always be grateful for their diligent work and all the time they invested, especially time spent reading my tedious drafts and chapters and providing invaluable feedback. Indeed, this would certainly not have been achievable had it not been for their incredible kindness, dedication, availability, support, and stimulation.

I would here like to thank mentors and colleagues at the University of Sussex, particularly Prof. Gurminder Bhambra for all her inspiring sessions, conversations, feedback, and continuous care, and support and the Sussex Centre for Colonial and Postcolonial Studies for being an engrossing hub of critical knowledge and growth. I would also like to thank the Institute for Advanced Studies at the University of Edinburgh for providing the needed space as I developed and refined this book and colleagues at the Al-waleed Centre at Edinburgh for providing generous feedback and engagement.

Prof. Mona Harb's long-standing support of my work and intellectual development—as well as her unparalleled kindness, availability, and encouragement—has similarly been imperative in developing this work and bringing this book into the world. Further, it is key to acknowledge the constant support and intellectual stimulation provided by Prof. Sari Hanafi from the earliest days of this project's conceptualization, as well as that of numerous mentors, colleagues, and friends at the American University of Beirut and across Lebanon and its diasporas. My thanks particularly goes to Dr. Anaheed Al-Hardan who has long supported my anti-colonial engagements.

Additionally, this book would not have been possible without all those who have engaged and read segments (or the entirety) of it at various points. Most importantly, my gratitude goes to Felix Mantz for his invaluable and thorough decolonizing engagement with my work. My thanks further goes to Prof. Sabrina Mervin and the Centre d'études en sciences sociales du religieux at the Ecole des Hautes Etudes en Sciences Sociales in Paris for their hospitality and engagement with my work. My gratitude further goes to Dr Giorgia Baldi and Dr Irene Zempi for their constructive and stimulating reading and feedback.

For financial support, I would like to acknowledge the Sussex School of Law, Politics, and Sociology's scholarship funding, the Arab Council for Social Sciences, the Carnegie Corporation of New York, and the Institute for Advanced Studies at the University of Edinburgh. I would also like to acknowledge the Institut Français du Proche-Orient for financing this project's fieldwork.

Prologue

Shortly after the 2006 war in Lebanon, one of my aunts began wearing a hijab. In a middle-class Westernized family with little to no religious observance, and ex-Maoist tendencies, the decision stirred much controversy as my first significant personal encounter with "Muslim dress" was that of a large dispute in an extended family that felt harmed and scandalized by one of its member's decision to dress "Islamically."[1] In 2010, I enrolled at the American University of Beirut (AUB) and, during my first week, met a hijab-wearing student to begin what was to be one of my undergraduate years' closest friendships. Having come from a French Catholic missionary school, she became my first hijab-wearing friend, ever. A relationship that brought forth many hitherto unknown realizations about a Lebanese "Islamic lifestyle," it was also a friendship that birthed tensions and distaste among my (mostly Christian) circle of friends. As the years went by and as encounters with this "Islamic" grew I became increasingly acquainted with Muslim dress as an "identitarian" object and of much contestations, disputes, and meanings.

In 2015, I was enthusiastic to learn of a graduate seminar titled "The Politics of the Veil" at the AUB Sociology Department as I was beginning my graduate studies. Interested and intrigued, I enrolled in the class, which offered a brilliant review of the academic literature on the Muslim dress.[2] By the end of the semester, I had come to realize the dissonance between the multiple assumptions and narratives underwriting the literature and what I had come to learn of the hijab and the hijab-wearing experience—as well as the wider Muslim experience in the country. I was particularly taken by the academic scholarship's unsatisfactory engagement with, and analysis of, what appeared to me to be the political role and meanings of Muslim dress and its life within the small complex conflict-ridden country. Steadily, Muslim bodily ritual for both men and women—from the hijab to male "Muslim" jewelry—appeared a key site of study for a critical contribution complexifying the distinction between the religious and the political and reexamining Muslim rituals' relationship to categories such as political activism, citizenship, and political behavior from Lebanon. Accordingly, I developed and began a research project examining (modern political) subject formation in its relation to

Muslim bodily ritual under complex multireligious multiparty "confessional democratic systems."

As I began fieldwork, I quickly realized that my concerns and interests did not align with those of hijab-wearing participants in particular as a significant discord plagued interviews. As I asked about political parties and political participation, hijab-wearing participants recounted experiences of exclusion and marginalization across spheres of Lebanese society. As I asked about the Lebanese state and political behavior, they explained the dissonance between the imagined ideal Lebanese citizen and their suspect identity. As I collected data, I became increasingly aware of a deep wound that particularly imbued Lebanese visibly Muslim women's world and tyrannized their being while it remained unrecorded, unacknowledged, and unaddressed in both academic and nonacademic circles. Putting aside some cries on social media and the occasional newspaper article, I came to recognize a largely invisible(ized) predicament. For participants, understanding *why*, *how*, *to what effect*, and *how to resist* this condition were the paramount questions that needed to be asked. The project reframed its questions, took a specific focus, and sought to meet the needs of those whom it needed. This book is one of the key outputs emerging from this movement.

1

Introduction: Thinking Islamophobia Elsewhere and Otherwise

Islamophobia has received growing attention over the past decades across public, media, and academic debates. From being analyzed through a security perspective to being explored in its sociocultural production and manifestations, much work has sought to define, situate, deconstruct, and disentangle the workings of a growing "industry" of Othering and assault (Beydoun 2008; Green 2015; Kumar 2012; Lean 2012; Saeed 2016; Tyrer 2013; Wolfreys 2016). Within this, mounting attention to the lived experiences of Muslims under escalating anti-Muslim hate has emerged to document and analyze the impact of such discrimination and contest its grounding narratives "from below" (Allen 2010, 2020; Bakali 2016; Carr 2015; Awan and Zempi 2019). Islamic dress for women emerges here as a key site where Islamophobia is studied and examined in its various entanglements with the Western nation-state, Western security, Western inequality, and Western modern sexism and misogyny.

Yet, while Islamophobia is often assumed to be limited to the West, research indicates its global prevalence. Despite this, its study has been "largely dismissed in Muslim countries" generally and in the Arab-majority region specifically as it has been presented as a "western phenomenon" (El Zahed 2019; Yel and Nas 2014: 568). For Muslim dress specifically, the standard narrative holds that "in a majority Muslim context, for example, a particular item such as the hijab is not a contested issue and therefore is not questioned" (Kaya 2000; Sandikci and Ger 2001; Smith-Hefner 2007; Wagner et al. 2012: 532).

Encountering the discrimination and assault plaguing the lived experiences of visibly Muslim women in Lebanon, this book specifically argues against such narratives. It will contend that rampant anti-Muslim racism exists in the small Arab-majority country—including within its Muslim communities. Showcasing this racism's echoes with anti-Muslim racism in Euro-America and thinking alongside various anti-, post-, and decolonial theorists, it will examine this racism's conditions, workings, and mechanisms of assault. Exploring its impact and reproduction, the book posits that anti-Muslim racism in Lebanon is structured by globally connected and contemporary Eurocentric modernity and that it functions as an apparatus of this modernity/coloniality's reproduction through both the erasure of the Muslim and the establishment of the Eurocentric modern as the only possible mode of knowing and being in the world. Pushing beyond reductionist and exceptionalizing narratives of Lebanon and the West Asia and North Africa (or so-called MENA) region, it invites a rethinking of anti-Muslim racism from the Global South and alongside the experiences of its wounded dwellers.

This introduction will offer some first clarifications as to what this book's story is, sketch its methodology, and develop its theoretical framing. By its end, the work might appear abstract, floating, and detached from its case study as little about Lebanon or the context of this work will be presented, with the project's empirical grounding and the voices of its participants remaining mostly missing. This, it is crucial to stress, is for pragmatic reasons of organizing the book and the multiple preliminaries needed for its coming chapters to make sense. The reader will have a very different impression, I hope, by the book's conclusion. Chapter 2 will elaboratly sketch Lebanon, while the remaining chapters will be empirically heavy as they strive to make the participants' own voices heard. In this, the reader's patience is asked, and an acknowledgment that this book, with its many limitations, only makes sense as a whole is needed.

First Clarifications and What This Book Is (and Is Not) About

Conducting research in Lebanon, I was told of exclusion, marginalization, pain, and aggression as conversations were loaded with instances, incidents, and debates around the visibly Muslim woman's abjection in the small country. Consequently, the question of the conditions that made possible, produced, and structured such experiences emerged inevitable. Accordingly this book is an attempt to understand, from and alongside participants' subaltern standpoint, the conditions and the movements that create, establish, and reproduce the various experiences of the daily lives they shared. From this analysis, the book will offer a series of theoretical and conceptual arguments and insights as a wider contribution to the study of anti-Muslim racism and of Eurocentric modernity/coloniality. The book accordingly works to contribute to an understanding of how racial formations are produced and reproduced, how they unfold, how they are lived, and what they do—including across the world and in the Global

North. It is, in other words, an empirical case study of anti-Muslim racism in a small country in the Global South that does not sit peripherally but rather feeds into the broader debates on understanding processes of racialization and racism, erasure, and coloniality.

This book will in this respect offer an in-depth exploration of lived experiences *as hijab-wearing*, focusing on the specific dimension of Muslim visibility in participants' lives. Surely, this is deeply entangled with other dimensions including gender, class, and sexuality, for example. Accordingly, the pursuit here is not a complete exploration and analysis of the visibly Muslim woman's lived experiences per se, for which other systems of power cannot be set aside, but rather a targeted exploration of the "visibly Muslim" within these experiences. Further clarification of the rationale behind this comes later in this chapter.

The operational definition of the "hijab" adopted in this book is that of any form of women's dress identified as "visibly Muslim" in Lebanon where the hair is covered. In other words, this term is used in line with how it is standardly used in Lebanese Muslim society and how it was used by participants during this research project. This includes the niqab as a specific form of hijab, as it includes various forms of "fashionable" dress. These differences will be explored in detail in Chapter 5, but it must be stressed that the word "hijab" is used as a nonhomogeneous umbrella term to refer to the various forms of women's Muslim wear practiced in Lebanon during the time of this investigation and identified by participants as thus without imposing any external terminology. The transliteration of the Arabic term, rather than the use of the word "veil," for example, was of particular importance as to stir away from ascribing to any orientalist assumptions and connotations, loaded categories, preexisting images, or circumscribed definitions that include specific forms of dress and exclude others. In line with this, the word *muhajaba*—translated into hijab-wearing woman—is operationally defined as the identity connoting those to whom such a term applies within Lebanese society. Surely, this is not a fixed or a binary category—particularly given the nature of Muslim dress, its varieties, and the fact Muslim women transition in and out of wearing the hijab or wearing specific forms of the hijab throughout their lives. Rather, *muhajaba* is an analytical category emerging from the field that remains complex, contingent, and contextual.

It is essential to note here that this hijab is *women's* dress. While this is standard, widely accepted, and seemingly evident, it is far from being problematic. Historically and across the Arab-majority region and West Asia North Africa, men's attire was itself aligned with a range of social norms and expectations. These included covering clothes, including covering of the head. Yet, with the impact of European imperialism, colonialism, and Westernization, the various local forms of men's dress were made to disappear as they were replaced with standard European and Westernized wear. Yet, this disappearance, both historically as well as in the contemporary moment, did not stir the controversies nor the pursuits that women's dress did. Most importantly, it never became a charged political topic the way women's dress did, nor did it become a major issue of public debate or scholarly reflection and analysis. Today, little remains of men's dress and covering the head has become unproblematically extinct with a few exceptions. No calls or demands for the return of these forms of dress, or for men to cover their hair, exist. The gendered, sexist, and patriarchal structures that have produced these vastly different histories and realties in relation to men's and women's bodies cannot be understated here. This book's focus on women's Muslim dress, as a sociological examination of this key case of Muslim visibility and the Muslim subject in Lebanon, must accordingly be situated within these histories and structures. It is these conditions that make Lebanon today a space where there is no significant men's Muslim visibility as women are doubly burdened, doubly wounded, and doubly erased.

This book is concerned with experiences in what it identifies as "mainstream Lebanon" taken as a category put forth by participants in the field. This mainstream, participants explained, cuts across sects, socioeconomic classes, and geography without meaning that it was unvaryingly standard throughout the vastly heterogeneous and plural country and its many divides or that it was not largely structured by a specific class, age group, sect, and geographic position. In this sense, the presentation of this "mainstream" approach must not be taken to be claiming the homogeneity of Lebanese society or monolithic experiences of the hijab-wearing woman within it. There are, surely, differences across regions, religious groups, geographies, and several other variables. Yet, a "national" view, a hegemonic standard discourse, was advanced by participants. The powerful experiencing of this mainstream is the object of investigation in this book, not disavowing, but also not examining here, other present competing experiences and constructions.

This book revolves around how hijab-wearing women themselves experience their lived dress in mainstream Lebanese society. In doing this, it does not emerge from an analysis of how Lebanese hijab-wearing women are understood, engaged, or perceived by/in mainstream Lebanon. Surely, this is not to negate the value of projects seeking, for example, to capture the Lebanese scene through working with different social groups, or ones pursuing an argument about the larger populations of which hijab-wearing women may be a part. Nevertheless, as an engagement with a wounded experience for its understanding this is not the pursuit here. Accordingly, this book does not claim to represent an external reality it has identified or the conditions of what is, but rather to listen and work with how the subalternized experience a specific aspect of their reality and its problems to understand its structuring and formation from their own position.

This project is not focused on an understanding of the hijab, particularly not on an understanding of motivations and/or meanings it has for its wearer as, I hold, these remain plural, complex, and wide ranging. Similarly, this is not a study of the emergence of the hijab in Lebanon, the factors structuring such emergence, and/or an analysis of how this emergence unfolds. Further, this is not a study of Muslim dress itself as a material object or of the dress from an Islamic jurisprudential and/or legal lens. Ultimately, a vast number of different projects can be pursued around the hijab and the hijab-wearing woman in Lebanon. The complexity of participants' lives, Muslim women dwellers of the Global South in a multi-sectarian (post-)conflict postcolonial (in the sense of being structured by the colonial) patriarchal society during the contemporary moment, meant that such a clear circumscription was needed to generate valuable insights and interventions.

It must lastly be noted that the analysis and argumentation in the chapters to come must not be taken to imply an ascription to binary terms of any debate or to clear unproblematic definitions, distinctions, divisions, or oppositions. Semantics are dictated by analytical utility. For example, the terms "West" and "Western" are used but such usage in no way implies an ascription to a homogeneous or monolithic West separate from the East, for example, as the "West" and "East" are themselves two imperial (Western) concepts that only exist in relation to one another. Similarly, Europe is surely a dissimilar space with myriad differences and, most importantly, multiple internal Others upon whom coloniality exercises its movement just as it exercises its movement on the rest of the planet. Yet, Europe (and its American settler-colonies) is here used as a category not connoting a geography but rather connoting a locus of enunciation and a self-fashioned imagined representation. Referring to hegemonic enacted epistemologies from culture to economy, its internal differences become analytically secondary. From participants' position, seen from the outside, deploying such categories is ultimately a relevant and strategic move. Further, Islam, the Islamic, and the Muslim are used not in reference to essentialized or presumed things that exist in themselves or transhistorically but rather as specific contingent constructions within specific structures that take on meaning within the particular space/place and time of the field (Asad 1983). Islam is accordingly conceptualized as a "historically evolving set of discourses, embodied in the practices and institutions of Islamic societies and hence deeply imbricated in the material life of those inhabiting them" (Asad 1986). In this sense, Islam is not engaged as an essentialized category or system of thought nor is it engaged at the metaphysical or theological levels. Rather, in line with Asad's "anthropology of Islam," it is engaged as it is lived by those who identify as Muslim—as it is constantly made and remade from below as a living and dynamic being. Later in this introduction, this will be further clarified as I set out the book's theoretical grounding and framing within anti-, post-, and decolonial thought.

Methods and Positionality

This book is based on research conducted across the Lebanese geography between 2018 and 2020 drawing on data collected with practicing visibly Muslim Lebanese women. Starting with preestablished networks and snowballing, photo-elicitated in-depth interviews and small-sized focus group techniques were adopted, with the project having 105 participants in total. Participants were diverse in terms of their demographics, socioeconomic backgrounds, occupations, and residence: both Sunni and Shia, from Beirut's upper classes to the Lebanese south's poorer populations, with an age range of eighteen to sixty-nine. Research was conducted in Lebanese Arabic, with the data then being translated and analyzed with the support of NVivo. The book's writing is done using pseudonyms, preserving participants' anonymity and not including unique identifiers.

Qualitative, interpretive, and reflexive, this case study of a small complex Mediterranean Arab-majority ex-colony sought to perform research outside of the Western academy's binaries, violence, and oppression. Based on the conviction that participants, and the phenomenon being studied, are "more than a collection of objective, measurable facts" and are in fact living beings who "are seen and interpreted through the researcher's frame" its methods seek to debunk oppression, exclusion, and erasure to theorize for redress (Mehra 2002: 20). To achieve this, I attempt to understand, formulate, enunciate, surpass, transcend, and make use of my own position, knowledges, history, and potentials, as I engaged, analyzed, and reported on experiences from across Lebanon's many (sectarian, regional, class, etc.) divides. Crucial to make explicit here is the book's approach as one upholding the subalternized's position to speak of, and against, the conditions of their subalternization. In this sense, this book is based on a decolonial listening exercise that attempts to make "visible the invisible" and analyze "the mechanisms that produce such invisibility or distorted visibility" through an exercise of engagement with the "invisible" people themselves (Maldonado-Torres 2010: 116).

Ultimately, and as social researchers, we cannot pretend or, even worse, be unaware "that the specific characteristics" of our understanding are "a point of view on a point of view" where we attempt to take the views of our participants and tell a tale about the world (Bourdieu 1999: 625), about my/their world. The most important challenge, perhaps, was not to fall into a failed listening where "women's voices themselves, their oral histories, with rich subtexts and eloquent voids and silences" are misunderstood and appropriated "by the interviewers zombified by Western scientific and scholarly principles" (Tlostanova and Mignolo 2012: 143).

Here, it is necessary to address the complex questions of legitimacy in this project. This is particularly salient in two key respects: gender and position within the Westernized university. In relation to gender, legitimizing this work begins with the rejection of any essentialist binary conceptualizations of gender alongside a commitment to advancing the conversation and the empathy across genders.[1] Importantly, sharing or not sharing a gender can have various impacts on research depending on the context, as it intersects with other variables, including ones that may be of more importance in specific contexts (Mazzei and O'Brien 2009; Stanley and Slattery 2003). In this respect, gender is one (important) characteristic, yet it is not the only one: religion, phenotypical race, ethnicity, class, and age, among others, greatly influence the subject, their interaction with the world, their knowledge-making as well as their experiences and expressions. Evidently, researchers are not required to share all these characteristics with their participants to conduct legitimate research (Ladson-Billings 2003; Walker 2005). Rather, what is needed is the sharing of key characteristics to permit rapport and understanding (Puwar 1997). As Ansell (2001) argues, it is the project's setting that determines the key characteristics in question. In this respect, Falen (2008) holds that the barriers to men conducting research with women "loom larger than they are," insisting that much stands to be gained through such a labor if it is oriented toward understanding and critical reflexivity without negating its challenges and limitations (Falen 2008: 164), as I hope this project further shows.

In the context of this study, I hold that the key characteristic was religion and, combined with multiple other shared attributes, sufficient identity identification to generate key insights and analysis was present. In other words, as a Muslim with an identifiably Muslim name and a mostly "Arab appearance," I shared dimensions of participants' racialization, despite the fact I did not share their gender or wear a hijab. Additionally, I shared their ethnicity and citizenship as well as language, accent, and cultural belonging, even though I was sometimes considered to have less of these than they did, given my upbringing and education or my residence in the UK.

This further relates to the second issue of relevance here: that this book is based on research, and is authored by a researcher trained and based in the Western(ized) academy. While this is a challenging question, its weight was alleviated by two main aspects of the project. The first is the project's questions and concerns while the second is my own identity and belonging. First, this project asks questions participants themselves first raised and is concerned with voicing their racialized experiences. As Zahraa stated at the end of our interview, "there is a lot to say, and to be told. Maybe these are the most important. There are things, that I would like to send." The coming chapters will labor to say, and send, what Zahraa and other participants said and sent cognizant of the differences between my positionality and their positionalities—differences that are approached as a site of generating insights.[2] In this sense, this is not a project confined to Western academia but is rather one shaped by encounters of/in the Global South. Second, my own position as a wounded racialized Muslim Lebanese subject is of significant importance here. Acknowledging and working through and against the significant impact of my own formation and position within the Westernized academy, this work stands committed to a more nuanced, reflective, reflexive, and honest engagement to expose oppression and exclusion—a key basis of this project's legitimacy. As disfigured knowledge and misunderstandings overflow in Western scholarship, this project ultimately emerges from a *need* to contest, including from within the hegemonic Global North academy.

My complex identity in this project in this sense formed the "framework of credibility and approachability" (Adu-Ampong and Adams 2020: 591) in relation to my positionality. Surely, the result is a complex insider/outsider balance where I both resembled and differed from participants. Blix (2015), discussing the insider/outsider "dilemma" in relation to decolonial research, explains that this must not be seen as a hurdle but rather as "an opportunity for the co-construction of new insights" where the researcher's performance can be constantly negotiated to understand the indigenous context at stake (Blix 2014: 182). As Enguix (2012) explains, "complete identity or identification with a subject of study is impossible, and it is not—and should not be—a prerequisite of knowledge or of understanding," inviting researchers to realize that the "construction of difference and the status of insider and outsider are shaped in the process of research through punctual interactions and negotiations among the actors, and are not aprioristic statuses" (Enguix 2012: 91). Rather, this difference itself can offer valuable benefits to the research process (Tinker and Armstrong 2008). In this sense, I argue that my own complex identity formed a key site where insights were generated, and where empathy and understanding were fostered (see Gair 2012).

As Said (2003: 94) eloquently said, "It is often the case that you can be known by others in different ways than you know yourself, and that valuable insights might be generated accordingly." Applied to this project, the fact that I have not lived participants' hijab-wearing experiences, and do not share participants' bodies in a sense pushes me to listen, hear, and see their lives in generative ways. Certainly, this means that certain facets will also not be seen, remain invisible, and such poses important limitations of this work that must be acknowledged. In this respect, it is hoped that this work will be the beginning of a conversation and that future research by researchers differently positioned will elaborate and explore the various issues that remain beyond its scope and remit.

My complex positionality ultimately held significant impact on fieldwork as both generative and limiting. This awareness was taken forward into the analysis and writing of this book. Indeed, while the risk of violence is (always) present, listening is our safest option in the necessary and urgent pursuit of dismantling structures of domination and objectification. So, while Eurocentric modernity is a "system that silences the Other, or better that produces the Other as silent, non-existent or as 'pure representation,'" this project has sought to listen and, through listening, to better understand and give voice to those who "have been denied dignity and voice" (Vázquez 2012: 248).

Eurocentric Modernity/Coloniality, Anti-Muslim Racism, and Theoretical Framing

While modernity is often understood as the latest stage in the long evolution of humanity that began, endogenously, in Europe with the Reformation, the Enlightenment, and/or the Industrial Revolution, this book situates itself in decolonial scholarship conceptualizing modernity as the historic and contemporary global "matrix of power" beginning in 1492 (Bhambra 2007; Dussel 2000). Then, as Granada was occupied and Islamic knowledge was being mass-burnt in Iberia, the extermination of the Americas' indigenous populations and knowledges began as Europe endeavored into its pillaging "development" through a barbaric process of labor extraction and a sophisticated economy of enslavement and assault. Accordingly, modernity is here understood as an inter-European phenomenon, instead of it being an intra-European endogenous one (see Bhambra 2007). Modernity's essence is thus conceptualized as a project of domination through the marking of all non-Europeans as "Others" and the "subalternisation of the knowledges and cultures [of] those other groups" (Escobar 2007: 184) for their ultimate erasure.

Consequently, modernity is not a historical phase, nor an idea and not even a process. Rather, it is a "Western" *project* of "civilization" that began with the "discovery" of the Americas to then expand to the world. Civilization here is an encompassing term that refers to the specific (contingent, nonhierarchized) epistemologies, knowledges, economies, and social orders of colonizing Europe.[3] In this, modernity, seen from the outside of Europe, is the colonial/imperial pursuit of a uni-versal world where Europe is claimed as the present of history and the geographic center of the world. Modernity is, ultimately, a rhetorical narrative concealing coloniality.

Coloniality has, in this sense, been developed specifically by the Latin American decolonial studies collective to refer to modernity's movement revolving around appropriation and representation as a "double negation" that both absences Others and consumes them and their worlds (Vázquez 2012). In this sense, modernity "names something you do not see that works in what you do see": something that is sensed through its effects (Mignolo 2018: 372). A movement built on an economy of exclusions in the metropole and an economy of erasure in the colonies, it is, therefore, a series of techniques: from violence and genocide to epistemicide (the erasure of all non-European epistemologies) and earthlessness (the break with the earth and its consumption/destruction). Through it, "the cultural, political, sexual, spiritual, epistemic and economic oppression/exploitation of subordinate racialized/ethnic groups [is exercised] by dominant racialized/ethnic groups with or without the existence of colonial administration" (Grosfoguel 2010: 74, 2002). Coloniality accordingly designates the denial and disavowal of all that belongs to the outside of the Eurocentric "reality" (Vázquez 2012: 242).[4] It is hence the ongoing movement toward the establishment of a monoculture and the negation of the pluriversality of the world (Grosfoguel 2012a; Mignolo 2012). Hence, coloniality is not colonialism: coloniality surpasses classical colonialism and its forms of administration and presence. Coloniality is modernity's darker side (Mignolo 2012: 17). It is "a heterogeneous historico-structural node revealing the underlying structure that sustains and governs, in the larger sense of the word, the order of knowledge and manages the order of being" (Mignolo 2018: 373–4). As elaborated on by Grosfoguel (2016) this is the matrix of the "capitalist/patriarchal western-centric/Christian-centric modern/colonial world-system." The modernity/coloniality coupling is used to indicate this.

The shifting of the onset of modernity to 1492 should not be read as a geocentric move that comes out of the Americas but rather a global, analytical, and necessary one for the understanding of our contemporary condition.[5] Even in itself, the "discovery" of the Americas was a colossal event in the history of Asia, Africa, and beyond as it shifted global geopolitics; altered commercial exchange, trade routes, resources, and commodities; and disrupted global power balances.[6] The year 1492 was indeed a colossal year for the Muslim world with the "Reconquista" and the ensuing expulsions, collapses, and erasures. Meanwhile, it was the birth of European colonialism that then transformed into a global phenomenon with its expansive nature. Eventually, the experiences of the Americas, from their earliest days, would be inconceivable without the experiences of Africa and Asia, just as the experiences of Africa and Asia would be inconceivable had it not been for the events in the Americas. Accordingly, from the enslavement of African peoples to the appropriation of various knowledges from Asia (from India to Muslim traditions), the project was deeply "global."[7]

The colonial matrix of power is a structure resting on a quest for the control of authority, sexuality, knowledge, and subjectivity. These four spheres are glued together by racism. Racism here is not "a classification of human beings according to the colour of their skin but rather a classification according to a certain standard of 'humanity'" (Grosfoguel 2016; Mignolo 2012: 55). "Race" is accordingly an institutionally produced and established structural phenomenon that anchors a "global hierarchy of superiority and inferiority along the line of the human" in various socioeconomic and political spheres (Grosfoguel 2016: 10). "Humanity" is not here "a transcendental and neutral essence that just anyone can appropriate and describe" but is rather a particular enunciation born out of the Western episteme and "based on epistemic and ontological colonial difference" (Mignolo 2009: 17). The category of the human is, in other words, "an invention of Western imperial knowledge rather than the name of an existing entity to which everyone will have access to": controlled by some, always denied to others (Mignolo 2009: 11). Within this system of modernity/coloniality, the condition of becoming human is becoming modern. Without becoming human/modern, one has little right(s) to claim(s) and remains outside, "different" and damned (Mignolo 2009). It is, indeed, a situation of all Others turned into *damnés*, who are always "either invisible or excessively visible" (Maldonado-Torres 2007: 257). Race is accordingly not conceptualized as a uniform category. Rather, it holds multiple articulations whereby different forms of racisms exist—coded by different racial markers and contingent on the specific case. In this respect, "colour, ethnicity, language, culture and/or religion" may all function as racializing dehumanizing markers, separately or in entanglement, in the contemporary world (Grosfoguel, Oso, and Christou 2015: 636).

On a related note, coloniality is a structure that is both Christian-centric and, simultaneously, secularizing. With its narrative since the seventeenth century, coloniality has identified humanity with "being secular bourgeois" where Christianity looms in the background (Maldonado-Torres 2014a, 2008; Mignolo 2009b: 14).[8] Moving from Christian modernity into a secularized modernity, "religion does not disappear altogether, but it acts in the complex union with nationalism and secularized racism, in fact, it acts through them" (Tlostanova 2014: 97). Here, secularism, entwined with a specific understanding of history and the past, with a specific European set of experiences, with a specific definition of meaning and rationality, is a structuring component of coloniality. Accordingly, a key site of dehumanizing racialization is that of religion, where Islamophobia can be understood as structural domination and hierarchization produced by coloniality and its reproduction in relation to the supremacy of the Christian, the secular, and the Western (Bayrakli and Hafez 2018; Grosfoguel and Martín-Muñoz 2010)—as the coming chapters will explore and elaborate. An important element allowing this racism to permeate Muslim communities is Orientalism and self-orientalism. A mechanism producing the colonized as inferior in their own eyes, it situates Muslims in a position and zone of internalized subordination eliciting within their subjectivity a desire to distance oneself from Islam constructed as an inherent deficiency, even by/for "practicing believers" (Bayrakli and Hafez 2018; Grosfoguel and Mielants 2006), as will be developed throughout this book.

On the other hand, gender and patriarchy are core sites of coloniality's functioning where Eurocentric modernity presents itself as championing women's emancipation while concealing its own deep patriarchy as it establishes and mobilizes gender inequalities for its hegemony (Brayson 2019; Federici 2014; Mignolo 2009). As Grosfoguel (2011) explains, key to modernity's formation is the establishment of "a global gender hierarchy that privileges males over females and European Judeo-Christian patriarchy over other forms of gender relations" (Grosfoguel 2011: 9). In this respect, patriarchy is a pillar upon which modernity stands, and is reproduced. With it, sexism permeates the colonial matrix and its functioning, from the coloniality of knowledge to the coloniality of being, whereby the modern order itself is a sexist one (Grosfoguel 2011; Lugones 2010).[9]

A decolonial understanding is eventually one that realizes how "race, class and gender are interrelated so that they cannot be understood as 'parts' of a reality, but as a network where they dynamically interact, either in a supportive or in a contradictory and conflictive manner" (Jiménez-Lucena 2006: 34). In this matrix, race has been argued to hold a central position as it forms "the transversal dividing line that cuts across multiple power relations such as class, sexual and gender relations on a global scale" (Grosfoguel 2016; Grosfoguel, Oso, and Christou 2015: 637).

In this sense, it is the racialized hierarchy of the human that "organizes the world's population into a hierarchical order of superior and inferior people that becomes an organizing principle" (Grosfoguel 2011: 10; Mignolo 2012). In other words, "gender and sexual hierarchical relations very much depend, in the modern/colonial world, on racial classification" (Mignolo 2011c: 16). This, Grosfoguel, Oso, and Christou (2015) argue, is crucial to realize in order to analyze modernity's structuring of the world as, within "the Western-centric imperial order of things, being an 'Other human' in the zone of being is not the same thing as being a 'non-human Other' in the zone of non-being" (Grosfoguel, Oso, and Christou 2015: 640). As Quijano (2007) states, modernity/coloniality has rendered the "social category of 'race' the key element of the social classification of colonized and colonizers" (Quijano 2007: 171). Quijano accordingly presents modernity by explaining that it "is based upon 'racial' social classification of the world population under Eurocentered world power" in a way that renders race "the cornerstone of this coloniality of power" (Quijano 2007: 171). This book's work and coming focus on anti-Muslim racism and the racialized dimension *as visibly Muslim* of its participants emerges alongside these theoretical and conceptual insights.

Book Outline

Before presenting the book's outline, it is key to acknowledge that the following chapters will elaborate a story that sits at the intersection of participants' lives, my own positionality, and various "academic debates" and theoretical arguments the book seeks to engage with and explore. While it will labor to convey participants' own stories, voices, and experiences, this labor remains limited within its, and my own, many confines and objectives as well as incomplete for future work to expand.

Chapter 2 begins by historicizing and framing this book's arguments. Its first section develops a brief reconstruction of Lebanon's colonial foundation, postcolonial condition, and the figuring of the Muslim and Muslim dress within it. Its second section turns to a historicization of Muslim dress as a lived experience focusing on the Global South and the Arab-majority and Muslim-majority regions in particular. Here, it argues that the hijab has long formed an object of colonial and modernizing postcolonial control and assault as it makes visible the long-standing deep entwinement of colonial aggression against the hijab with "modernization."

Chapter 3 assembles how participants experienced their identity as hijab-wearing women. It argues that the hijab-wearing woman is constructed as an Other in Lebanon and draws out the specific elements of this Otherness: a belated Arabo-Muslim difference in excess. This social form, I argue, is lived at the nexus of modern time, postcolonial national imaginaries, and global hegemonic imperial Western secular–liberal discourses entwined with patriarchy, sexism, and misogyny. The chapter posits that this Othering expulses the visibly Muslim woman from Lebanese citizenry as it situates her at the bottom of the hierarchy of the human. Based on this analysis, it concludes that the hijab-wearing woman is a racialized subject in contemporary Lebanon.

Chapter 4 sketches some of the *muhajaba's* daily lived experiences and brings to light ordeals of inordinate pain and suffering that largely go unrecognized. Four key spheres are drawn—public, domestic, market, and state—to discuss experienced exclusion and marginalization and the various rationales and narratives that wound and erase. In doing this, I explore the incidence of each sphere as I analyze the variables playing into the experiences of marginalization to offer insights and deduce specific techniques of erasure. Drawing out objectification, harassment and micro-aggressions, vulnerabilizing, devaluing and impoverishing, spatializing difference and bordering, and invisibilizing and cloistering, I attempt to extract each sphere's working in the postcolonial Mediterranean land as I demonstrate the similarities these experiences hold with anti-Muslim racism across Euro-America.

In Chapter 5, I explore participants' experiences with the various forms of Muslim dress present in Lebanon and their narrations of how these different forms dwell in the small country thinking alongside Frantz Fanon and Ali Shariati. Complexifying the very category of *muhajaba*, I examine what I term the *hijab kaleidoscopic spectrum*—differentiated on the basis of the dress's perceived modernity. Based on this examination, I propose "mummifying dilution" as a mechanism through which alternative more modern "less-Muslim" forms of the hijab are invented, differentiated in shape, and drained of content and effect upon conduct and being. Critiquing the very mode through which both the very categories of the modern fashionable hijab and the so-called non-modern hijab come into being in Lebanon, the chapter makes visible this presence's deep entwinement with Islamophobic modernity/coloniality and the specific, hegemonic, exclusive, and predetermined ways dress and practice can "modernize." The resulting mummified practices, I propose, serve the colonizer through their inertia in the practicing woman's life, testify against hijab-wearing women in rendering them an extreme excess, and stand emblematic as they offer a legitimization of the hierarchy of the human upon which visibly Muslim women are positioned. A "*less-Muslim more-modern* hijab," I conclude, is constructed to invent the *muhajaba* without appeal as a threatening belated *difference*, serving the reproduction of the conditions of her racialized and racializing anti-Muslim erasure, and beyond.

Chapter 6 is divided into two sections. The first pursues an exploration of the discourses of *difaʿ* (defense) mobilized by participants in reclaiming their Muslim dress and contesting their racialized condition. Drawing out four key strands—(parochial) universalism, (parochial) secularism, modern science, and anti-patriarchy—the chapter explores how *difaʿ* as negotiation mostly unfolds within Eurocentric modernity's epistemic territory, mobilizing its own terms and contesting it while and through ascribing to many of its underlying assumptions and categories. Away from a normative judgment, the chapter explores how participants' movement was itself implicated in the disavowal of the Muslim and the wider reproduction of anti-Muslim racism as well as wider modernity/coloniality. In the second section of the chapter, I turn to reconstructed elements of participants' accounts of their dress, and their relation to it, to conceptualize the hijab as a means through which participants self-form as Muslim subjects and establish a particular connection to Muslim ancestrality. The possibilities of being otherwise as well as the stakes of anti-Muslim racism in epistemological as well as lived and material erasure are accordingly made visible. The chapter closes by reflecting on the dissonance between what appeared to be the hijab's import to participants and the discourses they drew upon to legitimize their practice in reflecting on the experience of being a racialized Other under Eurocentric modernity/coloniality. The final chapter summarizes the book's key argument and offers some opening reflections. There, arguing that anti-Muslim racism is a globalized phenomenon, I ask what thinking anti-Muslim racism from Lebanon brings to the study of the country, the region, and Islamophobia scholarship more broadly.

2

Historicization and Framing: Lebanon and Muslim Dress

Informed by the need for an active and adequate historicization within a globally connected methodology (Bhambra 2007), this chapter begins by sketching Lebanon's historical foundation and a selection of relevant contemporary sociopolitical realities. It then turns to a historical outline of women's Muslim dress within the West Asia North Africa region of which Lebanon is a part. This allows the framing, grounding, and anchoring of the chapters to come and their analyses as this project's specific case and the site from which its arguments emerge are set. Further, this will be returned to in the conclusion in drawing out the book's larger contribution in interrogating and rethinking Lebanon, the region, and anti-Muslim racism more broadly.

Lebanon: Invention, Current Scene, and Muslim Dress

Lebanon is a small multiparty confessional republic classified as a "developing country" with high human development and a liberal (non-oil) economy located on the eastern shores of the Mediterranean.[1] The nation is believed to house around nineteen sects, twelve of whom are Christian and two (or three, depending on whether or not the Druze are included) Muslim (Shehadeh 2004).[2] In the words of historian Fawwaz Traboulsi, Lebanon as a nation "never existed before in history. It is a product of the Franco-British colonial partition of the Middle East" (Traboulsi 2007: 75). Before the First World War, during the days of Ottoman rule, there existed a *Muhafaza* (administrative division) within the Ottoman Sultanate called Mount Lebanon. Significantly smaller than the current country, Mount Lebanon was mainly a Christian governorate. The Maronites, the overwhelming majority of Christians in the *Muhafaza*, are a sociopolitical religious group particularly known for their great historical ties to Europe in general, and France in particular.[3] Indeed, it has been argued that Maronite loyalty and identity, the only Christian group in the East having supported the crusades, had long allied with Europe and the pope rather than with any local authority (Salibi 1998). With this, Maronite history is loaded with a contestation of Ottoman sovereignty and the pursuit of independence from the Muslim power with French support (Hakim 2013).

Historical evidence indicates that the *Mutasarifiya*, the name given to Mount Lebanon after the Ottoman nineteenth-century reforms, was itself a result of this power struggle as the Ottoman Sultanate ceded to a compromise: France would relinquish its project of an independent Christian princedom and the Ottoman Sultanate would relinquish its attempt to submit Mount Lebanon to its sovereign rule (Salibi 1998; Spagnolo 1971). As such, the *Mutasarifiya* was formed as a particular political unit of governance, with French and Christian missions dominating the sociocultural scene as French influence was as political just as it was (heavily) religious and cultural (Harris 2012). Indeed, even during France's most anticlerical moments, missions and support to Christians in Lebanon never waned as French Laïcité ended once the borders of the Ottoman Sultanate began (Tejirian and Simon 2012).

The regions surrounding the *Mutasarifiya* were heterogeneous: Sunnis as well as Orthodox Christians, Druze, Shias, and other religious minorities existed. Sunnis in both the *Mutasarifiya* and the surrounding regions had enjoyed a good position under the Ottomans, as the empire had a system that some have argued had culturally favored them (Makdisi 2000). Information about the other religious groups, particularly the Shias, is scant (Abidor 2012). Nevertheless, it has been argued that the Shias were a marginalized group at the time (Abidor 2012). Despite this, and notwithstanding political and legal restrictions, the sect's notables appear to have managed a fragmented form of localized power within, and perhaps through, their relegation (Winter 2010).

When the Ottoman Sultanate was broken down, Europe sought out a project of dividing it into smaller units in a supposed quest to create "European-style" nation-states. Accordingly, the idea of establishing minority homes gained much zeal. Pioneered by the French, and with a "Jewish" state being enforced nearby, a "Christian home" was to see light. Yet, Maronite leaders wanted a state that would survive without the need for support from Arab neighbors, and so the head of the Maronite Church (the patriarch) asked for the expansion of the *Mutasarifiya* to include a larger coastline, several major cities, as well as agrarian valleys.[4] As a consequence of the geographies included, this new land was to incorporate the Muslim populations of the surrounding regions, as well as a number of non-Maronite Christians (Firro 2002: chap. 1).

This "Greater Lebanon" with its "natural boundaries" was met with significant opposition from many within the Muslim populations (Makdisi 2000). Indeed, supported by a number of political actors throughout the Arab world, vast segments of the Muslim populations stringently refused this creation; and much unrest, from protests to violent attacks on the French, strikes, civil disobedience, and assassinations, erupted across the land (Hakim 2013; Traboulsi 2007). The Sunnis with significant power, from politics to commerce, voiced a particularly stern "Sunni nationalist" ideology and called for unity with Syria (Johnson 1986; Makdisi 2000).

Regardless, with European and expatriate support, Greater Lebanon was created in 1920 in spite of all opposition (Hakim 2013: 38). For the Maronites, Lebanon was seen as the natural product of the ties held between Europe and that "distinct Maronite community" of the Orient (Womack 2012). For the French, Lebanon was perceived as the beacon from which their project of enlightenment and modernization and their "universal" values of "rationalism" were to spread throughout the Arab world. France's "Lebanese project" accordingly came through: the metropole had obtained its "valuable conduit for imperialist policy" in the region (Verdeil 2006: 23).

This newborn country, as part of the larger political bargains in the world, had been put under a commanding French "Mandatory rule" (class A) (unlike many other realms of the previous Ottoman Empire) after the end of the First World War (Haddad 2002). Beirut was its (artificial) capital, a capital that had become a regional hub as it had been made into both a political and an economic center (Eddé 2013).

During the mandate time, the French attempted to establish a system of paternalism and to institute a bureaucracy and a hierarchy that would serve their interests, both in the region and beyond (Thompson 2000). To achieve this, different agreements were forged, and a multitude of oppressions took place. Most importantly, a hierarchized system of religious discrimination where the Muslims were placed at the lower end of the hierarchy was progressively and overtly institutionalized within the state's structure (Salibi 1998). This held especially true for the Shias, who lacked the regional support (political and other), as well as the historical infrastructure that the Sunnis enjoyed (Hazran 2009b; Winter 2010).

Accordingly, the various Christian and Muslim sects had unequally become the Lebanese where, in creating the nation, religion and religious divisions were strongly entrenched in a system where the state was, from the cultural to the economic, political, and constitutional, premised on Maronite dominance (Crow 1962; Firro 2002). Eventually, in their quest to establish "a colonial civic order rather than solely a colonial state" (Thompson 2000: 68) the French actively laid the foundation for a heterogeneous Lebanese citizenship and much of the country's contemporary contradictions. The French mandate established a (persisting) classification where individuals engaged the state both as citizens and as members of a distinct (religious) group as inequality and difference became defining features of the Lebanese order. In this respect, this colonial state was based on a dual legal system whereby "personal affairs" were referred to institutionalized and ossified state-sanctioned "religious law," further enshrining injustices, clientelism, divisions, and French paternalism (Mikdashi 2014; Zantout 2011).[5]

With these movements, the mandate days were characterized by a mix of economic and social flourishing with tensions, resistance against the French, and political instability (Longrigg 1958). This complex mandate only came to an end after the Second World War and the ensuing global repositioning that allowed for Lebanon's declaration as an "independent country." In this regard, Lebanese independence in 1946 was a complicated process. Key to realize here is that it was a result of larger political deals in the region in the wake of global shifts in power as well as local and regional politics. While the French had envisioned Greater Lebanon as part of L'Union Française, turbulence within the country and shifting politics within France, alongside the geopolitics between France and the UK as well as the United States and the Soviet Union forced the French to accept an independence, officially declared in 1943 (Clayton 1994). Naturally, it was only possible as a result of (some) Muslim leaders accepting this new home (which they diffidently did at times for economic and pragmatic benefits) and (key) Christian groups giving up their demands for "the annexation of Christian Lebanon by France" (Traboulsi 2007: 82). Accordingly, this new country was awkwardly brought into being through compromises, with multiple imaginaries coinhabiting the space declared as the Lebanese nation.

In 1946, a constitution was set in place, under French eyes and in emulation of French "secular" law (Abdallah 2003). Drafted by the French, the Lebanese constitution, which is mostly an (awkwardly) translated version of selected segments of the French constitution at that time, remains largely unchanged till this day except for the adjustments of the Taif Accord (see below) (Hajjar 2009; Semaan 1999). From its bureaucratic ordering to its institutional structure, the new state was molded on the European model with Christian preeminence. There, for example, only a Georgian calendar was (and continues to be) observed, with European holidays (Saturday and Sunday as weekend and Friday as normal working day, Christmas and Easter as the long breaks, etc.) and capitalist Westernized economic and social orders.

In the years following the Second World War, the now independent nation, at least formally, saw a period of relative stability where mass (Western-style) educational, (liberal capitalist) economic, social, and political modifications continued in line with the modifications of the mandate to reconstitute life for the Lebanese (Eddé 2013; Owen 1976; Salibi 1998). Yet, although the system put in place by the French remained mostly unaltered and the country seemed functional, the nation's social fabric and demographic constituency had been changing, and so had the region around it (Salibi 1976). With Arab nationalism on the rise throughout the West Asia region, the old order was becoming extremely strained and the Muslim masses' sense of marginalization was becoming ever more powerful (Harris 2012). Additionally, with the Palestinian-Israeli conflict escalating, the Lebanese system entered a particularly delicate phase. The rule of a Christian autocratic elite, which had largely turned to an alliance with the United States, was no longer sustainable (Traboulsi 2007).

With the 1967 Arab-Israeli war, and as the number of Palestinians pouring into the country grew, small civil wars began to break out (Salibi 1976). Sectarianism already well entrenched, and with a minor civil war having taken place in 1958 over rampant inequalities and the nation's "Arab identity," the country entered a protracted conflict that would not end until 1991 (Traboulsi 2007).[6] Beirut was soon split into Eastern Beirut where Christians were made to gather and Western Beirut where Muslims were made to gather by a demarcation line. But it is vital to realize that this was far from being the capital's only or even main line of division. Some of the many lines of division that ebbed and flowed throughout the conflict in Beirut, its surrounding regions, and beyond were between various Christian militias, between Sunni and Shia militias, among Shia militias, and among Sunni militias. Further, the combat between Palestinian factions, and between Lebanese groups and Palestinians, was also a major component of the conflict. Khalidi (1979), for example, identifies the Palestinians, alongside more than five Arab countries and three non-Arab countries, as "major actors" in the war.

A complicated process ultimately engulfing the majority of the Lebanese geography, the Lebanese civil war is certainly not to be reduced to combat among religious groups. The role of the economic cannot go understated in this, pushing some scholars to argue that it was a war of "capitalists in conflict"

(Hourani 2010, 2015). Yet, surely, much more than the "economic" was at play, from the geopolitical to the "identitarian." Examining and narrating this phase of Lebanese history ultimately remains underdeveloped and beyond the scope of this chapter.

In 1989, and under both regional and international political shifts, many, but not all, Lebanese faction leaders came together in Saudi Arabia and signed what came to be known as the *Taif* Accord (Abdallah 2003). The end of the civil war had begun. Of great importance is the fact that the accord established a new sectarian equilibrium where power was to be equally divided between Muslim and Christian groups while ushering in the Syrian Army as a guarantor of stability (Abdallah 2003). While before the civil war Maronite groups equated Lebanese nationalism with "Maronitism" the occurrences of the previous years with their military defeat and declining numbers as well as regional and global geopolitical shifts had forced them to relinquish this ideology and turn from a policy of domination to one of accommodation/compromise (Haddad 2002). As the accord asserted Lebanon's "Arab face" but not identity, it left large segments of the Lebanese constitution unscathed and much of the nation's colonially instilled structures and institutions, with their cultural foundations, intact (Abdallah 2003).[7]

Post-1991, all armed groups were disarmed, under the watchful eye of the Syrian army entrusted by the Americans, and most arms garnered from the militias were incorporated into the national Lebanese army with one exception: Hezbollah as a resistance movement considered not to have partaken in the civil war (Fadlallah 2014). The accord, only possible considering a Syrian-US deal with Saudi patronage, had succeeded in ending the conflict (Abdallah 2003). The result was an amnesty, with the exile of Michel Aoun and the imprisonment of Samir Geagea, two of the country's most powerful Christian leaders.[8] Then, Rafic Al-Hariri, Sunni business tycoon, became the prime minister with the support of regional (Sunni) power Saudi Arabia to usher the nation into a new age under the banners of reconstruction, modernization, and neoliberal capitalism (Baumann 2017; Salem 1994).

With backing from Iran, which had by then become an "Islamic Republic," the Shias were pursuing their own empowerment (Shaery-Eisenlohr 2008). Socially and economically, their (recent) appearance on the landscape of Lebanese mainstream society and state had allowed significant gains with a movement contesting their status of second-class citizens and allowing significant modernization (Deeb and Harb 2011, 2013). Meanwhile, the Christians found themselves increasingly disadvantaged. The amendments to the constitution did preserve significant Christian privilege, but this was perceived as a great reduction of their power and the realities of their situation meant their ability to exert political dominance had been limited. Despite this, especially on the social and economic scales, Lebanon's Christians held on to a diminished hegemony as neoliberal modernization pushed forth.

Lebanon remains a country with various distinct groups having vast differences in the dynamics governing their sociopolitical lives, their challenges, their hopes, and their dreams (Baytiyeh 2017; Cleveland, Laroche, and Hallab 2013; Farah and Samad 2014; Salamey and Tabar 2008). Nammour (2007) describes Lebanese identity as "complex and perplexed" where religious belonging, which is clearly distinguished from religious faith, rules supreme.[9] Lebanon's different groups, it is key to note, must not be reduced or equated to religious groups as the Lebanese scene is far more complex and composite, crossing and transcending the various religious and sectarian groups as these intersect and overlap in various ways—with class and geography particularly powerful. Indeed, Lebanon has no unified culture, with its various factions having been argued to live under different "value systems" (Bray-Collins 2016) but nevertheless said to have a "mainstream" overarching culture as one must not overstate these differences or absent the deep long-standing connectivity among its various regions and groups.[10] Here, a "Western-oriented Lebanese subjectivity" where cosmopolitanism, tourism, and the habitus of merchants are prime (Maasri 2016: 138) structures a cultural scene revolving around a Westernized set of practices across the country: from Zahle in the Bekaa and Marjayoun in the south to Jounieh, Anjar, and Batroun among many other cities, towns, and villages. The result is a growing mainstream Lebanese scene imagined as being *in* the Arab Middle East but not *of* it as "expensive cars line up behind one another in Beirut's never-ending traffic" where "restaurants and shops of Hamra bustle all day" with extremely high prices "meant for those who can afford it" (Nair 2013: 11).

A distancing from the Arab world and a rapprochement to the European continues to characterize the Lebanese founding myth and the Lebanese contemporary scene (Nammour 2007; Stone 2008).[11] Accordingly, the claim that Lebanon is not an Arab country but, rather, a particular nation in the Arab East, or a Phoenician one, for example, continues to be made and echoed across Lebanon's (sectarian as well as other) divides (Kaufman 2004; Maasri 2016).[12] With a powerful "political desire to evoke Lebanon's particularism in the Arab East" as well as its linking to "ancient Phoenicia," Lebanon's capital Beirut itself continues to push for a reclaiming of its status as "Paris of the East" where a tourism economy pursues a narrative of continuity with a cosmopolitan thriving civilizational past drawing tourists, investment, and Lebanese expatriates—even if unsuccessfully (Maasri 2016: 134). A "city of lines" and material consumption, Lebanon's capital, like the rest of the country, continues to be a space of boundaries: religious, sectarian, class-based, and ideological. Omnipresent and often unspoken, these lines demarcate Beirut and its inhabitants with, for example, the movement from Beirut to its southern suburb, being one where Lebanese taxi drivers "rarely agree to venture [in]to" as it is a movement between two places that appear "a continent apart" (Nair 2013: 11). As Lebanon faced socioeconomic and political crisis starting from 2019, such dynamics have only exacerbated and intensified.

A note on language is due. Arabic is Lebanon's official language as the country remains a member of L'organisation Internationale de la Francophonie. Formal Arabic is nearly non-present in the country as colloquial Lebanese Arabic continuously recedes in favor of French and English. Indeed, in Lebanon, language is a potent social marker and its historical and continuous role in reiterating the old Lebanese self-understanding of a country with a regional "civilising mission ... as a Mediterranean country that looks both East and West" cannot be missed (Salameh 2010: 187; Womack 2012). With it, the "the belief among many Lebanese, according to Suleiman (2003), in Lebanon's civilizational mission in the East" survives and persists (Esseili 2017). While Lebanese Arabic contains a large number of French and (to a lesser extent) English words, widespread foreign language proficiency today functions as a marker of religious affiliation (mainly the fact that most Christians are francophone in both education and daily life while also being conversant in English, while most Muslims, including the Shia, are far more likely to be conversant in English and to speak little French). While the question of the Arabic language in Lebanon, from the claim that Lebanese Arabic is a language of its own to the calls for its writing in Latin script and its persistent decline in usage in favor of English and French (Salameh 2010; Shawish 2010), is beyond the scope of this book suffice to note its power and Lebanon's continued imbrication in the persistent Westernizing order.

Crucial to realize from this recounting of Lebanon is that the small country was established as a colonial project where hierarchization through religion with a special connection to Europe was foundational. Institutionalized and imbuing the state's identity, this resulted in an exclusionary approach to citizenship where the nation's colonial founding largely stood on the disavowal of its Muslim population in favor of its (Maronite) Christian one. As decades passed, the balance of power in the country has changed to witness a gradual and eventually significant sociopolitical and demographic emergence of its Muslim population to become a nation of distinct separate coexisting groups as the Lebanese state continues to be colonized by corruption, warlords, and inefficiency. Segmented and fractured, the Lebanese, I would say, is a failed enunciation. This failure has certainly not been mitigated by Muslim ritual, especially the most visual of them: women's dress.

One of the first known references to "veiling" in Lebanon comes from an Assyrian text, dating back to the thirteenth century, showing that specific modes of "covering dress" were a sign of social status: they were worn by certain women and prohibited for others, including "prostitutes," for example (Keddie 2012). Scholarship then seems to go quiet on the issue of women's dress in Lebanon and little can be found about such dress's status before the late eighteenth century where, in contrast, calls for the abolition of (Muslim) dress were being strongly made under modernization agendas with the echoing of "male 'feminist' Qassim Amin's advocacy from Egypt in his book *Tahrir Al-Mar'a* (The Liberation of Woman)" (Dhanda 2008: 54). In 1928, a young Druze, later accused of treachery, published a book about (face) veiling to condemn the attire as a patriarchal tool, asking the French high commissioner to intervene and save the region's Muslim women.[13] The book caused much debate, but little beyond debate (Thompson 2000). Zeineddine, the book's author, continued writing and advocating for the "liberation" of women from Muslim and "oriental" practices and customs for many years.

Reports as well as anecdotal evidence claim that the number of hijab-wearing women in Lebanon has been on the rise during the last few decades (Le Thomas 2012: 10) and, simultaneously, that around half of the Lebanese population thinks that women should not wear the hijab in public (Moaddel 2013). With this, the hijab has been recorded in local media outlets as a serious handicap for employment in several economic sectors, particularly in state-run administration, the banking sector, and security forces (Abou Ammo 2012; Mereeb 2017).[14] This is also the case in spheres such as the media sector, where a number of news agencies are known to refuse to employ hijab-wearing women, especially as broadcasters (Kassem 2013). Further, some academic work has alluded to or mentioned the hijab as an object connoting a lack of education and "backwardness" within mainstream Lebanese culture (Deeb 2006; Itani 2016).

In Lebanon's contemporary political scene, only two hijab-wearing women have ever been high-profile public figures: as parliamentary members or ministers (the same two women have been both). The first was Bahia Al-Hariri, sister of Rafic Al-Hariri, who was not hijab-wearing when she entered politics but began wearing a light scarf on the head, which gradually became more hijab-like, after the assassination of her brother in 2005. Interestingly, it was Bahia Al-Hariri who introduced the hijab to Lebanon's political sphere as the first hijab-wearing woman to hold public office in the country's history. The second is Inaya Ezzeddine, who became a minister for the *Amal Movement* in 2016 (Rizk 2016) and then became a member of parliament in 2018. The analysis of such entry remains to be done, and this book will attempt to present a number of insights in the coming chapters toward such work.

While little has been written on both Muslim dress and the lived experiences of those wearing it in Lebanon, the dress has attracted significant interest across the Global North and Global South. The next section sketches the historical scene of the Muslim dress beyond the colonial confines of "Lebanon" while focusing on the West Asia North Africa region in preparation for the chapters to come.

The Hijab in the West Asia North Africa Region: Eurocentric Modernization

Across the West Asia North Africa region, the history of Muslim dress and its wearers has long been characterized by a deep entanglement with the history of colonial control and assault. Women's dress has particularly figured in this at the intersection of patriarchies and sexisms. Indeed, it is key to note here that what could be conceptualized as Muslim dress for men, often including covering the hair and most of the body, has too been made to disappear across the Arab-majority world in particular in deep entwinement with the region's colonization and "modernization." Yet, this disappearance did not transform into a public or political issue, nor into a serious question of academic, intellectual, or even Islamic debate and scholarship. Rather, it developed with seeming ease and is now largely standard and hegemonic across the region. Little scholarship has examined this change, a change that is of little if any political or social relevance today. The gendered and patriarchal structures in place are here key, greatly determining knowledge production and discourses. This book and this chapter remain constrained by this—even if at the request and alongside Muslim women themselves.

In Egypt under British rule, for example, Cromer and others led campaigns to "liberate" the Egyptian women from their hijab and Europeanize the nation through various social, cultural, legal, and institutional means (Ahmad 2001).

In Algeria, a brutal and systematic French effort worked to eradicate the Muslim dress where unveiling Algerian women became synonymous with French control over the land. Indeed, as the colonizers pursued "destroying the people's originality, and under instructions to bring about the disintegration, at whatever cost, of forms of existence likely to evoke a national reality directly or indirectly" the efforts, resources, and forces of French colonization seemed obsessed with eradicating the Muslim dress (Fanon 1994a: 37, 1969). Through techniques as varied as staged unveiling ceremonies, collective hijab burnings, media propaganda, and enforcing (European) Muslim family laws, the French pursued a systematic effort to avow modernity through the control of women's appearance and practice (Macmaster 2009; see Boittin, Firpo, and Church 2011). Accordingly, the movement against the hijab and its wearer was "one facet of a much broader and repressive attempt to expand state power in the name of a particular kind of modernity" loaded with patriarchy and gendered control (Cole 2012: 219). Here, it is important to highlight the sexual dimensions of this control and the fashioning of the colonized nation as a feminine space for the constructed masculine colonizer's (sexual) gratification. This colonial effort fixed the Muslim dress and objectified its wearer, stripping away "the plurality of meaning and performative outcomes" that had long imbued it for its forging into a "monolithic and static symbol" (Baldi 2017c: 44).

This aggression did not end with the end of formal colonization. Rather, it continued and persisted, rebranded under various banners and pursued through various actors (Ahmed 1993; Aljouhari 2007; Cooke 2010; Saadawi 1997; Shaaban 1995; Shaheed 2008).[15] In this movement, postcolonial nation-states emerged as the most powerful and aggressive agent where a (gendered) secular–religious binary emerged as an essential element of modernizing postcolonial nation building (Al-Ali 2000; Kandiyoti 1991).

A key example of such a movement is Turkey, the Ottoman Sultanate's previous home. There, starting but not ending with Atatürk, the hijab appeared in political discourse as one of the central elements in an all-encompassing project of refashioning Turkey into a glorious and powerful nation for the future (Kasaba 2010). At the core of this project was a pursuit of modernity explicitly understood as European and Western and a desire to distance the Turkish nation from Islam (Kasaba 2010). With this, a large question of public concern arose, with "Turkish" history, law, and morals all colliding to construct the Muslim dress as a sign of the past that needed to be overcome. Indeed, in the post-Ottoman moment, the creation of a modern Turkish state became powerfully dependent on the bodies of women expected to be the site of "the formation of the enlightened, modern Western-style nation Turkey aspires to be" (Saktanber and Çorbacioğlu 2008; Shively 2005: 46). From that moment on, those who chose the hijab were, in this frame, rejecting the state's governing ethos and violating its core principle: these were hazards and "violations that require state regulation" (Shively 2005: 46). Eventually, the dress emerged as a site of gendered nation-state control and affirmation as the newborn sovereign pursued a mimicry of its creator, spreading its control across its newly found citizenry and enforcing an agenda of modernity on and through the bodies of women.

In the 1980s, the tides began to change in Turkey as a result of complex geopolitical and internal shifts while state policy began to gradually pursue a project of religion's de-privatization and revalorization (Yeğenoğlu 2011). Yet, it must be made clear that the hijab stigma proved powerful and long persisted at the intersection of national belonging, women's emancipation, the security of the nation, and its planned progress and modernity, all constructed in opposition to Islam and the Muslim (Kasaba 2010; Shively 2005). Indeed, the hijab continued to be constructed and projected as a lacking, as a threat: a threat to the Kemalist legacy, the secular identity of the nation and, eventually, to the modern Turkish republic itself. In light of these realities, the relegitimization of the hijab was no smooth process (Turkmen 2012). It was only in 2010 that, for example, the ban on the hijab in universities was lifted, as new spaces where the dress was included complexly emerged in a manner that "belies attempts to delineate clearly bounded spaces, subjects, and ideologies [regarding the hijab] that have become vital to secular modern, nationalist, and orientalist representations" (Gökarıksel 2012: 4).

In another key example, Iran in the first half of the twentieth century witnessed a state-run all-encompassing program of Europeanizing the people by the *Shah*, with the hijab, again, at the center (Chehabi 1993). Through "sartorial social engineering" Iran, like Turkey, was taught by European colonizers that "government could form new people" and sought to erect the modern nation-state through processes of standardization and domination (Chehabi 1993; Sedghi 2007). To this end, "civil society" institutions were invented and put in place, with the "Lady's center" in Tehran being a prime example, producing a discourse of an interlinked women's emancipation and a shedding of "religious traditions" where dress figured prominently, if not primarily. Meanwhile, the state relentlessly introduced laws, official bodies, and various discourses pushing for a break with the Muslim and mimicry of the European (Chehabi 1993; Sedghi 2007). In either case, across the years, in Iran as in Turkey, the hijab stigma might appear to have been dismantled as the dress spread and reclaimed legitimacy and standing.

In accordance with this, particularly post-1936, systematic state efforts sought to construct the hijab as backwardness, as tradition, and as renounced religiosity: all in opposition with the required civility, modernity, and progress of Europe (Rajaee 2007; Zahedi 2007). Accordingly, the "modernizing discourse" adopted focused on the emancipatory effects of gender heterosocialization. Through its desegregation policies "the state sought to modernize Iranian women and transform them into publicly visible citizens" (Shahrokni 2013: 3). The modernization of women, the narrative claimed, stood deeply contingent upon unveiling as official policy and law sought out a shift of dress "to modernize Iranian women—or rather, an attempt to exhibit them as signifiers of Iran's modernity" (Shahrokni 2013: 4). In reflecting on the period of the Pahlavi regime, Chehabi (1993) summarizes thus: "'modernization' was literally staged, with directors who had not fully understood the play and actors who had not volunteered for their parts," in a movement erected on the "plight of ordinary people" for a trifling return (Chehabi 1993: 229).

These policies, going against much cultural custom and beliefs, stirred great controversy and were met with significant opposition from the Iranian masses. Albeit dependent on variables including geography and class—with urban populations, especially in Tehran, and the upper middle class appearing to relatively accept the new rules—many throughout the nation mobilized in multiple forms and contested the imposition (Chehabi 1993; Yeganeh 1993). The issue soon turned into a grave security one with police raids, shootings, and fatalities as the effort to enforce the new code of Western dress persisted (Amin 2002; Talachian 2004). Here, the state stood its ground and the crusade against the Muslim hijab was gradually institutionalized with the support of various non-state actors (Chehabi 1993; Talachian 2004). Eventually, constructed as a political contestation of the Pahlavi vision and program of returning Iran to its past (pre-Muslim) glory, the hijab-wearing woman was criminalized and greatly confined as European wear became the norm.

Ultimately, this was nothing but a potent manifestation of "Europeanization" forced on a population that attempted resistance, a resistance to be violently stifled by the colonially invented and sustained "sovereign" nation-state. While the question was not systematically or explicitly framed as being a question of women's emancipation, the state did present its all-encompassing policy using the language of rights and claimed that its actions were to relieve "the plight of ordinary people" through offering modernity and development (Chehabi 1993: 228). The result, as usually is in "modern" projects of "relief," was the wounding of large masses (particularly of women) and the breach of the most basic of rights.

When Ruhollah Khomeini overthrew the regime and established the Islamic Republic in 1979, the dogma changed. Then, an entire system of modesty was to be put in place and, at the center of it, laid the Iranian woman as "the hallmark of the new Shiite nation" (Mottahedeh 2008: 2). The matter did not stop there, and the hijab was actually used, transformed into an icon through which Iran would attempt to shatter the image of the downtrodden Eastern woman and present a hijab-wearing political activist engaged in military exercise, demonstrations, social debates, and public issues (Mottahedeh 2008). Of special relevance was the entry of the Iranian woman into the armed forces, presented to the world through a media overflowing with *chadoris* (women wearing an Iranian-style loose black cloak) undertaking military training. Nationally, the hijab became law and all women were required to cover their hair, or face legal repercussions. Here, the gendered European fixing of the dress under the modern state persisted as the state sought control (Baldi 2017c; Sedghi 2007). Across the years, in Iran as in Turkey, the hijab stigma might appear to have been dismantled as the dress spread and reclaimed legitimacy and standing.

In Tunisia, as an Arab example, a highly similar process unfolded building on the long colonial effort to push Tunisian women to abandon the hijab. Indeed, after "independence," the state adopted a modernizing project and pursued an anti-hijab agenda as the dress was constructed as being in contrast with the desired and needed modernity. The state in this followed the colonizer and adopted the strictest of measures enforced with significant violence and intolerance: "during this time wearing hijab in public, urban areas was unwise" (Hawkins 2011). Indeed, as the Tunisian nation was being erected, its orientation was clearly "the West" and the anti-hijab policy specifically sought "to show the West that Tunisia was committed to secularism and democracy" (Cotton 2006: 3). In this respect, throughout post-independence Tunisian history the hijab has been constructed as, fundamentally, "a physical manifestation of Islamist support," threatening both state and nation and requiring strict control and prevention (Cotton 2006: 4). Throughout, "Tunisian women" have been forced to navigate these conditions at the political, social, and domestic levels where both "localized structures of patriarchy" and Westernizing modernizing ones continue to aggress their experiences as they pursue "liberation beyond emancipation and secularization" and the alienating "forced feminism" they are pushed into by the Tunisian state (Cotton 2006: 37). Since then, and until the Tunisian uprising in 2011, an anti-hijab public, policy, and legal structure remained in place with the pursuit of modernization where "within the Tunisian state ideology of modernity, hijab by its very nature cannot be modern. It is something different" by virtue of being something "Islamic" (Hawkins 2011: 52). After the 2011 uprising, a sense that this has abated has significantly emerged, albeit much contestation and disruption persists.

Another key example is that of Egypt where a powerful unveiling trend during the first half of the twentieth century was inspired by the discourse of modernity, as unveiling became "an emblem of an era of new hopes and desires and aspirations for modernity" as the hijab became a rare sight, even in rural areas (Ahmed 2014: 39).[16] This, as ever, was significantly a continuation of the colonial phase where Muslim dress was constructed as backward and oppressive (Ahmad 2001). During this time, the hijab-wearing woman was stigmatized as a regressive person who refused to modernize, as the colonized, and then the postcolonial, nation pursued a semblance to Europe and a distance from the Muslim. This shift, data indicates, greatly unfolded through the introduction of European fashion, with newly introduced clothing stores across urban centers invading and controlling the Egyptian market. With this alteration in the norms and habits of dress, the hijab was affirmed and reaffirmed as an object of "vulnerability or promiscuity," while veiled women were increasingly harassed in the streets at the intersection of sexism and "modernization" (Baron 1989). The important role of the privatization and control of both sexuality and religion under the modern postcolonial state, as Mahmood (2012, 2015) elaborates, is here essential.[17] Consequently, and in a short time frame, the dress gradually disappeared from schools, institutions, and the public sphere (Baron 1989; Fay 2012).

Yet, this was not to last, as it did not last in Turkey and Iran. According to Ahmed (2014), Muslim dress returned in the second half of the twentieth century after multiple phases of its erasure, including a phase where the state and its Arab nationalist ideology heavily intervened. At this point, the era of unveiling was "being quietly erased from Muslim memory, and even Muslim history," to be portrayed as "a secular age" that the nation had awoken, and repented, from (Ahmed 2014: 74). These nations are said to have therefore come full circle: "All women (Muslim and non-Muslim) were veiled before 1925. By the 1950s, a veiled woman in the Egyptian cities was a rarity. In the 1970s, the veil started reappearing in the streets, but it was by then a strictly Muslim product. At the dawn of the twenty-first century, unveiled women became a one-off" (Saleh 2010: 34). Here too, one is left with the impression that the Muslim dress has been relegitimized, normalized, even esteemed and rendered a requirement within the contemporary cultures of Muslim-majority countries.[18]

Based on this, the contemporary history of the hijab within the West Asia North Africa region can be characterized as an assaulting violent history of Eurocentric colonization and postcolonial modernization where the "Islamic" is systematically aggressed and abjected. Most importantly, the examples presented here illustrate how the newly established postcolonial nation-states of the region both sought to mimic and continue the legacy of the Imperial powers as they pursued the construction of their citizenry in the image of the imagined civilized modern European.

In the contemporary moment, this assault on the Muslim is standardly argued to have ended as both "modernization" and state building have departed from their strictly Eurocentric and colonial legacies and formations while Islam has "resurged." Based on this book's arguments, I will return to this narrative and the cases outlined here in the coming chapters as well as in this book's conclusion to complexify the position of Islam and the Muslim in the contemporary Arab-majority and Muslim-majority worlds and the standard narratives dominant both within and outside of academia today.

3

Racialization at the Intersection of the Local and the Global: From an Expulsion from Citizenry to Dehumanization

This chapter sets out to explore the hijab-wearing woman's construction as an Other based on conversations with hijab-wearing women themselves. I will group the experienced characteristics and traits shared by this project's participants into two sets: those of an "Arabo-Muslim difference in excess" and those of "belatedness"—each explored in one of this chapter's two sections. Together, they show how the hijab-wearing woman is Othered at the intersection of the local and the global through an expulsion out of Lebanese citizenry as well as an expulsion out of the modern human.[1] Based on this analysis, I hold that the visibly Muslim woman in Lebanon is racialized and subjected to anti-Muslim racism.

Experienced Exclusion from Citizenry as an Arabo-Muslim Difference in Excess

I will begin with what appears a straightforward note: the prime association of any hijab-wearing woman in Lebanon, according to participants, is the assumption of her being a Muslim. While this might appear as unproblematic to many, it was expressed in many interviews with much disapproval and irritation. For a significant period of time, I had some difficulty understanding the objection to this association and could not comprehend why participants grudgingly opposed people counting the hijab-wearing woman as a Muslim. Eventually, I realized that the issue was not in the assumption itself but in its persistent corollary. As Naila, a young upper-class Shia translator living in the Southern suburb of Beirut (Dahieh), and an older Shia participant in a focus group in this same suburb clearly explained,

> Lebanon is different from all others: plenty of sects and religions and all. And the social, there's a ladder: people hierarchised, and are perceived that way. Regardless of whether this is right or wrong. So where the hijab comes from, what religion it belongs to, this definitely influences the way the hijab-wearing woman is perceived. On this ladder of hierarchy, the hijab-wearing woman is ... she's ... this is not something I normally like to talk about ... but you have Christians and Muslims and the hijab means Muslim. And then Muslim means follower of that [hand gestures to indicate inferior] group. (Naila)
>
> Hijab means Muslim, and they don't want any of this. That is why we have all this [discrimination]. (Markaz focus group 2)

Being visibly associated with Islam was a deficiency. Participants were all religious subjects and they were nothing but religious subjects—subjected to religion. Indeed, they were subjected to the lowest religion on the hierarchy today under globalized modernity—Islam. Accordingly, the very identification of the hijab-wearing woman as Muslim was where the problematization of the hijab begins as being associated with Islam meant being placed low on the hierarchy. It was, at its core, a series of disavowals: disavowed from being Christian, disavowed from resembling the Christian, and, consequently, disavowed from desirability under the "Western-centric/Christian-centric" world order. Naila aptly situated this "problem" within the Lebanese context: a country birthed as a Christian home in the East and institutionalized on Muslim's inferiority.

The issue participants expressed was not just in Islam as a deficiency, it was in the hijab, as practiced Islam, as a *problem*. What might appear, at first, as a frustration of being identified as Muslim thus becomes clear: it was being an excess of Islam by (just) being a hijab-wearing woman. Reem and Madawi, two older lower-class Sunni Beirutis, described it thus:

> **Madawi:** Like now with the whole terrorism thing too, they're scaring people. That someone hijab-wearing is too committed, a zealot ...
> **Reem:** They simply don't like Islam! [Reem and Madawi]

The rendering of Muslims as an extremist threat and the resulting assault on visibly Muslim women (Magearu 2018; Parvez 2011) clearly echoed in Lebanon. As this excerpt indicates, it was a question of zealousness and of being "too committed." Islam had become an adjective—Islamicness and Muslimness—and a quantifiable good, a light dose of which could be digested but a stronger one becomes too much to handle.

Explaining how her professor at a university in Hadath near Beirut had studied in France and was "so influenced by that culture," Sara, who is a young middle-class Sunni, for example, stressed that her professor's problem was with the hijab as a practiced Muslim object and recounted stories of his overt expression of refusal and disdain of "Muslim culture" and/or practices:

> When I first put [the hijab] on, he expressed resentment, very bluntly. Like he would come to me and say: "what have you done to yourself, what is this," and all that. And then, after a while, I told him that I stopped shaking hands [with foreign men] and he said that it was too much: "you keep deteriorating," he said, "instead of developing, forward, you keep getting worse." (Sara)

Sara went on to assert that his issue related to "the Lebanon he wanted," a "want" that made this kind of treatment "quite common" among faculty members "trained in Europe." The global connected and entwined with the local, participants' shared experiences and thoughts made clear. It was, I would suggest, the Westernized elite (Grosfoguel 2016) performing its colonizing role. In this role, the imagined horizon of Lebanon and its construction as a beacon of (French) civility loomed large.

Already, by simply wearing the hijab and becoming visibly Muslim, a Muslim presence, participants seemed to enter a grim space of being in excess *because of* their Muslimness. In that space, they would be constructed as an object of dislike, an object of repulsion, and an object in decline. Additionally, they risked falling into being an excess of excess. Not shaking hands with the hijab was "too much."

Rima, a middle-class Shia participant from Beirut, was among those who echoed this:

> Let me give you an example, I wear this [fashionable hijab] usually, but sometimes if I'm just jumping to go somewhere I quickly put on the *khaliji* cloak. The same person, Christian, when I was wearing this [fashionable hijab] they were Ok with me. When I went in wearing the cloak, she said please don't come this way. She said: "please don't come this way, please you look too Muslim like this." That's exactly what she said. It's even worse than that. Once I was putting on *Oud* [the perfume, with the hijab], someone said: "that is too Muslim, please don't put that smell on." (Rima)

Rima, working in Beirut's central district at a UN agency, the "first and only hijab-wearing woman" as she explained, came from an upper-middle-class background and had to live the hijab's marking: if it is accompanied with social practice, if it becomes too "covering," if it is worn with an Arab perfume, it becomes "too much." It should be noted here that while Rima spoke of being "accepted" in her fashionable hijab, the shift to a rejection so extreme as to reach a formal and urgent request of change reveals that the case was one of tolerance, rather than of acceptance (see Brown 2009). But tolerance can only go so far in the modern space of metropolitan Beirut. The question accordingly appeared to be one of difference—a difference from an ideal and imagined modern liberal secular subject where geography becomes secondary under the globalized Eurocentric modernity that renders hijab-wearing women an inferiorized excess.

Shariati (1986) explains that this question of excess is crucial—a key means through which colonization works "to overcome the influence of religion" where a movement against "fanaticism" was invented and propagated so that the religious may be "crushed and humiliated" to forcefully produce a state where "the one who identifies himself with it feels also crushed and humiliated" (Shariati 1986: 63). It was, as Sayyid (2014) has well elaborated, rendering the Muslim subject position impossible. And so, indeed, were participants.

This anxiety permeated the Lebanese sphere, and was exacerbated by the hijab's Arab connotations, as Rima went on to elaborate:

> Look, we can't deny that the hijab is not yet part of the image of the Lebanese woman ... We are hardly an Arab state: we are a state with an Arab face. There are portions of the Lebanese who don't see themselves as Arabs but as Phoenicians. There are many Lebanese who if you ask them about who they are, they wouldn't say Arab. They wouldn't even accept to be compared to Arabs. Like an Arab like the Syrian or the Iraqi or anyone like that. We are the Lebanese, the Phoenicians, we are very different from all Arab countries. We live among them, but we are different. And this continues to exist. And this isn't just about Muslim and Christian, I know Muslim families who don't accept the hijab. (Rima)

> There are stereotypes, expectations, she's hijab-wearing woman so they think she is interested in eastern things or stuff. But it's not true! (Marah)

> [The Lebanese woman] is that person who's ... first ... they think you have coloured eyes, super pretty, very funny, very outgoing, partying all night ... The Lebanese is coloured, hair, eyes, they are different from the other Arabs, they are very fashionable. This is the ideal Lebanese woman you hear about all over. The hijab-wearing woman is [outside]. I don't know why ... I guess it's from the mandate. It's the French system, that we're not like the Arabs, that we are developed, that we are Phoenicians, that we are all these things and not that. It must be that. (Maya)

Looking back at these quotes, I am intrigued by the oppositions participants drew and, then, drew on. While I had made no mention of "race," skin color, or eye color, and no mention of ethnicity (i.e., being Arab or Phoenician), I found that many participants referred to such categories when trying to tell of mainstream Lebanese society's construction of the hijab. To understand the dress, it appeared, I needed to think of phenotypes and ethnicities as these questions consistently made their way into interviews and focus groups despite the fact they did not figure in interview schedule or plans, not even in my own expectations.

The entry of phenotypical features complicated my understanding of the circulating discourses and indicated the racialization of the hijab-wearing woman as an equivalent to a phenotypical category, which stands in contrast to that of non-Arabness: lighter skin and colored eyes. Eventually, it appeared that, for participants, the will to distance Lebanon from a particular set of races, ethnicities, and cultures was central in the problematization of the hijab and the ensuing rejection of the hijab-wearing woman as the country pursued its colonial invention under global Eurocentric modernity. In this sense, to explain why the hijab-wearing woman is not the "ideal Lebanese woman" as imagined by the larger Lebanese community, participants drew upon the very imagined nature of the Lebanese nation as non-Arab, Western looking, "progressive," "civilized," and "liberated" (see Kaufman 2004; Maasri 2016). While the hijab-wearing woman is an Arab, a Lebanese is not. At least, she is not "that Arab." It was this differentiation that extended into a differentiation between the Syrian and the Iraqi, for example, on the one hand, and the Lebanese, on the other hand, which made the hijab-wearing woman an outsider to the small country. The persistent imagined nature of the Lebanese nation as a secular liberated beacon for the Arab-Muslim world to follow accordingly here intersected with global discourses of Eurocentric empire and white superiority.

Further, this phenotypical distinction is linked to an ethnic and cultural belonging: from Euro-American fashion to (most specifically Western-style) parties. These, in turn, are contrasted with another ethnic–cultural belonging: an interest in "Eastern stuff" (which participants were swift to reject). Accordingly, this juxtaposition of the hijab-wearing woman, on the one hand, with her Arab phenotype, ethnicity, and culture, and the ideal Lebanese woman, on the other hand, with her Western(ized) phenotype, ethnicity, and culture reveals a major nexus of the hijab-wearing woman's lived experiences. Consequently, the hijab connoted both loyalty and belonging to the Arab East, which was automatically thought to negate the belonging to the imagined West as well as to Lebanon. Consequently, the hijab connoted the (rejected) placing of Lebanon within the Arab world and its distancing from the Western one. Here, just as the hijab was produced as a symbol of Otherness in the West, so too it was produced as a symbol of Otherness in Lebanon. It is in light of this that stories such as Maha's, a young Sunni from Beirut, made sense to me:

> And then at university [we were looked down upon], and then when I did an M.A I did it in *Ashrafieh*. We used to hear a lot of talking. A lot of scorn and sneering. When they first saw that we were hijab-wearing women, there were a few of us [hijab-wearing women] in class who came together, the Christian girls were really bothered. At first, they would not talk to us at all. When we try and talk to them, they would speak to us in disgust [chucks]. Yeah … it stayed that way. We tried to break the barriers many times, but unfortunately, that's how human beings are. Whenever we would want to do a research project they would go like: "Oh you want to do a research project in Arabic, of course, right? Are there books in Arabic? Are there references in Arabic? Arabic is backwardness!" And Arabic this and Arabic that. (Maha)

Ashrafieh is a predominantly Christian region. Maha went on to explain how her exclusion in Ashrafieh was not one she was unfamiliar with in wider Beirut, but it surely was more intense. Ashrafieh, it seems, was more aggressive in preserving itself from the hijab-wearing woman and more powerful in enforcing its imagined image. I will return to this heterogeneity in the following chapters to critically engage with its workings.

The assumption that hijab-wearing women students would want to study in Arabic (which was the case in this instance, as Maha explained) and the fact they were scorned for it reveal the constant production of the hijab-wearing woman as "Arabness." It was, I would claim, a question of threat to the difference: the presence of the hijab-wearing woman in the university and their practices, especially in a majority-Christian region, threatened the space, pushing it from being a sphere of sophisticated Francophonie into one of Arabness as backwardness. The global powerful inferiorization of "Arabs" (Massad 2015) had a clear reverberation in Lebanon. The hijab-wearing women, who "dared not" enroll in the university until they knew they could go together, were the embodiment of this hazard: a source of disgust, of worry, and of threat.

Throughout, the multiple, varied, and complex reasons for which Lebanese women chose to wear the hijab appeared irrelevant and inconsequential in participants' experiences of mainstream Lebanese society. Eventually, the gendered patriarchal misogynist and sexist European mobilization of clothing to operate "a visible differentiation, a boundary, a clear-cut dividing line, between citizens and foreigners and between the different classes of citizens" in continuation with a long Christian/secular tradition (Baldi 2017b: 678) appeared to have been globalized, with Eurocentric modernity producing a racialization in the Global South entwined with a persistent colonially structured national identity. Just as the hijab-wearing woman had been produced as the "enemy within" across the west and just as France's Indigènes de la République have been excluded from citizenry despite often being formal citizens, the hijab-wearing woman was produced as the enemy within Lebanon despite formally being a citizen and regardless of it.

In Turkey, Yel and Nas (2014) posit that a "peculiar image of Islamic lifestyle, which is hierarchically positioned lower than the representations of secular lifestyle" continues to permeate Turkish society to structure rampant anti-Muslim inequalities (Yel and Nas 2014: 569). They accordingly argue for the reading of the ongoing modernist, secularist, and capitalist Turkish project—regardless and despite of the Justice and Development Party (AKP) rule for many years—as one of systematic anti-Muslim racism in the cultural sphere and beyond. Accordingly, they affirm Islamophobia's prevalence in the Muslim-majority country where the wearers of Muslim dress are relegated to second-class citizenry and "are considered as the signifier of Islam and the anxiety that stems from it" (Yel and Nas 2014: 578; also see Auerbach 2017; Eum 2017). Similar dynamics seemed at play in Lebanon where the production of the postcolonial nation-state's patriarchy and sexism mapped the nation's invention on the bodies of women, and at their expense.

What first appeared to be a straightforward association of the hijab with Islam and with the Arab comes to represent a huge branding of inferiority for hijab-wearing women—a branding they tire to struggle against. This branding was first imbricated in the global order of inferiorizing Islam and the Muslim as well as in the colonial founding myth of Lebanon and its identity. The association of the hijab in contemporary Lebanon with an Arab profile, which implies a phenotype, an ethnicity, and a culture, consequently, racializes the hijab-wearing woman as an inferior Other and forms the site on which her exclusion and marginalization play out. In this sense, the argument I wish to take from this is that the hijab-wearing woman experiences a production as a Muslim excess and as an Arab: a *difference*, an Otherness, in an inferiorization that must be understood within the attempt at distancing Lebanon from particular (disavowed) affiliations. This, in turn, gains depth and meaning in view of Lebanon's founding myth and imagined colonial identity within contemporary global Eurocentric modernity/coloniality.

The Lebanese civil war of 1991 ended with the *Tai'f* Accord establishing a new sectarian equilibrium in the country where power was to be "equally" divided between the Muslims and the Christians. These post-Taif changes to Lebanon and the ensuing limiting of Christian dominance with the rise of Sunni and Shia political and economic force have not changed the colonial order and the country's imagination. The visibly Muslim signifier was still not Lebanese, and its wearer was still a hazard. The colonial construction withstood change in material and political conditions to strive despite them in deep entwinement with the contemporary global order. Having established religion as the problem, this aggression eventually revealed itself as an adamant phenomenon beyond national politics' sphere of control within a global order of Eurocentric dominance.

Experienced Expulsion from the Modern Human through Muslim Belatedness

The Arabo-Muslim difference in excess discussed above does not encompass the entirety of the experienced Othering of the hijab-wearing woman; there were many more traits, many more detailed tangible traits, that emerged in the field. Through a selection of illustrative quotes, taken from a vast number of interviews, I will try to draw some out in the coming paragraphs:

> [They say] backward, retard, know nothing, [stuck] in history, if she speaks then it's like "Oh shame on you why are you speaking." What, do I not have a voice? (Maha)

> In Lebanon, as a hijab-wearing woman, for example, there are assumptions that have to do with hygiene. There are people who think the hijab-wearing woman does not care for herself, or her looks, does not go to aesthetic and care places. In Dahieh ... like there are people who have these ideas, I go to a place in Ashrafieh to take care of myself. I am giving you details about my life but it's useful. As soon as they see a hijab-wearing woman entering the [beauty] institute, it's an anomaly. They all stare. They start asking [questions]. There are people who really don't accept. They ask the institute owner "Why is she here?" She is my friend, she told me. They keep saying; "Why is she coming here?" (Rima)

"They all stare." They do not ask her questions; they ask the beauty institute owner. They do not engage her in speech, they engage the institute owner. In Ashrafieh, with her, all they do is stare. But the stare was more than sufficient. Loaded with import and directed at a body already "saturated with significance," they were no different from the stare directed at the Black body: "not one of nonengagement but rather one that already positions the black body as unworthy" (Bogues 2010: 44). These stares were therefore not expressive but productive. It was her production as unbefitting, as unclean, as a stranger in the land of beauty and self-care. As Nadine, a young Sunni from Beirut living in an upper-class urban neighborhood, explained,

> And then, if they see it [the hijab], they will have these stereotypes: these are ignorant people, these are poor people. They would assume less educated, less achieving too. Someone whose priorities are her husband and kids, which is not necessarily a bad thing! Someone who is old-minded, traditional, not modern, not progressive. (Nadine)

> The Lebanese society, I think, really sees it as a symbol of oppression. This is the only word, like I always really feel that people have this way of looking at it. That it's oppressive. Like they ask you: "why did you put it on" and "was it your parents or your husband?" Like it's always this thing that is necessary and oppressive. This is how I see people looking at it. They express that she's oppressed. And you feel it's full of mockery a bit: these are the people still in their cocoons, and stuff like that. (Sara)

"Your parents or your husband?" Sara who lived in Tarik El-Jdide, a predominately Sunni Muslim region, echoed Nadine's argument. Despite her residence and work in a region often claimed to be the archetypal (lower-class) Sunni area of Beirut there was no choice of her being the one who "put it on." Autonomy was not her trait in a clear echo of global discourses on the hijab as an object of oppression, subjugation, patriarchy, and proclaimed "Islamic misogyny" (see Grace 2004; Okin 1999; O'Neill et al. 2015). Often, participants told me how people they met would rarely believe the hijab to be their choice: from parents to partners, the agency was never to be found in the hijab-wearing woman herself. As a (global) symbol of oppression and subjugation (Brayson 2019; Magearu 2018) the hijab could not be reconciled with agency and will: those belonged to the modern subject while the hijab belonged to the premodern self that is ruled by tradition. In this sense, the hijab-wearing woman was always already ascribed a position of subjugation, weakness, and humiliation.

The word "modern" in these quotes is not my translation. Participants used it, expressing it in either English or French. Indeed, the word "modern" emerged and reemerged, in both these colonial languages, to delineate what the hijab was not.

> A2: There will always be that understanding, maybe outside of our community a little, that the one wearing a abaya, or wearing a hijab like this [points to conservative dress], that she is unlikely to be

>
> educated, or has a career, or is cultured. She is treated as that ignorant simple old lady. We really feel this, even inside of our society.
>
> A4: The hijab-wearing woman is seen as backward, has nothing to do with civilization, development or progress or culture. Hijab-wearing woman means limited culture.
>
> A3: Well put, limited culture. This is even in our environment, regardless of Lebanese society. Take your son to a doctor, see how he speaks. We live this thing. He speaks to you as a *hajje*, as an ignorant woman, he speaks in that way. If, later, for some reason, he discovers you have that [good] job or you do that [important thing], his way of speaking changes. It becomes different. Once I asked a doctor a question and he said: "Like the question you are asking me, now if I answer it, will you understand?"
>
> A1: "Do you know?" I left a doctor for that word. … [It was] 10 years ago now. He said: "Like, what can I explain to you? Do you know?" I was in a abaya then. (Markaz focus group 2)

As this focus group with mostly middle-aged Shia women conducted at a Muslim NGO center in Beirut's southern suburb reveals, by pushing any and every hijab-wearing woman into an Othered collective, practicing Muslim women felt that mainstream Lebanon as well as their own "Muslim societies" have a clear understanding of who they are: they all, always, belong to that Arabo-Muslim difference in excess and an accompanying clear set of traits. Uncivilized, oppressed, dirty, unclean, smelling, stupid, unlawful, monolingual, lacking education, illiterate, monolithic, barbaric, and backward were some of the traits echoing, in various forms and shapes, throughout interviews. Indeed, transcripts contained all the narratives one could think of: from intelligence, civility, and merit to hygiene and "neatness." The hijab-wearing woman manifestly experienced a clear set of descriptors: derogatory and loaded with offense. The ensuing wounding imbued transcripts, notes, and the direction of my work: from participants in tears to participants at a loss for words, passing by women who could not forget what was said to them "10 years ago now," their being was subjected to massive Eurocentric modern/colonial wounding.

The majority of the hijab-wearing woman's characteristics had to do with the imagined past: these were traits from the proclaimed premodern past, a past the hijab-wearing woman was situated as belonging to and resembling under a hegemonic global order of linear time and (Eurocentric) progress (Vázquez 2009). Eventually, they were words from the fallacious imagined precolonial past thought to be lacking in bathrooms, formal education, freedom, and science later exported to salvage the East from its claimed ignorance and darkness. From being unclean to needing education, I would argue that "backward" was not a trait, among others, but was rather the trait that incorporated all others. It was Bhabha's (2004) time lag in its full might.

Eurocentric modernity can be thought of as a project of "the redrawing of geographical borders and their simultaneous transformation into temporal stages of rationality and Modernity" (Bhambra 2007; Mignolo and Escobar 2013: 224). The result is situating colonial Europe in a locus of enunciation, which allows it to fashion itself as the apex of reason and as the present while the rest of the world drowns in darkness and backwardness (Mignolo 2011a, 2011b). This Otherness, this difference, becomes henceforth negatively marked as the before, as the less, as the dispensable. The result includes the creation of "ontological differences hierarchically organized in colonial forms as part of the modern civilizational order" (Maldonado-Torres 2017: 123). In this sense, an ontological colonial difference as an outside "that is constructed by the inside (civilized, imperial)" is established by a process of hierarchical Othering. Thinking through this colonial difference, retellings such as these came to make sense:

S3: There is that thing of "oh, hijab-wearing woman and you have a Facebook page?" But what is wrong with it!
S4: Or the hijab-wearing woman who speaks English!
S2: Or being a niqabi and going to a restaurant, they think all this is not ok. But why?! (Saida mosque focus group)
W: Well first, it [the hijab] gives this back-off message. One, because it's associated with sadness and grief, you'd feel it's someone strict. Before you see them or get to know them or even look at the face you feel this is a strict person, frigid, has many walls around him. That the circle is big, in terms of stay-away. And then there is this horrific contrast walking in the street … it's very powerful … it's something black and long … not just black … even if you're wearing full black, you feel like you're different not like everyone else just as a colour, so what if it's a colour and a shape … the shape is very different … (Maya)

In the Saida mosque focus group—constituted by a combination of older and younger women with one participant wearing the niqab—I was told of how Muslim dress was woundingly experienced as *different*, as rejected. If a hijab-wearing woman represents a historical "pre," a backwardness, it is only normal for people to express surprise when she displays knowledge or tells of her (even basic) use of "modern technology": the example of communication and social media (Facebook) is a stark illustration. Further, it was this logic that explains the situating of the hijab-wearing woman as the stay-at-home housewife with no career, no self-fulfillment, and consequently no "joy." Such was the presumed premodern norm. It was only normal that it appeared to be assumed for someone made to live such a life to be "frigid." The sexist assumptions inherent here become evident as anti-Muslim racism's gendered nature emerges and reemerges. This *frigidity*, it is worth noting, was not unique to Lebanon. Bowen (2008), for example, has recorded a similar sense in France as a key element of the white French citizens' reactions to hijab-wearing women wearing black in public spaces as participants' experiences echoed across north and south.

> They think they [hijab-wearing women] are vulgar, they eat with their hands, don't speak French … they [the Christians] like really really are not exposed to Arabic language and things like that … it's seen as a taboo … the Christians, they stereotype the hijab-wearing woman like that … (Marah)

While one might think that there is no reason for Marah, a young Sunni middle-class Beiruti woman, to jump from vulgarity and descriptions of "primitive" habits to an issue with the Arabic language, she did: a clear example of coloniality's rendering of Europe as the real and civilized and the Arab as the negation of this where language is central. Lebanon's age-old colonial invention as a beacon of European "civilization" into the Arab East haunted the hijab-wearing woman in various forms and at various scales.

Clearly, such is only possible in light of a very specific understanding of time and of the past. Fanon (2001) explained,

> Colonialism is not simply content to impose its rule upon the present and the future of a dominated country. Colonialism is not satisfied merely with holding a people in its grip and emptying the native's brain of all form and content. By a kind of perverted logic, it turns to the past of the oppressed people, and distorts, disfigures, and destroys it. (Fanon 2001: 209)

Here, it was this distorted, disfigured, and destroyed past that was made to haunt the hijab-wearing woman and powerfully structure perceptions and practices. This haunting is particularly powerful given hegemonic narratives of secularism as Eurocentric modernity has long identified humanity with "being secular bourgeois" while Christianity "looms in the background" (Maldonado-Torres 2014a, 2008; Mignolo 2009b: 14).[2]

Leen, a middle-aged and middle-class Sunni participant, told me that even her best attempts at the most fashionable hijab in the northern city of Tripoli could not be tolerated by those around her: as long as it was identifiably Muslim, it was rejected. Instead, she was advised to "wear a hat" and would consistently be told: "You don't need to go into religion that much, there is no need for that. Stay normal like people." The hijab fell outside of the natural, the normal. Indeed, within the context of linear time and Arabo-Muslim belatedness, the hijab-wearing woman's inferiorization meant it fell out of the modern human:

> The hijab in general, in general, for those people who are not committed, they see the hijab as backwardness. As soon as they see a hijab-wearing woman, she is classified as a backward person. When they speak to her, and start knowing she is cultured and knows things, they get shocked and don't believe it. That she has a thinking mind, no way. But why? We are human beings, like you. (Maha)
>
> They see the one without a full hijab, she might be normal, like other humans, not from another planet [laughs]. (Fatima)
>
> I would love for them to realise that I am not a human being that different from what you are … that I am like you. But it's done for them, they consider that I am not like them. I do not dress like them, I do not speak like them, I do not act like them. You know? (Hanin)

Fatima is a middle-aged Shia Muslim activist living in Beirut's Shia-majority southern suburb while Hanin is a middle-aged lower-class Shia living in the southern town of Haret Saida. Maha was younger than both, Sunni, and middle-class Beiruti. The difference between Shia and Sunni participants across social classes in lived experiences of discrimination and subjugation appeared negligible as stories echoed across Lebanon's divides.

The layer upon layer of racialized Othering amassed to produce an experienced marking of colossal wounding: a dehumanization. In this sense, these experiences were not (only) lived as expulsion from the potential of being Lebanese: it was an expulsion from being modern and, by consequence, from being fully human. It was the production of a clear "them" and "you." The "you" was an Otherness, an Otherness of inferiority and lacking in humanity: a lesser mind, lesser ethics, lesser knowledge, lesser culture, and so on. The resulting wounded consciousness is one of difference, of being from another planet and from a different world. It was the marking, the consciousness of their subject position. It was being made to feel "like someone else, like not a human like them."

Beginning with the expulsion of the Arabo-Muslim from the Lebanese imaginary in deep entwinement with global discourses of Muslim inferiority this lived experience swiftly arrived at its expulsion of a belated Arabo-Muslim excess from humanity. The rejection needed to be understood under a different paradigm than the one offered by the literature in analyzing Lebanese identity and identity politics within the frames of sectarianism, it appeared, and needed to be situated within dehumanizing global Eurocentric modernity/coloniality.

In line with the conceptualization of racism as a "global hierarchy of superiority and inferiority along the line of the human" (Grosfoguel 2016: 10) and based on the discussion presented throughout this chapter, I posit here that the hijab-wearing woman's Othering was a dehumanizing racialization and an articulation of anti-Muslim racism in the country.

In this respect, participants' experiences were those of a sealed subject position: a religious premodern self with a specific habitus located at the very bottom of the hierarchy, at the very bottom of the colonial difference and subject to anti-Muslim racism. This was a position participants clearly abhorred, expressing pain and cynicism; they felt they had little power in changing the status quo as they expressed their intent to continue trying. Nevertheless, the ruling sense here is that of the hijab-wearing woman, as long as she is hijab-wearing, constructed as a lack in humanity that cannot be mended: it was not only a question of things they did not have but a question of things they could not have as a consequence of their totalitarian racialization:

> A3: Now there is more acceptance yes, things have changed from what they were yes, now despite their beliefs, like they [still] consider us to be backward, retarded in this hijab, or not, whatever. They accept us.
> A1: It's only because of politics!
> A3: But there are still many places where the hijab-wearing woman would go and she would draw looks. To this day.
> A1: We would definitely draw looks.
> Me: Is she still considered as different?
> A1: Oh, I did not say she is not seen as different! But they acknowledge her existence, that, yes, there are hijab-wearing women who exist.
> A4: And the looks are different.
> A1: Even the abaya [is sometimes acknowledged to exist].
>
> (Markaz focus group 2)

> They think like they can't come close to me. That I am associated with terrorism or something. This has happened to me. I had friends, like from another sect, and they thought this. They stayed away from me. In Lebanon, you get this all the time. They think that they can't come near us so that they don't become contaminated. Even the parents, they think like this and they tell their kids to stay away. It happened to me. Of course, this influences everything [in life]! (Bana)

... but if I imagine myself walking in there [Lebanese government building] in a abaya, I would feel it would be ... VERY ... odd ... very. Even if people appear OK with it, you'd feel ... like ... like when I told you about having one hijab-wearing woman only in a group of 25 people you'd feel like one out of the whole circle and I would be, like very happy if someone can do this because it doesn't take away your qualifications or anything, but it's a very strong ... contrast ... exactly ... the contrast is huge. (Maya)

The abovementioned quotes from Maya, an upper-middle-class urban planner from the south of Lebanon now living in Beirut, and Bana, a young lower-class university student from the north of Lebanon, illustrate the wounding sense of *difference* that has become a part of the hijab-wearing woman's daily life. The focus group with middle-aged and older Shia women with a majority lower-class and two middle-class participants further evidenced the commonality across age groups, sects, regions, and social classes. Surely, this is not claiming a homogeneity of experience but is rather arguing for a commonality that forms the basis of a shared experience, a shared dehumanization that cuts across divides under a powerful anti-Muslim racism.

Within the UK, Zempi and Chakraborti (2014, 2015) have identified hijab-wearing women as "'ideal subjects' against whom to enact Islamophobic attacks" specifically for their "perceived difference" (Chakraborti and Zempi 2012: 276; see Mondon and Winter 2017). "Neither seen nor heard," they conclude that Islamophobic attacks on women in Muslim dress produce harm "far more than ordinary crimes," where "it is victim's intrinsic identity that is targeted" as the wearer and their family are pushed into a detrimental state of isolation and exclusion (Zempi and Chakraborti 2015: 53). Allen (2015) similarly discusses the "demarcation of difference" that plays out differently in different spheres to explore the gendered aspects of Islamophobia, offering a grounded analysis of hijab-wearing women's lived experiences. This *difference* was not limited to a Western context but extended to the eastern Mediterranean and Arab-majority worlds. In Lebanon too, the *muhajaba* experiences an agonizing predicament imbricated in the global order of inferiorizing the Muslim as well as the colonial founding myth of Lebanon and its identity.

Here, the hijab-wearing woman's racialization pervades and looms, felt and encountered in myriad ways and in myriad places. Such is the impact of anti-Muslim racism: the Muslim signifier's delineation was so hegemonic that many of its elements were internalized by the hijab-wearing woman's body. In this sense, her branding has become a structuring component of a "wounded habitus": being different is not something the hijab-wearing woman realizes by being hailed as different; it is not something the hijab-wearing woman comes to discover by being interpellated as less, it is something she has come to sense and internalize irrespective of direct external stimulus. The hijab-wearing woman, raised and socialized in Lebanon, is not like Fanon who comes to discover his Blackness: her Muslim visibility has long been inscribed into her. This habitus of difference and lack by women becomes unavoidable and tyrannical from a young age.

There, she was joined by those who resemble her: marked as closer to specific racialized and oppressed groups and, by consequences, as farther away from specific privileged groups:

Fadia: Outside [the committed community], oh yes [there are assumptions]. In the company [I work at], they all have that idea that all Muslims are the *m'atarin*, they have no money, each one gets 15 kids.

Manal: Like beggars, lowly vagabonds, *shrarih* [derogatory Lebanese term connoting uncivilised people].

Fadia: Yea really, we were talking about his, how you see all these hijab-wearing women on the street begging each with 4-5 kids. The Christian one I was telling you about, she started telling me that they should do, like … uhh … awareness campaigns, for the Syrians, how they shouldn't get kids because they're turning them into beggars. (Fadia and Manal)[3]

With Fadia and Manal, two older lower-class Sunni women living in one of Beirut's poorer areas, unsurprisingly perhaps, the Syrians systematically made it into our conversation. Indeed, Syrian refugees figured across so many other conversations in the field. Throughout, they emerged and reemerged as the most present personification: the epitome of disdained Arab marginality in all its proclaimed lack, ugliness, malignancy, and nuisance (see Thorleifsson 2016; Yasmine and Moughalian 2016; Suleiman 2006). Given their status as (one of) Lebanon's racialized internal Others I should not be surprised. Often, they were accompanied by the vagabonds, the beggars, and the scroungers: those groups embodying what is to be inferior, rejected, and prevented from *being*.

This, indeed, had a clear class dimension. It was evidently the attributes of those belonging to the lower classes: the hijab was made into a garment of the poor and the hijab-wearing woman was to be marked as lacking in economic status. This was further elaborated: stereotypes held that the degree of conservatism was directly proportional to the level of poverty. Indeed, in the field, I encountered stories of families who claimed to have chosen the *abaya* because it made life cheaper: "you only need one *abaya*, you wear it every day and you save a lot of money." Inferiorizing stereotypes therefore held that the dress was no object of agency, no object of religiosity, and not even an object of social accommodation: it was a simple materialization, by-product, of a lowly economic status.

Deeb's (2006) description of the hijab as a stigma in Lebanon, which was eventually a stigma of nonmodernity, can be affirmed as being much wider than she had held, much more rooted, much stronger, much deeper. More than fifteen years after her fieldwork, it stands firm, perhaps firmer than ever, as it strives both within and outside of the Shia (and Sunni) communities both within and beyond the questions of cultural, political, or even civilizational backwardness to, aggressively, wound in humanity.

While some data presented here points to some form of lessened discrimination, this book's later chapters will return to this to explore and interrogate these questions. For our purposes here, it must be realized that overwhelmingly, systematically, and pervasively the hijab-wearing woman experienced delineation as an Arabo-Muslim subject of the past. Worse, she is constructed as a threat to the coming of the present: the present of the West in Lebanon, the present that is the future. Such was her mark: an inexorable branding of racialized inferior humanity mobilizing global discourses and constructs fertilized by colonially invented national(istic) patriarchal and sexist imaginaries—as I will continue to explore in the next chapter.

The hijab connoted an identity. What I have explored in this chapter is not how this "identity" is standardly presented, interpreted, or analyzed. Maybe it was because so much of the scholarship on Muslim dress was thinking of ethnic or religious majorities–minorities. Maybe it was because so much of it missed the experiences of being and living, of being pushed into experiencing, a colonially invented racialization. Maybe it was because it did not understand identities and their production as producing and reproducing a specific ordering of the world through the production and reproduction of a colonial difference of inferiorizing racialization. It should have thought about Westernization. It should have made us realize that Islamophobia was not a question of being different because one was *in* the West, as a migrant. It should have told us that it was a question of being different *from* the imagined (Christian secular) West. It should have told us that it was a question of practicing Europe's Othered religion. It should have situated the patriarchy and sexism it identifies within Eurocentric modernity/

coloniality. It should have told us that it was a question of practicing religion, a remnant of a past that must be overcome for the Eurocentric future to come.

Conclusion

The experiences of participants that I have engaged and reflected on in this chapter showcase and analyze the construction of the hijab-wearing woman in contemporary Lebanon as a belated Arabo-Muslim difference in excess. The analysis presented shows how, through an unrelenting assault, modernity's Muslim Other is lived and erased at the violent intersection of postcolonial national imaginaries, global hegemonic Imperial Western secular–liberal discourses, patriarchy, sexism, and modern time. This, in turn, reveals a wounded habitus produced by a series of disavowals and expulsions. Most aggressively, this was a racialized hierarchy of humanity where the hijab's inferiorizing rejection was an articulation of anti-Muslim racism in Lebanon.

With these accumulating experiences, participants were victims of a stigma that both preceded and followed them. The result is severe aggression, uncivil violence, inflicted on the hijab-wearing woman's body, mind, and soul, by modern patriarchal "civilization." Additionally, this data has shown that the lived subordination of coloniality's Other was not undone through the shift in political power within the nation, as it has shown that this subordination is far more pervasive, profound, and wounding than is suggested in both scholarly and public understandings focused on sectarianism and "intercommunal" conflicts.

I am here ultimately presenting an argument that is not about the hijab but rather about the experiences of racialization, Islamophobia, and erasure within the so-called "Middle East"; about the conditions of Arabness and of Muslimness; and about the hierarchy of belongings and of human beings, which can be unraveled through listening. In this sense, I am arguing that the hijab-wearing woman must be understood as a racialized subject inferiorized along the hierarchy of the human through a complex construction. Produced for these women and lived by them, in a small postcolony, this anti-Muslim racialization dictated social anguish and suffering across life's various fields. In the coming chapters, I will continue exploring how this racialization manifests itself and materializes in lived daily experiences.

4

Domestic, Public, Work, and State Spheres: Lived Anti-Muslim Racism and Its Workings

This chapter presents and thinks alongside the lived experiences visibly Muslim women participants in Lebanon shared. Exploring various forms of assault, discrimination, and exclusion across social spheres, it analyses anti-Muslim racism in Lebanon and offers a series of insights into its workings echoing with anti-Muslim racism across Euro-America. For purposes of presentation and analytical clarity, the chapter is divided into four sections covering the four spheres of lived experience that emerged in the field: the domestic, the public, the market, and the state. Participants' experience certainly remains, it is important to note, far more tangled and complex as the trends extracted greatly overlap, diverging and converging.

Domestic Sphere

Across fieldwork, hijab-wearing participants shared experiences of exclusion that began inside homes, in daily interactions with their Muslim families and within one's most intimate relationships. As one participant in a focus group with young working-class and lower-middle-class hijab-wearing women working in the aid sector in Saida explained,

> Some people wear the hijab in a supportive environment. Some find an encouraging environment. But I didn't. For me, it was a fight to wear it. When I did, no one in the family spoke to me for a week. My dad didn't speak to me for two weeks. So it was this atmosphere where everyone was saying: "*Uf*, why? What happened? What are you doing? How will you even find a job? How will you get married?" How and how … I had, for three years, this was in 2002,

I kept thinking about it for 3–4 years before I could take the step. And that wasn't because I was thinking about it. I knew I wanted it, but I was thinking about how I can do it without getting into a confrontation with the community around me. But I did end up with a confrontation. And to this day, it's ongoing [confrontation]. (Saida, NGO focus group)

As the focus group participant went on to clarify, her family considered her choice to wear the hijab as one that will "doom" her to failure and, simultaneously, one that will be understood by the community as a manifestation of failed parenting. In this sense, her choice harmed her family and, at the same time, harmed her own future prospects. Her family's behaviors, she explained, were only a result of the "ideas they had" and their will to protect her, to salvage her. Ghada, an older lower-class Shia woman living in Lebanon's south, explained,

So I wore the hijab … I used to be beaten every day at home. Not once, multiple times. My mother would take off my hijab, and I would wear it. She would take it off and I would put it back on. She used to say: "I don't have girls who wear the hijab." I stuck to it by force … And I kept suffering … Yes, I went through a lot with my mother. A lot, a lot, a lot of suffering with my mother because of the hijab. Generally in the family, they don't like the hijab, they see it as backward. (Ghada)

Ghada, like many other participants, explained how her experiences were "justified" by her mother through an insistence on the inferiority of Islam and the East and on the need to look like "Europeans and Christians" and "civilized people." Otherwise, one would never "develop" or "progress in life." The hijab, Ghada's mother believed, doomed her daughter's future, and negated what she herself had strived to build for both herself and her family. Distinguishing between other "private" religious practices such as prayer and fasting, on the one hand, and the "public" hijab, on the other hand, many told of how their parents asked them to practice their faith "as you like" but to "keep it between you and God." The family sought, in other words, the (enlightenment-inspired) privatization of religion for the protection of their children—of their daughters—in an evident manifestation of the secular liberal ethos and its universalism dictating that religion must remain in the private realm if it is to be tolerated (Brown 2009).

S: I come from a family that's not very religious. I always get comments like "Now if you take it off and wear a hat what difference would it make?" I'm like, why don't you guys drop it, I'm happy, just leave me alone. But they won't, they're always saying things like "it's prettier if you wear a hat," and "you should wear a turban instead." But I'm happy the way I am!

A: Like thinking of my own experience, every day, every day, I hear a comment. Something like: "When will you take it off already?" Three or four times, a day. And things like "it's enough now [take it off]." Or things like "give her a year and she'll give up." Or like: "what is it [the hijab] for?" These are from my own family, and also neighbours and friends. Daily, every day, 3–4 times. At first, I would be really nice and make an effort and I would try to explain that there are reasons for it, that I was not forced to wear it, that I am convinced and all that. But now my reaction is: just go away. There's no point. You have to keep justifying and each time you need to find convincing reasons, which are stronger than what you said before because what you said before did not convince them.

S: They're never going to be convinced, that is it.

A: They really aren't. (AUB focus group)

Argumentation and reasoning were unsuccessful given the hijab-wearing woman's racialization discussed in the previous chapter and when faced with an evident and unquestionable reality of being visibly Muslim's detrimental effect on lived experience. From parents to close friends and neighbors, the hijab-wearing woman's error appeared both manifest and palpable, pushing her concerned social circles to seek redress. This wounding racism, therefore, began with the Muslim family and the closest of social circles.

In a modern world of secular hegemony, the rejection of the hijab becomes both "natural" and common sense in and of itself as well as a practical need, a necessity, an inevitability. Discrimination was here care, exclusion was motivated by love, erasure was benevolence. The responsibility of parents to equip their children with the necessary forms of capital, with the necessary norms, codes, and practices that could render them successful in the modern world, had become powerful drivers of anti-Muslim discrimination and assault. These experiences of discrimination, this immersion in the experience of hijab-wearing women revealed, begin with one of the key agents of socialization as it mobilizes and infiltrates the Muslim family in a mechanism that remains often absent and neglected in the northern-centric literature on anti-Muslim racism. I would suspect that among many migrant communities in the Global North, especially middle-class ones, similar dynamics do unfold.

Most participants expressed the impossibility of seeking support when faced with exclusion or discrimination. That would only lead to further accusations along the lines of "you have done this to yourself" and requests of removing the hijab. The hijab-wearing woman was in this sense deprived of family and close support if (or when) she faces discrimination or oppression in "public" areas, at work, or in the state. The hijab-wearing subject-position, it appeared, had much solitude to it as anti-Muslim racism sought to isolate the visibly Muslim.

In addition to the parental home of the nuclear family (the standard hegemonic norm in Lebanon) the aggression persisted throughout the hijab-wearing woman's life. Particularly, it moved to one's marriage. A middle-aged lower-class participant in a focus group in an NGO in Beirut explained,

> Me, you know, in my husband's family, I'm the only hijab-wearing woman. There were many problems and a lot of fights with their side, for me not to wear the hijab. I got married and I wasn't hijab-wearing and then later I wanted to wear it. There was the explosion in the Iranian embassy and I had just been on the [same] street and I didn't die. So I felt that life is empty and immediately thought that what am I waiting for to become a hijab-wearing woman and all that. So yes. My husband's mother went hysterical. To this day she wears sleeveless shirts and things like that and keeps telling me things like "what have you done to yourself?" … My husband at first was not convinced at all … he left the house for over a week … because I put on the hijab … and then with time things rebalanced. But I don't know where God gave me all that strength from. I was so insistent, I said there was no way for me to take it off. No matter what. No matter where I was going to reach, even if it was divorce. I hung in there. (Khaled association focus group)

The themes of husbands concerned about their image and families who found Muslim dress distasteful were pervasive throughout the field. Indeed, even beyond my own interviews, I encountered myriad stories about women who wanted to wear the hijab but could not as it would "destroy their marriage." Their choice in a modern patriarchy was not theirs, it appeared. This further seemed to hold a class dimension where, particularly, middle- and upper-class men found Muslim dress unattractive and unpleasant. Further, for such men a hijab-wearing wife could threaten their social standing, social circles, and even occupation. Calling for significant attention, this too seems largely overlooked in the literature. Ultimately, it appeared that this assault on the hijab-wearing woman was carried on into marriage where a colonial patriarchal system transfers "responsibility" from parents to husbands. Throughout, the need to preserve social status and prestige, playing out and aggressing hijab-wearing women, their bodies, and their will, ruled. The result is rejection, prohibition, and violence where under a world of modernity/coloniality the hijab transforms into deviance and the hijab-wearing woman into a willful subject to be disciplined by her colonized and enforced guardians for erasure.

Starting from this realization that the discrimination faced by the hijab-wearing woman pervaded her most intimate of spaces and was exerted by Muslim family and friends, I further hold here that this cannot be reduced to sectarianism or interreligious competition. Looking at these accounts, one realizes that the wearing of the hijab is a constant battle and struggle: inside one's Westernized home, within one's Westernized family, across one's Westernized life.[1] It was not, it appeared, only the work of a Westernized elite but rather that of Westernized relatives across divides under powerful hierarchizations.

As Bayrakli and Hafez (2018) show, self-orientalism and self-hate are powerful mechanisms within anti-Muslim racism that produce the colonized as inferior in their own eyes. In this sense, this internalized racism situates Muslims in a position and zone of adopted subordination eliciting within their subjectivity a desire to distance oneself from Islam constructed as an inherent deficiency, even by/for "practicing believers" (see Bayrakli and Hafez 2018; Grosfoguel and Mielants 2006). As fieldwork revealed, Lebanon contained ample self-orientalism and self-hate with a powerful desire to distance oneself from the Muslim. As a visible ritual that directly negated this distancing, the hijab is aggressed and its wearer powerfully assaulted. For some, this means physical pain: a process of daily beating that would reach the extent of "fainting." For others, it was psychological: an ostracization where family members simply ignored one's presence, or left. For many, it was a combination of both, complemented by a bombardment of aggressive and hurtful comments, attacks, and insults. Anti-Muslim racism's patriarchal mapping of itself on the bodies of women in Lebanon was a violent and aggressive process. Eventually, as a practice outside Western modern discourses, the hijab-wearing woman requires a divine force to keep the hijab as her unconcealable marking constantly triggers serious and severe harm and injury. While the psychological effect of this is beyond my scope in this book, it cannot be understated. In the following sections, this will be further evidenced.

Public Sphere

While many families seemed to want the hijab-wearing woman to stay at home, invisible, the hijab was a public object by its very definition—its exclusion necessarily moved into the "public sphere." This "public" Islamophobia has been documented across the West. Iddrisu (2019), for example, shows how hijab-wearing women in public spaces "encounter several discursive situations where strangers perform rhetorics of public spatialization that construct the veiled Muslim women as security and cultural threats" (Iddrisu 2019: 78). Through intersecting discourses, a spatialized experience of exclusion and assault consequently emerges through biopolitical rationales of control and discipline (Iddrisu 2019). The result of this is a situation where "women who have for long worn a head scarf can no longer function in the societies where they have lived for a considerable time" due to their aggressing production as the enemy within (Afshar 2008: 424). Accordingly, hijab-wearing women in the Global North today are standardly "facing the burden" of Western anti-Muslim hate, as "their movements, their postures, their gestures, and their attire become objects of intensified surveillance" and aggressive assaults (Mageau 2018: 136). In this public sphere in Lebanon too, Muslim dress is a powerful object of ostracization. I will be listing quotes from participants, for they must be voiced:

> The other day I was driving and someone was driving in the wrong direction. I opened the window and simply said: this is the wrong direction. Then I got [yelling]: "Hijab-wearing woman and talking!" What, do I not speak? And then they said: "Hijab-wearing woman, be quiet!" This always happens, they say this or they say: "Oh you have a voice!" It's not like I had cussed at them or anything, I would have just pointed it out. Yes. Yes, there is this. (Hoda)

> A lot [of discrimination]![painfully] Like out of the things I've heard is: "Oh you've put on the diaper!" For example ... "so, you're diaper-wearing now" ... you hear that. (Markaz focus group 1)

> There is this small café shop, very nice, at night it flips to a bar. Not a full-fledged bar but just a bit. But if you go there you will hear talk. Once my sister went and stayed for [just] a bit late, she got swear words, for her hijab. (Salma)

> I4: A few years ago, like before the Syrians came, I used to go to Bliss street, where AUB is, I would really feel as if I was in another planet when I'm there, really. People would be "What is this? Who is she and what is she doing here?"

> I3: Yes, of course, you feel like a total stranger! (Iman focus group)

> The other day they had this march, for women. And all the organisations went to march together demanding women's rights. But one of the signs they were holding, said something like "You will not oppress me with your hijab," like saying be free of the hijab, you are oppressed, something like that. We're outside. (Maya)

Not long ago there was this public beach that prohibited the burkini, in Lebanon. I'm not talking in Niece, in France where this can happen, no, it happened in Lebanon. And people started saying that no, there wasn't a municipal decision, and yes, there was a municipal decision and there was a debate about all that. Regardless! This is outrageous for me! Me going to a beach, public, and having one of the municipality workers come to me and say: "No, Syrians and hijab-wearing women are not allowed." This happened! So this is something. And then even private beaches. If someone is wearing a burkini, she can't go to most private beaches in Lebanon. So, no. there are many things, rights, many things missing. In terms of rights. (Sara)

Hoda is an older upper-middle-class niqab-wearing woman from Beirut, Salma is a young middle-class Shia from the south of Lebanon while Maya is an upper-class Shia architect from the south as well, living in Beirut. The Markaz focus group 1 was held with middle-class Shias living in Beirut's southern suburb, while the Iman focus group was held with lower-class Sunnis from Beirut. As these quotes from across Lebanon's geography, social classes, and sectarian differences powerfully illustrate, saying that Muslim dress is not accepted in much of Lebanon's public sphere would be a dire understatement. The parallels and similarities with anti-Muslim racism across not only the Global North but also the Global South were unmissable. Going over these quotes, I was particularly reminded of women in Turkey and in Pahlavi Iran (Rajaee 2007; Zahedi 2007) during the past century as well as various other parts of the Global South (Cole 2012; Macmaster 2009): the aggression against Muslim dress and visibly Muslim women was an ongoing historical phenomenon, a phenomenon that would not yield to the modern logic of linear progress. In the case of contemporary Turkey, Auerbach (2017) identifies a key role for space where a "policing [of] the borders of cultural territory and reinforcing the symbolic significance of a particular cultural orientation to a particular place" pushes the hijab-wearing woman into a position of exclusion through "neighbourhood pressure" (Auerbach 2017: 228). For her participants, this primarily involved negative looks and comments from family, peers, professors, neighbors, and strangers (Auerbach 2017: 229). Despite this spread, the majority of experiences are reported to occur in public spaces and with strangers as the hijab-wearing woman emerges as the object of much marginalization as she did in Lebanon. As Parvez (2011b), Zempi (2016), and Bruck's (2008) practicing Muslim participants shared across Euro-America, it truly was a global phenomenon of systematic aggression and assault. France, in particular, powerfully loomed. The practices of the colonizer were today continuously reproduced in the (ex)colony: from burkinis and beaches to marches and social movement mobilizations.

From streets to shops, the visibly Muslim woman is consistently subject to insults and disrespect, to harassment and rejection, subtle and explicit, overt more than covert. As many participants explained, Muslims are prohibited from buying homes in a number of Christian-majority regions across Lebanon—often through formal municipal decisions. While this is a phenomenon that is not limited to the hijab, the dress—even if just as a future possibility—figured within it as participants explained how many did not want their "Muslim sight polluting the scene" as they recounted stories of blatant discrimination and policing.

Objectified and degraded, the visibly Muslim woman is always at risk. Unable to participate in the demand for "civil rights," unable to practice in leisure activities, unable to complain when she is wronged, she lives in paralysis. As Mira told me, as a abaya-wearing woman, she could not teach at the university, she could not get employed, she could not even exercise on the street because "I was considered not to have the right." Indeed, the hijab-wearing woman lives with very few rights. She lives "outside." Unable to tread on some streets, with her habitus of Otherness, horrific insults and words that wound, the hijab-wearing woman in Lebanon would appear imprisoned by, and in, her inferiorization. Muslim dress was indeed a prison, but not because of Islam but because of a powerful exclusion of the visibly Muslim.

This rejection was not homogeneous but was rather subject to two main variables: geography and perceived conservatism of the dress. For geography, participants explained that there is a limited number of regions (among those regions where the majority population is Muslim) that have acquired a certain degree of Muslim identity over the past two decades and that, as one moves away from them, discrimination aggravates.

> Let me tell you this story. Once we were, in the summer, in Zahle. So my kid and I got out of the car to get some ice cream from [shop name]. When I first walked in, I asked for ice cream. He said they don't have any. And the ice cream was right next to me! I was like: "But it's here, that's ice cream." He just repeated that they don't have any to sell me. (Iman focus group)
>
> A: Like in Ashrafieh or Dekweneh, if you're a hijab-wearing woman and walking on the street ... like ...
> N: That's not accepted ... (AUB focus group)
>
> Once I was doing research work in Ashrafieh and there were some Syrian refugees [sitting] on the street there, hijab-wearing women. They have some there, apparently. Everyone there insisted that

I was Syrian and treated me in a way that was not acceptable. Like not acceptable at all, at all! They [strangers on the street] said they wanted to call the police, that I was taking pictures. And this guy, who had nothing to do with anyone, like a nobody, took me to the notary [office], and he started … like in a very unacceptable way … He insisted I was Syrian. I was like, "What is wrong with you? I don't have a Syrian accent to begin with!" And I feel that if I weren't hijab-wearing, he wouldn't like … never said I was Syrian! Right or not? But maybe for him, the hijab-wearing woman in that region is Syrian. You know? Maybe because the Lebanese hijab-wearing women don't go there. (Rabab)

There is that discrimination. You find it. It's especially obvious in some regions. Like even the way people stare at you and give you looks. Even though I don't wear that [conservative] clothing, I wear modern [hijab]! (Saida NGO focus group)

In many regions, your mere presence and the simplest act of walking on the street were "not accepted." Ashrafieh, the archetype of Lebanon's right-wing Christian-majority regions, emerged and reemerged. Zahle, another archetypical Christian-majority town in the Bekaa, was similarly aggressing. This rejection was not subtle: it was vocalized, expressed, enforced by everyone; from shop owners to pedestrians, as the association with Syrians echoed throughout. Not unlike "Black ghettos" and anti-Black racism across the Global North, space had plenty to say in discrimination.[2]

This, it appears, does not yield to the logic of the capitalist market, for example, as the hijab-wearing woman would not be admitted as a client in commodity exchange. Similarly, the hijab-wearing woman is not innocent until proven guilty where she could not be detained with no evidence. Rather, she is evidently guilty until proven otherwise, marked with as many markers as possible in great echoes of exclusionary migration regimes and bordering practices (see El-Enany 2020). "Good citizens" felt a strong moral responsibility, a duty, to police the hijab-wearing woman into erasure and preserve the purity of the common space—of the street. Here, erasure was rarely mobilized under the banner of preserving the hijab-wearing woman but was rather advanced under the banner of preserving the space from the hijab-wearing woman's stigma, contamination.

Lebanon is no homogeneous place but rather one where religious difference is largely mapped onto geography, with distinct majority regions for different religious groups. These different groups have differing histories, differing imagined horizons, and relatively differing relations to Westernization, imagined Lebanon, the Muslim, and the Arabic-speaking world. As the hijab-wearing woman moved throughout the Lebanese space, she entered and exited areas where she was different, and where she was differently engaged. She indeed moved across gradients of exclusion and marginalization from spaces where she would be inconspicuous in public to ones where she could be asked by the municipal police to leave. The hijab-wearing experience was accordingly a spatialized one where different regions approach and engage the hijab and the hijab-wearing woman in different ways. Whereas in Zahle the hijab-wearing woman could not be allowed to buy ice cream, in Ashrafieh and Dekweneh she could hardly walk on the street; this level of expulsion was not uniformly encountered across the Lebanese space. In some other regions, her abjection meant being badly spoken of, or receiving "kind advice" to remove the dress, for example. In yet others, the public sphere caused little aggression as erasure remained concealed from the public space, and was rampant across the domestic, the work, and the state spheres as later sections of this chapter will continue to explore. Lebanon's different histories and identities were key in these assaults where Lebanese sectarianism entangled with religion, class, and cosmopolitanism of specific spaces to dictate the most blatant, most violent public discrimination.

This spatialization was reproducing Lebanon's colonially instilled heterogenous citizenry, inventing its separate communities, and enforcing the hierarchy of belonging and the unequal citizenship established with Lebanon's very postcolonial foundation where Muslims were relegated in favor of Maronite Christian supremacy—a superiority given their "proximity" to Europe. As the hijab-wearing woman could not move across the Lebanese space she could not belong to the Lebanese space but rather needed to be cloistered in her belonging to the specific—inferiorized—community of which she was a part. Under a global order of the Muslim's inferiority and entwined with Lebanon's (postcolonial) history of sectarian struggle, the hijab-wearing woman was kept at bay as the nation's postcolonial identity and divisions as a space of difference, as different spaces, were reproduced in deep entwinement with anti-Muslim racialization and assault.

In either case, for the hijab-wearing woman, where she can and cannot go are clear as part of what could be termed a *wounded habitus*—a habitus that is split, fractured, and multiple as one inhabits multiple worlds and is violently subjected to modernity/coloniality (see Kassem 2022a; Silva 2016). Her experiences established what Itaoui (2016) has called mental maps of exclusion, which had great impacts on her mobility and ability to navigate space and place. In the case of the Lebanese hijab-wearing woman, as many of the project's participants elaborated, the "can areas" are well known, everywhere else is "cannot." Such a learning was not, participants explained, "too difficult" to understand and was "to be expected" given Lebanon's "makeup." As Zahraa, an older Shia resident of Beirut's southern suburb (Dahieh) explained,

> Of course, I have been through harassment! But not inside Dahieh, once you're outside of it. You hear words, *toltish [degrading cusses]*. (Zahraa)

This naturalized spatial ordering of discrimination in Lebanon echoed the spatial ordering of anti-Muslim discrimination and racism more broadly across the West as well as the spatial separation and ordering of indigenous and colonists in conventional forms of direct colonial regimes. Ultimately, the hijab-wearing woman in different geographies, and among different communities, did not experience discrimination in a uniform way but rather faced it with a complex variety of its lived and material manifestations. Surely, this itself entangles with a number of other factors, such as class and education, to produce a complex intersectional lived experience that remains beyond the scope of this chapter's analysis. This spatial ordering was eventually one where those (very few and very well-defined) regions where the sociopolitical Muslim religious community has established a strong presence were the hijab-wearing woman's havens of acceptance. Here, I am mainly referring to most of Dahieh, some regions in the north (parts of Tripoli and some surrounding villages), and scattered villages in the Bekaa and the south of Lebanon.

I would here argue that this spatial dimension does not make the scene in Lebanon any less horrid. On the contrary, it aggravates the sense of entrapment, of cloistering, and of imprisonment. Within a narrow space, the hijab-wearing woman is pushed to the brink of suffocation as her difference becomes enshrined, physically mapped, and codified, and her contrast accentuated. In a situation where the hijab-wearing woman and those around her are pressured to learn how to navigate the space and "their limits" (otherwise, they would only have themselves to blame, I was told) this space of *tolerance* was itself a tool, a technology, of the visible Muslim's policing and erasure. Through this, the sight of the hijab-wearing woman in "mainstream," "cosmopolitan," touristic, or most upper-class regions was further anomalized, and her absence was further standardized. It was a clear incident of absenting (Vázquez 2012): of invisibilizing the hijab and the hijab-wearing woman, of policing, control, and discipline for erasure.

This is further made clear as one examines the stereotypes as well as conditions of these regions. Given multiple factors including the historical supremacy of Christians most Christian-majority regions in Lebanon are generally more "developed" and affluent: from infrastructure to aesthetics. Many Muslim-majority spaces are, on the other hand, often "underdeveloped" and lacking in planning and infrastructure, overpopulated and marginalized particularly given Lebanon's ongoing unequal development and the various sociohistorical formations of regions such as Dahieh (see Harb and Deeb 2013). Consequently, this spatialization of exclusion was a powerful means through which the hijab-wearing woman's racialization and inferiorizing associations as explored in Chapter 3 were themselves reproduced. From stigmas and stereotypes as lacking in hygiene to lacking technology and from claimed disorder to unlawfulness, many of the regions in which the hijab-wearing woman was cloistered were regions that she was said to resemble and to resemble her.

On another (entangling) level, a second factor that plays into this experience is the position of the dress on the imagined spectrum of (Eurocentric) "modernity." The rule appeared simple: the more "conservative" the dress was deemed to be, the more non-modern it was and, consequently, the more extreme the incidents were. For example, a woman choosing to wear a *abaya* (long black cloak) in a focus group with Shia women living in Dahieh recounts,

> We would pass by places and people would yell: "Look at the ninja!" Or things like: "Look at the black garbage bag!" The words would be that harsh, they would say those things to us. (Markaz focus group 1)

Of insight is the fact that the insults, the words, were often not about the hijab. They are about the hijab-wearing woman. She was not wearing a black garbage bag. *She* was a black garbage bag. This was objectification at its most vicious. Fanon's (2008: 82) writing, "then I found that I was an object in the midst of other objects," took on a different meaning. For those wearing the face-veil, the situation was drearier, as Hoda, an older Beiruti niqab-wearing woman, and a niqab-wearing working-class participant from the focus group in Saida, explained:

> [Chuckles] … they still don't accept me. I would be walking in the street, the stares, it's unbelievable. Especially when I drive … Like, they would look in this way, and they almost get into a car accident just because they keep staring at me and giving me looks. And this is the easy part. There are those who say things … I used to stay quiet, but not anymore … Like "ninja," this is the least [bad] word, ninja. And they swear at me. Some have even tried to run me over when I'm driving. There was this one time, here, I was crossing the road and there was this

woman, old, like really old, and I was driving, so I stopped for her to cross the street, it was a turn and I felt that no one was going to let her pass, so I stopped to let her cross the road, and then she just stood there and started yelling at me and threatening me. She said: "You know just wait, tomorrow they are going to take it off your face, they will force it off your face!" I looked in shock, I was just letting her through, I hadn't said anything! And then she crossed while she kept giving me bad looks. (Hoda)

Loads of times, I'd be walking on the street, and I see kids yell out and start screaming to their moms [scared of me]. But who is behind this? Why is he scared? I [try to] take him to the side and show my face, or give him a lollipop. Or anything. Just to show him that I am human like him. (Saida mosque focus group)

With stories of how people would, upon seeing a niqab-wearing woman, move to the other side of the street, exit shops, and change their seat in a bus to "sit next to the window" the situation held powerful affective elements as it held practical ones. The similarity to, for example, Mason-Bish and Zempi's (2019) or Zempi and Chakraborti's (2015) explorations of anti-Muslim racism in the UK was resounding: the experiences were the same as the movement from "first world" to "third world," from north to south, changed little. It was not, it again appeared, simply about migratory status or a threat to the West by "foreigners." It was about a difference from the imagined modern subject. It was a terrorizing threat to the globalized Eurocentric modern/colonial horizon.

The last recount mentioned above had happened on the streets of Saida: one of the country's most "conservative" Sunni cities in the south of Lebanon. I left that interview with the unequivocal sense that the question was not of safe regions or safe cities and towns. It was not even a question of safe neighborhoods. The best that can be said is it being a question of some parts of some streets where the situation is likely to be better than others. As a threat, the hijab-wearing woman was a subject of hate, of hate crimes. Stares, as they did with Fanon, figured powerfully. While walking on the street aware that people do not approve of you is one thing, walking on the street aware that children are frightened by merely seeing you is another.[3] The niqab-wearing woman was, by walking, experiencing herself as a source of fear and pain while also experiencing fear and pain as global discourses of "Muslim terror" resonated throughout. One participant, a hijab-wearing woman, explained how she once got off a bus when a niqab-wearing woman got on as she was worried "she would be a terrorist." She would do it anew if it happens again, she explained with no feeling of guilt or wrongdoing. Two other hijab-wearing participants, Sunni and Shia, expressed similar concern and fear when encountering niqab-wearing women in shops or events. The internalization as well as normalization of anti-Muslim racism was resounding.

The condition, strongly reminiscent of pandemic apartheid, of systematic hegemonic racial segregation as a global phenomenon indicates that this discrimination was a material and lived experience that functions by ostracizing Eurocentric modernity's Other from presence, mapping her movement, controlling her being, and signaling her exclusion. Mobilizing the specific context and its unequal development, this spatialization itself reproduced the racialization and its inferiorizing characteristics. Marked, the hijab became the threat, the subject to be aggressed, wounded, erased by social actors and agents across "public life" where all citizens become responsible (anticipated) agents toward the achievement of this erasure in an ironic form of citizen, community, and civil collectivist "police," "watch," and "protection." Accordingly, anti-Muslim racism functions by mobilizing a multitude of social actors, from vendors to civil society organizations and to random citizens in a crusade waged in the invented public sphere against modernity/coloniality's visibly Muslim Other. The more *difference*, the more brutal the attacks—as the following chapter will more fully explore. With this, a (physical) space of accommodation was thus established where the hijab-wearing woman was (relatively) permitted to roam in a powerful mechanism of policing, control, and management that anomalized and established the public nonappearance, the absence, of Muslim dress and its wearers.

Work Sphere

While hijab-wearing women were subject to hate speech, micro-aggression, and blatant discrimination under various justifications and in different social spheres the question of employment emerged as particularly prominent and pressing. Indeed, "the market" has been recorded as a key site of anti-Muslim racism across Euro-America (Koura 2018; Mahmud and Swami 2010). In the US context, research on discrimination based on religious attire presents "direct evidence for both formal and interpersonal discrimination and low expectations of receiving job offers among Hijabis" (Abdelhadi 2019; Ghumman and Jackson 2010; Ghumman and Ryan 2013: 692; Strabac et al. 2016). In France, "laïcité, post-feminism and neoliberalism" have been found to intersect and imbue the workforce to racialize and "erect barriers to Muslim women's employment opportunities" (Rootham 2015: 983). Accordingly, and aware that the market is often drawn out as a distinct social sphere with its own logic and with the magnitude of experiences shared by participants focusing on the labor market I choose to reflect on participants' shared experiences within it in a separate section:

> And then about work! When you apply to work it's the same thing. They look for you to be non-hijab-wearing. I studied psychology. And some of the things, when you apply, you hear: "How can you be a psychologist in a hijab? They don't work, no way, we won't have our psychologist be hijab-wearing" Why? No. (Bahia)
>
> S1: And there is more. There are companies and job ads, they put a flagrant specification: not hijab-wearing.
>
> I2: Yes, yes there are those. And there are places when you call them, they immediately ask "Are you hijab-wearing or not?" And if you say you are, they would say "No that doesn't work for us."
> [verbal agreement]
>
> I3: I applied to a school once. From the start of the interview, she said to me: "Look, miss, to say this as it is, we don't hire hijab-wearing women. And that was that. (Iman focus group)

The hijab-wearing woman was filtered out of employment in clear continuity with her racialization as a belated Arabo-Muslim difference in excess in Lebanon. The racialization destroying women's employment opportunities across the West was a global phenomenon, my research powerfully indicated. In a country where state provisions, welfare, and social security are alien concepts, this exclusion from the workforce is suffocating, pushing the hijab-wearing woman into myriad challenges. In some respects, particularly given the small country's economic realities, some participants argued that the effects of this discrimination in Lebanon could be "more harming than they are in much of the west," at least for citizens of Euro-American countries. While this remains unclear, this dimension of hijab-wearing women's exclusion was particularly violent:

> Me as a hijab-wearing woman, I suffered so much to find a job, and you can't not … I once applied, a C.V., to go work in the Gulf, in a company, through a Lebanese recruitment agency. I arrived before my appointment, and sat there. And then my appointment time arrived. People were sitting in there, one by one going and having their interviews inside and my time came and passed. And I

was still sitting, waiting. She didn't call my name for the interview. And I just kept sitting there, 5 minutes, 10 minutes, 15 minutes, 20 minutes … and then eventually I went up to her and told her I had arrived before my appointment time and it had passed but my name was not called for an interview. And she said: "Apologies but you are a hijab-wearing woman, and they don't take hijab-wearing women." (Maha)

Later, Maha told me that the recruitment agency was "Christian" and that she knew they would never employ her. Yet, she was hoping that the fact the recruitment was for a company in the Gulf meant she would have a chance. It appeared she did not. This was because "Lebanese people are controlling this," she explained, and Lebanese people would never want others to "see them as hijab-wearing because such was not how they wanted their nation to be." The postcolonial imagined identity of Lebanon as a bastion of empire and a Western-looking space powerfully aggressed. As Fatima, a middle-aged Shia Muslim activist, stated,

> They specify "non-hijab-wearing woman," on job applications or advertising jobs. They write: non-hijab-wearing woman as a condition. The hijab-wearing woman does not go well with them, the Lebanese. (Fatima)

The issue here was that of postcolonial Lebanon and a social category Fatima identified as "the Lebanese" who had obstinately decided that hijab-wearing women were always already disqualified from obtaining employment. Both within the country and in sending (skilled) labor abroad, particularly to the Gulf, the hijab-wearing woman was being excluded and expulsed. Here, the invented nation was drawn on again and again in entwinement with global discourses imbricated in colonizing racist structures. This stands in clear continuity with practices explored throughout this book where women's bodies become key sites for the stigmatization of wider communities and are instrumentalized to embed a social hierarchy. Rabab, a young upper-class Sunni living in central Beirut, recounted,

> I was already [working] in the same company in the Qatar branch, where I didn't see this [discrimination] at all. The human resources department [in Lebanon] in specific … their treatment was really really different with me. And my manager explicitly told me that, because you are hijab-wearing, they didn't want to get you, but I forced them to recruit you, but they didn't want to get you because you are hijab-wearing. He [the human resource manager] even lowered my salary. I had an agreement, with the company owner, my relationship was with the owner

and I had agreed through my manager with the owner to a salary, and I came to Lebanon on that basis. When I went to sign the contract I found it was 400$ less. That's a lot. From 2000$ to 1600$. I asked why and he said he didn't know me yet. And I was like "What do you mean you don't know me, I work for you! You are the regional human resources, not just for Lebanon, for both here and Qatar! You can't say you don't know me." He said he wants to try me. Eventually, I said no and that I won't accept it. Then he said he could add 100$ and I wasn't going to accept it, but the manager spoke to me and said that it would just be for a while and that it was because of the hijab only, and that they'll fix it [later], but it never got fixed, of course. (Rabab)

Prompting (different kinds of) research on wage inequalities in Lebanon, Rabab clearly evidenced the role of the labor market in reproducing the colonial order, an order in which the hijab-wearing woman's labor held less value. Gupta (1996: 15; 2006), in her classical work on Canadian racism, explains that devaluing labor is an essential technique of structurally racist social ordering where powerlessness is established and that, in this technique, "the labour of women of colour is evaluated in a doubly negative manner because it is based on an intertwining of sexist and racist ideologies." Theorizing this, she explains that it occurs in continuity with the history of slavery and is based on "reinforced common notions about 'race,' 'racial difference' and 'racial inequality'" where citizenship, immigration, and legal status were key (Gupta 1996: 15; 2006). In Lebanon, there was no such history of slavery or questions of legal systems, immigration, or citizenship. Further, the issue at hand is one of a recent emergence as the hijab appears to have figured little as a contested issue in the country's history. The question was, nevertheless, one of difference and manufactured inferiority for inequality. The establishment of powerlessness, it became clear, was a global(ized) phenomenon that could be manufactured in any place and time under modernity/coloniality and in relation to the colonial difference: any difference from the European, to racialize and establish dwelling in the zone of nonbeing.

As with the exclusion in the public sphere, this colossal subjugation, exploitation, and alienation was again subject to variables. In this instance, geography, the identity of the institution, as well as the conservatism of the dress all figured prominently. The level of employment was similarly there.

First, in terms of geography, participants expressed a sense that this exclusion is eased in some specific "Muslim regions." Zeinab, a young Shia student in Beirut, articulated this clearly:

> Most of these banks, if I go to their Hamra branch, there's no way I can get a job. If I go to the Dahieh branch, they've started leaning a bit to reality: no, you find one hijab-wearing woman. Of course, there are particular clothes only allowed, so yes, it's a baby step, but it's a step. It's still that a girl in a abaya; no way she can work in a bank, this is a big X. A girl in an *isharb* [conservative hijab], no way. But they have gone past their hijab phobia there. It's a good thing. (Zeinab)
>
> I once applied to a job and the guy flat out told me that "you are hijab-wearing woman and I want someone who's not." It was a car sales exhibition. And I have a friend who went to a real estate office and he told her that it just doesn't suit him to have a hijab-wearing woman. (Abbesiye focus group)

A participant in the Abbesiye focus group, held in a municipal center in the town of Abbesiye in the Lebanese south, recounted this incident and insisted that this phenomenon existed across the Shia-majority southern towns of Lebanon. "Muslim regions," it must be restated here, are not regions where there is a majority Muslim population. Rather, they can be thought of as regions where the cultural norms have shifted, mostly through "Islamic political" movements having established a strong presence. Often, these are regions dwelling on the margins of the Lebanese nation, on the margins of modernity. Practically, when it came to employment, this definition seems to further shrink to extend very little beyond (most of) Beirut's southern suburb. But, as I came to know, even there, it appeared that this mitigation was limited. As Zahraa, an older Shia resident of Dahieh, and both Shia and Sunni focus group participants, identified,

> The question of work, there is a serious problem there, it's very rare for them to accept. In Dahieh, you find both [acceptance and non-acceptance]. But there are harassments when it comes to work everywhere. Like if she wants to work as a saleswoman [in Dahieh], there is a particular dress which is forced, or banks. And the make-up, and the tight clothes and the pants ... even when they accept the hijab-wearing woman there [in Dahieh], they accept her on their conditions. And a abaya wearing woman? It's beyond rare for her to be accepted. And if we see her we get surprised: "Oh, she really got that job? It's so good they accepted her!" (Zahraa)
>
> M3: There are even institutions in Dahieh that are not accepting. Not outside only. They are requiring that she be non-hijab-wearing woman. Why? Because they are considering that the employee needs to be presentable and chic and the hijab is ruining that. There are institutions, in our regions, having it as a condition. It's a policy thing. (Markaz focus group 3)

A3: Even our religious community, inside of Dahieh, would prefer that she not be wearing a abaya because it is more comfortable for him.

A1: It always happened, once she arrives at an interview, they go: "We apologise."

A2: And we had this centre for children with special needs [in Dahieh] and this girl wearing the abaya, they told her: "We accept you but you must take off the abaya because this appearance reflects something negative on kids …" (Markaz focus group 2)

Even in Tripoli, which is this very conservative Muslim place, you don't see hijab-wearing women in the banks. All those at the bank are non-hijab-wearing woman. Where did they find them? Really, it's so bad. (AUB focus group)

In Shia-majority and "Hezbollah-supporting" Dahieh some Lebanese hijab-wearing women were so excluded as to be made to feel a "negative" sight for children and a tarnishing of the employer's reputation. The marking of a belated Arabo-Muslim difference in excess pervaded and rendered the hijab-wearing woman a form of contamination, pollution, which threatened the employer and their image, their success, their belonging. The hijab was not presentable, it was not tolerable. Hezbollah's "Islamic milieu" (Deeb and Harb 2011) was a difficult exaggeration, it appeared.

Mira, an older psychologist living in the southern Haret Saida town, for example, told of how "committed Muslim men [employers] choose non-hijab-wearing women" because they feel "they simply cannot" choose otherwise if they wish to attract customers and preserve their commercial interests. Surely, sexism was a powerful factor in this as the hijab-wearing woman was excluded at the intersection of sexist ideologies and Islamophobic forces in line with what Mason-Bish and Zempi (2019) had shown in the UK. Ultimately, this exclusion was not only normalized but also rendered necessary, an inevitable strategy dictated by Lebanon's "diversity" and "economic interests," as Mira explained. Endorsing diversity, it appeared, meant the concealment of Muslim difference and a push to homogenize the shared space into the European universe. Employers, regardless of their identities or their beliefs, needed to yield to this logic if they are to preserve their economic interests. The market had an omnipotent invented racialized and imagined logic that cannot be understood independently from racism's establishment across the various spheres of life. When it came to employment, vulnerability and exploitation yielded little, I came to conclude, to geography.

The last quote above also brings to light the second variable: the nature of the institution. First, there are particular institutions, primarily banks and tourism-related ones (hotels, travel agencies, high-end restaurants, etc.), where it appeared nearly impossible for the hijab-wearing woman to find employment regardless of geography. Such work, that of the major sector of the Lebanese economy (the services sector), was simply not for the hijab-wearing woman. Such work that represented modern Lebanon as the tourism hub, Lebanon in its "golden days," Lebanon as dreamed was not for the hijab-wearing woman.[4] The image of the ideal Lebanese echoed again and again as the policing of who belonged in "modern" spaces such as banks and hotels wounded.

The question of an institution's position on the local–global spectrum also emerged as important: "internationally affiliated" institutions were presented as more likely to reject hijab-wearing women than local ones. The following quotes from a focus group with older Shia women living in Dahieh, Sunni women living in Saida, and a young Sunni from Beirut living in an upper-class city neighborhood illustrate these trends:

> A4: And there are shops [names shops], in Bir-al-abed [neighborhood in Dahieh], they don't take hijab-wearing woman employees. And this is in our region!
> A2: Yes, yes of course.
> A4: I think it's because it's an international firm, they wouldn't take her there. (Markaz focus group 3)
> The [hijab-wearing woman] lady is facing many obstacles in some places, like in [shopping] malls … like the places which are not from Lebanon, the international ones, the ones with brands in many places around the world. (Saida mosque focus group)
> The hijab is a problem, in any place, except in Dahieh or Tarik eljdide. But even there, all international chains, even ones like [names restaurants] … I don't know … But all those shops [they don't take her]. (Nadine)

In Lebanon, a prime instance of the neoliberal order, the marked hijab-wearing woman is perceived to be unfit, below the standards set by modernity and anti-Muslim racism, to reside within the global neoliberal market. The mall, as a space of modern globalized consumption and leisure, as a space for the modern subject, was naturally unwelcoming. The hijab-wearing woman was better off trying her luck in "shops" and "small places" as she was largely excluded from many erudite or socially respected professions. Echoing direct colonialism and north–south economic colonization, those places deemed to be "not from here, the international ones, the ones with brands in many places around the world" were here key agents of anti-Muslim racism and the hijab-wearing woman's erasure.[5]

In the market, both the dominant logic of exclusion encountered in the home and the dominant logic of exclusion encountered in the public sphere converged where the role of globalized consumption in reproducing anti-Muslim racism was astounding. This data, accordingly, points to the complicity of global consumer capital through its various institutions in anti-Muslim racism and the ensuing colonization of lived experiences for erasure—in the coloniality of *being* (Maldonado-Torres 2014).[6]

Among local institutions, there was also the question of the relationship to the Muslim: was it an institution overtly identifying as "Muslim"? From the literature (such as Le Thomas 2012) and from hearsay in the country, I was aware of incidents where some Islamic schools, in particular, required teachers and students to cover their hair as part of their uniform and of how "backward" the practice was thought to be. With such incidents in mind, I was under the impression that "Muslim institutions" would be safe for the hijab-wearing woman. Expressing similar thoughts, many participants suggested that hijab-wearing women should, and do, feel comfortable "there":

> I feel [the hijab cannot find a job] in banks too. It's very rare [for a hijab-wearing woman to find employment]. Unless it's an Islamic bank, yes, you get a hijab-wearing woman there. But other banks they prohibit the girl from the hijab. (Saida NGO focus group)[7]
>
> In communication, it is hard for me to find a job in communication because I am hijab-wearing woman. I don't even work in communication now. I feel most hijab-wearing women work like in Islamic institutions, like that keeps them in the same circle, so they don't fit in society. (Nadine)

Nadine expressed a clear reading of this invention of a labor space to cloister the hijab-wearing woman as a mechanism of control, of erasure. It was, as she very well explained, absencing through concealment: of "keeping" hijab-wearing women away from "society," of keeping society beyond hijab-wearing women as inferiorizing attempts to exploitatively make use of some of their labor were made. Nevertheless, she went on to express a sense of comfort, of relief, in the welcoming space these "Islamic institutions" offered. Yet, as I gathered data, the conditions under which this unfolded revealed themselves to be not as favorable as I thought, as some of the project's participants thought.

First, I soon came to realize that "Muslim institutions" only meant a very narrow subset of those institutions self-identifying as publicly and unequivocally

Muslim (mostly some local NGOs and schools). In Lebanon, these are a frail minority. Further, I soon realized that the embrace was ambivalent, even in the most "Islamic" of these institutions. The following quote from a middle-aged lower-class Sunni teacher living in Beirut is an example:

> Even me, as a casual hijab but long dress, if I went to an institution … like this is a personal experience: I went to an institution, an Islamic one [names institution], a while back, they told me you are wearing a hijab which is the dress of nuns. I told him this is my Muslim dress and you are free to hire me or not, but I will not give it up. And they didn't take me. And this was an Islamic association! (Farida)

The issue was that Farida's hijab was too conservative, signaling an identity the institution did not wish to project within Lebanese society as it would "push people away" and even raise fears of extremism and terrorist violence. The institution Farida named is one of the country's most powerful "Islamic" networks. While she was wearing a long plain dress during our interview with a casual bright headscarf that was put under her dress, her plight struck me as exceptional. In either case, this experience, I came to realize, was not too exceptional.

While such incidents echoed with participants in various forms of Muslim dress, my research clearly evidenced that the degree of exclusion was correlated to the degree of perceived conservatism. In this respect, the niqab-wearing woman was the most wounded:

> But the niqab, the Lebanese Muslim society, in particular, rejects it. [With much pain, in tears] How do we know this? I first came as a niqabi to the [Muslim] school. They said "Yes sure, but inside the school, you must take it off. Ok, for young kids, I take it off, but when I am asked that even in parent-teacher meetings I need to take it off? You, as an Islamic institution you did not help me, you hurt me! And this isn't new. This has nothing to do with ISIS, it has to do with the profile of the school. Parents are registering their kids, if they see a niqabi, they won't like it, they'd get scared. The purpose of the school is to gain, gain students. (Farida)

In tears, Farida, who had given up the niqab completely by the time of our interview, told me how she was asked to remove her niqab and her ensuing sense of violation. The "Islamic institution," I realized, was wary of excess in excess. The institution, I realized, did not want to be *too Muslim* and was, actually, particularly worried and actively working against the threat of being labeled as "too Muslim." Women's bodies seemed the evident space on which a "moderate" Islam could be projected outward. The patriarchy at play, and its reproduction, resounded. This, I came to find, was a trend in the country—a trend echoing global patriarchal Islamophobic trends as explored across both the East and West. Discussing employment opportunities as I was conducting a focus group at an "Islamic NGO" in the city of Saida, one of the participants confided,

> Us here, the institution, one of the girls who work here, she applied to wear it [the niqab] and we had something like ... like ... not reservation but ... like what would others think of us? We are a centrist institution, we work with different groups to serve society and we admit that in this region there is cultural variety, and even sectarian [mentions examples of groups they work with]. Ok, we have our [Muslim] personality, but we can't go to the extreme. Also, once we had a niqabi who applied, we really discussed it for a very long time and dragged on and in the end, it was that she had applied to a job where there were so few candidates, so I told them to just accept her and eventually we did. (Saida NGO)

As a "centrist" institution, they could not go to the "extreme." Their identification as a "Muslim NGO" made this particularly important. The construction of a "moderate" Islam and its opposition to an "extremist" and "threatening" Islam (see Haddad and Golson 2007; Khandaker 2017) was, again, clearly not limited to the West and woundingly existed in the so-called Middle East. Indeed, in this quote, the hegemony of the rejection of Muslim dress manifests itself in full might: even women wearing a conservative form of the hijab and even Muslim institutions in "Muslim regions" have great difficulty and trouble accepting the niqab due to its powerful social stigma under anti-Muslim racism's global narratives of backwardness, extremism, and fear. It was the impossibility of the Muslim subject position (Sayyid 2014) at the level of market institutions within the so-called Middle East, within the Arab-majority world, on the eastern shores of the Mediterranean.

The niqabi accepted in this incident was fortunate to have obtained a clerical position—a position many participants described as "in-the-back job," a job where the niqabi would "not be seen"—to which "very few" other candidates had applied. With all of the above in mind, by the time I left the field, my take on "Islamic institutions'" relation to Islamophobia was quite indecisive. Not only did these institutions represent a marginal part of the economic sector but even within them, the acceptance of the hijab-wearing woman was adulterated, precarious.

Ultimately, this mitigation of the hijab's exclusion by geography, by the nature of the institution, and by the appearance of the dress was violently creating a segregated space for the hijab-wearing woman—establishing the rest of Lebanon for the non-hijab-wearing woman. Further, it was creating a space that regulated, disciplined, and governed the hijab and its wearer. It was, as in the public sphere, the demarcation of a very narrow space where the hijab-wearing woman is pushed to suffocate in her racialization. Feeling that they themselves are part of the reproduction of the dominant norms, of the constraint of the hijab-wearing woman, of her appeasement, my sense was, again, of circumscription, of imprisonment.

Further, in exploring the collected data, a most worrisome observation overwhelmed me: many participants expressed an "ability to comprehend" why hijab-wearing women are not given customer-facing jobs—where "she would be seen" as many phrased it—but not why she is rejected even in those jobs where "no one would see her." For example, refusing the hijab-wearing woman any employment in any bank seemed unacceptable, while rejecting her employment at the front desk seemed much more fathomable for a great many hijab-wearing woman participants. Reflecting on those statements, I wondered what it meant for someone to accept that they were unfit to be seen, that the best they could fight for was to be given a job in the backstage, that they were not "presentable." Fanon's words plagued the field: "shame. Shame and self-contempt. Nausea" (Fanon 2008: 88).

Across both the East and West, the hijab-wearing woman was and continues to be discriminated against in the work sphere. Contemporary Lebanon was no different as the hijab-wearing woman's invisibility becomes normalized and her subjugation becomes justified for erasure. Physical and material concealment was a key technique of anti-Muslim racism in Lebanon. This was, I would argue, another powerful instance of absencing (Vázquez 2012) in the realm of the coloniality of being (rather than power/knowledge) where the non-modern is concealed as the modern claims itself the totality of the real. Here, by preventing her appearance, by pushing for her non-presence, the image of Lebanon was preserved and the imagined identity could be (re)produced, enunciated, perpetuated in/through an Islamophobic labor market.

Before moving on, a final factor must be highlighted: the nature of the work being done. First, this related to the degree of interaction with clients, as was illustrated and explained in many quotes presented above where the hijab was subjected to practices of concealment, which became more extreme as the perceived conservatism of the dress increased. The second was regarding, quite expectedly I would say by now, the rank of the employment. The following quotes present this:

I4: Some companies accept hijab-wearing women for certain jobs.
I1: At AUB hospital, all the cleaning people are hijab-wearing women. When my mother was in the hospital. All of them, one after the other. Very rare to have a non-hijab-wearing woman cleaner.
[agreement]
I3: You feel like that, that inferiority.
I1: Maybe we're over-sensitive, but you feel it! (Iman focus group)
Like now you go around, you might find hijab-wearing woman people, but even if you look at faculty members at universities, you don't get many hijab-wearing women. Very few. The ones who work and are hijab-wearing woman are the cleaners, or security. Like it raises questions … Of course there is a hijab-wearing woman who is qualified to be, like an administrative assistant! I don't know. I think, I don't know. In general, they think it's more presentable [not being hijab-wearing woman]. (Nadine)

I do not know why Nadine, a young Sunni from Beirut living in an upper-class neighborhood, paused before giving her example. I do not know why she said "I don't know" twice. I do not know why she said "administrative assistant." Yet, I would claim that the way she expressed her idea and the fact she did not pursue her example and say "qualified to be a university faculty member," for example, is highly indicative of the hegemony of the discourse inferiorizing the racialized visibly Muslim under dominant anti-Muslim narratives. As Maha, a young Sunni participant, evidenced,

> The hijab is really a "no," in so many organisations and companies. And if it so happened you found a hijab-wearing woman in a particular [good] position, it would be that she was not a hijab-wearing woman and then wore it while she was already there. She might get fired, they might stay after her until she leaves, they might postpone or demote her. This happened to my brother's wife. She wasn't hijab-wearing woman and when she wore it they kept after her. She used to work in a bank. She was the assistant to the director and they kept demoting her until they eventually appointed her as data entry. So she got upset and left. And this is despite the fact that she has no work with customers, she is not in the front! (Maha)

In this sense, if an employee decides to wear the hijab, the employer did not need to fire her as he could, among other racist everyday strategies, simply keep devaluing and demoting her until she, of her own will, left. The standard celebration of women's presence across public and economic spheres in

Lebanon, often presented as an indicator of the country's progressiveness and liberties, required ample nuanced debunking to reveal it as the concealing narrative it is. It was not Lebanese women, but non-visibly Muslim women who enjoyed such privileges. Shia participants in a focus group in Dahieh confirmed,

> Even if you have the brightest student who worked with the greatest doctor and got a PhD, universities wouldn't appoint hijab-wearing women. [I have this friend] they told her that if you wear the hijab, you can't stay here [employed as a professor in a university]. They felt it, at [names university]. So she didn't wear the hijab. They still don't take the hijab-wearing woman as a doctor, in many places. They can accept her as a student, or maybe as a researcher or something, but not a doctor. (Markaz focus group 2)

The hijab-wearing woman, it appeared, when employed, must be employed in a position of weakness, in a position of subjugation. The hijab-wearing woman, it appeared, cannot, should not, occupy the "master" position. The hijab-wearing student can be tolerated, she might even be accepted as a subject to be emancipated. But the hijab-wearing woman in a position of power cannot. It was, it is, institutional and systemic racism (entangled with sexism) at its finest (see Carter 2003; Khattab and Hussein 2017).

Consequently, while this prohibition of the hijab-wearing woman was not (mostly) codified in law as it was in France, for example, it was a de facto hegemonic control pushing anti-Muslim erasure. In facing this reality, it was claimed, many women who wanted to wear the hijab did not, could not. In parallel, many participants expressed how they had to settle for unemployment to keep their dress. The market as both a site and a process of anti-Muslim erasure powerfully worked, I came to conclude. Indeed, many participants claimed that employment, more than any other factor, was keeping many women from wearing the hijab and, consequently, allowing a Muslim presence and visible being in Lebanon. Bana, a young lower-class university student from the north of Lebanon, affirmed,

> Work, for example, in banks, they don't hire a hijab-wearing woman. They think it's a shame. They don't give opportunities. Many girls don't wear the hijab just so that they can find a job they would like and which would suit them. (Bana)
> I have many friends who work who wish they could wear the hijab, but they can't because they work and don't want to lose their job.
>
> Me: There is a chance they'd lose their job?

Ne: [It's] not a chance, of course they will, of course. I have many friends in Lebanon, from Beirut, Sunnis, like they would really love to. They are very committed, don't wear revealing things, only go to women's beaches, don't wear short things but wear long sleeves and long things, but they can't become hijab-wearing women. They know that they'd lose their jobs. They tell me I am so blessed because I don't work and could put it on. That she couldn't, she'd lose her job. One is in an insurance company, one in a software company, they sell ... so, yes. And there are many hijab-wearing women who can't find work because they are hijab-wearing. (Maryam)

Maryam is a middle-aged upper-class Sunni from Beirut whose husband is a well-off businessman. She has the "luxury" of not working, she explained. In her narrative, she said it was that privilege that allowed her to wear the hijab. It was also that privilege that made her choice difficult: she was seen to be giving up on "prestige," becoming an object of "spooking people" and having to go through significant changes in lifestyle. Despite these, she did make the choice, execute it, and now continues to struggle to show most people around her that, in her words, "It's enough, it's not that big of a deal, it's normal. Like you can talk to me [if I am hijab-wearing woman]." It was a clear example of the relationship between privilege and power, privilege and capital, where anti-Muslim racism intersected and entangled with wealth and financial status. It was also a clear example of privilege with a colonial (and patriarchal) curse.

In any case, the noninclusion of non-hijab-wearing Muslim women in fieldwork means there is very little I can say about this. I would, nevertheless, note that some informal conversations with non-hijab-wearing Muslim women confirmed these statements. Still, an additional point can be made here: rarely was the abstaining from wearing the hijab for a need for employment condemned by participants. Rather, it was always justified, presented as an acceptable solution to an intolerable racist condition. Additionally, some proposed a compromise in the face of anti-Muslim racism's attempts at concealing and invisibilizing them: wearing the hijab outside of work and removing it within. Religion needed to be privatized, the neoliberal labor market needed to be secularized, and some hijab-wearing women had no choice but to yield. And indeed, participants explained that this was something some women, including close friends and family, have chosen to do. As Leen, a middle-aged Sunni participant from the north, acknowledged,

There is a huge problem for the hijab-wearing woman in getting a job. I know a lot of people who take off their hijab, go to work, and then go out of work and wear it. This is here in Lebanon, here in Lebanon yes. I've seen this with my own two eyes. Especially if they are working with people. I've seen this. Yes, yes, yes, yes. And they [the employers] know she is doing this. Especially the ones in contact with customers, like not behind offices or working in administration or that, no, the ones at the front. Of course, there are types [of employment] more difficult to get into [than others]. (Leen)

None of the project's participants held that this was their own experience, or that they had to do this at any given point. I do not know if that was because none of them had, or because none of them felt comfortable speaking about it. I never asked; it was not a question I was willing to ask. Either way, they did tell me that such an experience cannot be anything but "devastating." Hoda phrased this as "nakedness," saying "the feeling of nakedness would be unbearable." Additionally, it was presented as a baffling phenomenon, as the hijab is something to be practiced, to be committed to, in the presence of nonfamily individuals. It was presented, ultimately, as extreme assault. What does it mean when someone is not allowed to practice their belief, forced to feel naked, violated for display to resemble the imagined ideal because they need a basic income to survive? Anti-Muslim racism had a different set of priorities, it appeared.

Anti-Muslim racism held vast power within the labor market, a neoliberal market that was a powerful site and tool of this racism's establishment and reproduction. Indeed, mobilizing precarious economic conditions, the need for employment, and the necessity of being "employable" anti-Muslim racism powerfully erased and absenced visible Muslimness from the Lebanese space. Those who, despite this, choose to wear the Muslim dress enter a never-ending struggle, a constant battle, which aims at the eventual *exhaustion* of the visibly Muslim pushing her into removing the dress. In this manner, visible Islam is systematically combated, averted, and obstructed through the Lebanese neoliberal work sphere where techniques of material concealment and invisibilization enforced racialized erasure.

The State

Beyond the domestic, the public, and the work spheres, the Lebanese state was drawn out as an equally excluding anti-Muslim space by participants. The following quote from a discussion among lower-class Sunni hijab-wearing women in Beirut illustrates this:

W3: Of course, because the state here is not a Muslim state. It's a state following something else …

W1: Even the army, the security forces. Everything. You can't if you're hijab-wearing. I know a lot of people.

W2: You know, but the other day I saw a woman wearing the military clothes, the army, hijab-wearing.

W1: She would have worn it during … like after she joined. If she had already joined they might accept. But before joining, no way. Like I know a relative, she's excellent, great in the university, tall and a great body, but because she was hijab-wearing, there was no way for her. (Khaled association focus group)

For participants, the state's exclusion was an evident facet and a core element of its very constitution. As a state "following something else," Lebanon was presented as a structure that was itself inherently incompatible with the hijab. Tala is an older lower-class Shia social worker while Maryam is a Sunni upper-class Beiruti. They explained,

> [The state is] so excluding. Like now, where have they opened [employment opportunities]? In the military, internal security, it is only now that they have started allowing her to wear a hijab. But what is happening in there? What kind of dress does she have to wear? What have they opened for her? As a soldier? As what? (Tala)
>
> Now, the hijab doesn't really fit well with them in the Lebanese state. Like they can't hire her. (Maryam)

In this respect, variables again influenced the exclusion of the hijab-wearing woman with the question of the dress's conservatism and the shape of the hijab, which can be accepted emerging as key. In continuity with the market and the public sphere, both the level of the employment and geography figured. In this sense, a heterogeneity of lived experiences emerged. Anti-Muslim racism imbued the practices of the state despite this heterogeneity. As a focus group participant in Lebanon's north asserted,

R: The Lebanese state wants the non-hijab-wearing Lebanese woman. Why do you exclude me? Why do you discriminate against me? I am Lebanese like you! The people in Tripoli don't want the state, don't engage with it, don't belong to it. People are very marginalised and disadvantaged by it. (Tripoli focus group)

It was a cry of pain and wounding, a serious statement of statelessness, of homelessness. The state and its institutions were not welcoming of the hijab-wearing woman, particularly as an employee. Participants felt the weight of this. The hijab-wearing woman was, certainly, not their intention, not their hope. Similar to Muslim women in the Global North, participants experienced a "criminalizing [of] Islamic dress [that] evidences the attachment of the colonial past to the present and future" where the nation-state functions toward specific political imperial agendas (Brayson 2019).

For reasons of this project's focus and this chapter's space and especially as the methods used, the nature of the data and who fieldwork included with very few interviews with women who had sought work in the state, I will not elaborately explore this issue. The question of this postcolonial state of the Global South and its institutions in their relationship to the racialized hijab-wearing woman's social interaction and life is worthy of a separate project and a serious and elaborate exploration that is beyond the scope of this book. Rather, I will limit myself to making three points.

The first point to be made is that the state, which might be theorized as the institution to protect hijab-wearing women from the racism they face in other spheres, is, to the contrary, an institution that magnifies their racialized oppression and marginalization, indeed one that underwrites it. With this, no participant mentioned the police, the law, or any state institution at any point in our interviews as a source of protection, of rights, or of any form of claims-making. This is an important distinction, with significant effects on how resistance to anti-Muslim racism can be imagined and to how it has been imagined in scholarship focusing on Euro-America (see Kassem 2020).

It was a clear sense of expulsion, and a fracturing of the relationship with the nation, where women expressed an inability to belong in a space where they needed to struggle to be considered human beings. Anti-Muslim racism was here revealed to work by neutralizing sources of legitimacy, of protection, and of resistance, and by building on the imagined patriarchal nation to further establish its exclusion through state apparatuses and institutions. As a Shia focus group participant from Dahieh said after a long debate about feelings of belonging and the relationship to both the nation and the state, "This country has rejected me. With all due love … How much can I belong to it after that?" (Markaz focus group 1).

Second, it can be inferred that the state through its various apparatuses rejects the hijab and the hijab-wearing woman in terms of employment, with similar trends to those encountered in the market: geography plays a role, the conservatism of the dress plays a role, and the type of state institution plays a role. For instance, a "moderately hijab-wearing woman" can find employment at a state school more easily than she can in the army, for example, while one in more "conservative" forms of the dress has little chances in either. If, and when, she is accepted, she is accepted on the terms of the employing institution, with the senses of debt, deficiency, precarity, and threat looming large. Political parties emerged as significant agents here, separate and distinct from the state:

> The hijab-wearing woman is excluded, in her relationship with the state. Us, if we did not belong to these [political party] institutions, and had jobs, the state gives us nothing. (Khaled association focus group)

Eventually, although participants stressed the pressure they lived in as a result of their exclusion from state institutions, many expressed that this exclusion "is not very present" (Markaz focus group 3) and that they only feel it in those instances when they had to be in direct engagement with the state—which are not too frequent. Indeed, some participants stated that the state's racist exclusion is mostly felt by those who attempt to, or wish to, join its institutions and that this was a small minority of hijab-wearing women. Most other people, I was told, lived with little interest or engagement with the state, be it in regard to the hijab or the vast majority of other issues. Surely, this must be contextualized within the historic and ongoing marginality and specific modes of functioning within the Lebanese state, but I contend here that it holds across other geographies as it invites us to reconsider state-centrism from the perspective of the racialized in the study of racism and anti-racism. In this sense, the public sphere, the family, and, most importantly, the market were vastly more wounding while the state's absence resounded. In other words, a reconsideration of some key conceptualizations of the unfolding of racist politics where the state structure is centered requires interrogation, especially when exploring lived experiences outside of the West.

The last point I wish to make here is that the state's position has been undergoing challenges and contestations. Yet, this in itself is a very complicated development beyond this book. Nevertheless, one can assert some impact. While I was conducting fieldwork, the Lebanese prime minister asked state institutions to stop discrimination against hijab-wearing women, especially in terms of employment, in a televised call. While this resonated very well with participants, it was felt to be the beginning of a long struggle and the kind and shape of hijab, the conditions and extent of its existence, and its continued denormalization remain to be seen. Indeed, aware that Hezbollah has failed to produce the normalization of the hijab within its Dahieh "stronghold," cognizant of escalating global Islamophobia, and realizing the heightened divisions in Lebanese society as the country's conditions collapse the scope of this movement's success in subverting colonial structures and discourses that ground anti-Muslim racism remains uncertain. The arguments that will be developed in Chapter 5 where I explore the emerging acceptance of some "modern" and fashionable forms of hijab will allow a more critical and informed reflection around this change and anti-Muslim racism's reproduction.

Ultimately, in respect to the state, the hijab-wearing–state relationship is structured by many elements beyond the dress itself: from corruption and underdevelopment to a lack of provisions and a history of war and sectarianism. When one of the Sunni participants yelled "I am not politically active, I do not vote, I do not believe in this Lebanese state!" (Mona) or when another said "the state is long dead" (Tripoli focus group) I understood these within a much broader context. I would expect similar answers from many non-hijab-wearing women, as well as many men. It was the "people in Tripoli," in this example, not only the hijab-wearing women whose relationship with the state was broken. Many others across Lebanon sought out the state and called on it to take its responsibilities, even if they were not very optimistic that it would. What can be made of the state under such realities that have greatly exacerbated since this book's fieldwork?

The state was not the source of protection many might expect it to be. The judiciary, the rule of law, were neutralized through the very establishment of the Lebanese imagined nation-state, established in a way as to never be mobilizable by Eurocentric modernity's Others. Within this, the "weak state's" oppression did not appear the key element, the most pressuring agent, in anti-Muslim racism in this small nation of the Global South. Here, the state appeared to complement the racism, rather than be its core, in significant contrast to anti-Muslim racism in Euro-America (Brayson 2019; Ezekiel 2006; Mancini 2012; Navarro 2010). Nevertheless, the state in Lebanon did reveal itself as a site of exclusion and marginalization: the state in the so-called Middle East too appeared as an apparatus of anti-Muslim racism under global modernity/coloniality. Eventually, while the issue went well beyond the question of the hijab, it certainly engulfed it as state institutions from within the logic of anti-Muslim racism and modernity/coloniality joined the market, the public, and the family for erasure.

Conclusion

This chapter explored anti-Muslim racism across the various spheres of social life in Lebanon. In practice, the data suggests four key spheres where anti-Muslim racism was experienced through a process of material and lived aggression. The first is the home where it ravages under various pretexts, including care and love, to preserve prestige and guarantee the family's, and the women's, interests. In the public sphere, a collectivist bottom-up aggression unfolds mobilizing everything from civil society institutions to random citizens to preserve the country's image and push toward its anti-Muslim and Westernized projected future. In the work sphere, pragmatic economic motives as well as ones relating to Lebanon and its desired image pervade with rampant structural Islamophobia. The state, as an institutionalization of the imagined Lebanese postcolonial nation, was produced as an additional site of exclusion: unimaginable as a source of protection. Thinking through these four spheres and the data, the market is suggested as the most potent agent of anti-Muslim racism and the most effective aggressor while the state is suggested as a complement to the market's functioning in a curious manifestation of the neoliberal logic. Further, across these various spheres, the same variables emerged as structuring: the geography, the conservatism of the dress, and the social status attached to it. These structuring variables, in turn, reveal themselves as mechanisms of racist control, of policing, discipline, and management. In this structuring, anti-Muslim racism mobilizes different spheres in different ways and to different extents in different spaces.

Based on this, a number of techniques through which anti-Muslim racism functions in a non-Western Arab-majority setting can be suggested and research developing these techniques is raised as necessary. The first is the omnipresence of cumulative converging pressure through various forms of harassment and micro-aggression and directed from various social institutions, actors, and spheres working toward exhaustion. The second is systematic vulnerabilizing, devaluing, and impoverishing the objectified racialized Muslim at both material and non-material levels. The third is a spatialization of difference and the establishment of invented imagined borders for cloistering across both geographies and institutional spaces in continuity with established colonial practices of past decades. Here, epistemic absencing meant material and lived physical concealment, a cloistering away from the public eye in negating existence. In this respect, the Fanonian zone of nonbeing revealed itself as painfully heterogeneous and, as this research shows, its heterogeneity was even within the same (one) marker. As with the difference with the non-hijab-wearing woman, a difference between the different forms of hijab pivoting around similarity to the imagined West dictated the degree to which hijab-wearing women had a semblance of "life." In Chapter 5, I will return to this difference.

Eventually, anti-Muslim racism reveals itself not only as a structure of power at the epistemic level but also as an epistemic and material structure of power that reproduces itself by mobilizing everything around the contemporary world's dwellers subsuming all difference under one logic. The ultimate result is a deep wounding, a deep hemorrhaging wound that is social and psychic inflicted on the hijab-wearing body and being.

My knowledge of academic scholarship on Lebanon, especially works such as those of Deeb (2006), had prepared me for a Lebanese field where the hijab was deeply stigmatized, where hijab-wearing women were considered backward, inferior. In the field, the situation revealed itself as far more complex than expected. Indeed, my own experiences in the country would have, I thought, helped prepare me. Yet, during research, the experienced anti-Muslim racism revealed itself as far more exhausting. In fact, I came to realize that I was profoundly unprepared. Ultimately, anti-Muslim racism was forcing erasure in a manner I could not have been prepared for. Both the project's participants and I, as subjects identified as Lebanese Muslims, experienced "a feeling of inferiority? No, a feeling of nonexistence" (Fanon 2008: 106).

5

A Kaleidoscopic Spectrum of Muslim Dress and the Reproduction of Anti-Muslim Racism

In Chapter 3, I explored the visibly Muslim woman's racialization as a belated Arabo-Muslim difference in excess. The lived impact of this racialization within participants' everyday experiences across social spheres was made visible and analyzed in Chapter 4. Throughout this analysis, Muslim dress's heterogeneous scene was identified as was the heterogeneous scene of this dress and its wearer's lived aggression and assault. Thinking alongside Fanon and Shariati, this chapter examines the lives of the various forms of Muslim dress in Lebanon, their emergence in deep entwinement with the conditions of anti-Muslim racism, and their implication in (re)producing this racism as it complexifies the very category of the *muhajaba*. Specifically, it explores how a higher association to the Muslim, the Arab, the historicized means increased aggression while a distance from these racializing traits means lessened assault to examine the relevant dynamics at work in participants' shared lived experiences.

The objective of this chapter is to explore the various forms of Muslim dress's effects, rather than to classify or sketch the forms of Muslim dress in themselves. In turn, these effects are not stipulated in relation to material form/shape—essentialized or claimed to hold inherent or independent properties—but rather to situatedness within a specific context and space. Consequently, the effects discussed here can differ from one context to another, shifting from particular shapes of dress to other shapes, while the underlying *dynamics* that this chapter examines woundingly persist. While the chapter speaks of "fashion," "modern," "non-modern" and "committed" hijabs, these categories are not essentialized nor taken as fixed, intrinsic, or (trans)historical but rather used as they were used by participants in the field. Far from being discrete, neat, or binary identifications they are co-constitutive and imbued with meaning within the worlds of this project's participants where they are always being contested, made, and remade as they converge and diverge in complex and layered ways. As conceptual and analytical classifications, they are surely far messier and overlapping in the lived reality of Lebanese society. These categories are indeed used specifically to critique them—to show how "non-modern," "modern," and "fashionable" hijabs as forms of "Muslim dress" only exist and dwell in relation to modernity/coloniality emerging through it and implicated in its reproduction. Accordingly, the chapter is invested in thinking the specific—and only—ways through which the dress is made to change and "modernize." The consequent argument is the need to liberate Muslim practices and allow them to *be* living, dynamic, and pluralistic beings beyond the tyranny of modernity/coloniality.

The Kaleidoscopic Spectrum and Muslim Dress's Possibility

This chapter will not develop a typology or a cartography of the various forms of Muslim dress present and practiced across the Lebanese space. Indeed, in the field, I rapidly realized that the varying multiplicity and complexity of forms, shapes, sizes, and associations in which the hijab came meant any classification or typology was difficult, if not counterproductive.[1] Rather, the chapter will seek to identify a heterogeneous scene to examine and analyze its entanglement with anti-Muslim racism in Lebanon.

In line with the data presented in previous chapters, participants articulated an overarching sorting based around "modernity," with "fashion" deeply associated with it in identifying various forms of Muslim dress practiced in the country.[2] As both Rima, a Shia participant from Beirut, and another Shia participant in a focus group in Dahieh, presented,

> P3: What counts [is that] you have the fashion, the *shar'e* and the abaya, which is the full cover.
> [Group verbal agreement]
> P4: And all [different shapes] in-between. (Focus group Markaz 3)
> There is a gradation. In general, we speak of two [main]
> categories: very committed: abaya, then *shar'e* and the long shirt and scarf, these are the really committed where there are certain habits forced vs. the less [committed], the more modern, the one who shows the neck with pants for example and tighter clothes. And it keeps going. (Rima)

For participants, the different forms of Muslim dress could be sorted, placed on a spectrum going from what is constructed as most unmodern to most modern while passing by the various degrees of what was presented as a measurable modernity. On this spectrum, the abaya-wearing woman emerged as situated at one pole of lived experiences while "fashionable hijabis" wearing pants, a shirt, and a headscarf (or sometimes a turban) emerged at the other.[3] The abaya-wearing woman was the most "committed" in the sense of being the one most adhering to Muslim jurisprudence and requirements of Muslim dress as per most participants' (and wider) beliefs in the country. Most committed, in this sense, meant most religiously observant as well as closest to the Muslim identity as standardly perceived in Lebanese society. In between, a variety of shapes, forms, sizes, colors, and cuts existed. The *shar'e* was one of these, connoting a form of dress wearing a long skirt and a long covering shirt with a long loose headscarf in a manner deemed "modest."

Importantly, these signifiers of modern, fashion, committed or modest do not refer to one form of dress but rather to a "set" of forms. There is no straightforward linear and methodically sequential variation from a specific signification into another specific signification. The scene appeared, rather, extremely complex and multifaceted composed of many elements with no preset or unambiguous removed boundaries. Thinking through these multiple dimensions while also wary of falling into ideal-type fallacies and circumscribed or clear-cut categories (see Bhambra 2007) and attempting to convey lived experiences that are never fixed, always in process, I refer to this as a *kaleidoscopic spectrum* structured around modernity.

Maha, a Sunni participant from Beirut, and Sana, a Shia participant in a focus group in South Lebanon, argued that there existed an important correlation between the growing public appearance of the hijab in Lebanon and the emergence of the modern and fashionable hijabs:

> I think this makes it [modern hijab] fit more with the society now, the age we now live in. It's beautiful, and we can all resemble each other with it, and that's very important. (Sana)

> The contrast is huge ... that's why ... maybe ... like what I said ... what is getting the hijab to be accepted more is that it's become diluted more. You are now wearing the clothing of casual people but with the hijab on your head. It's becoming more, like ... these are hijab-wearing and these [women] are not [hijab-wearing] and the difference is that [only] one specific thing now ... but if

you were to see someone wearing the *abaya*, you're seeing someone completely … like … different. (Maha)

Casually stating that an abaya-wearing woman cannot possibly be imagined walking into or even standing in front of a government building, Maha described how the hijab was differentiating into "normal" dress—away from its Muslim identity. By decreasing the difference and contrast between the *muhajaba* and the standard (modernized) Lebanese woman, this differentiation, she argued, constituted a different improved social experience. The result, she went on to explain, was the spread and proliferation of this "modern hijab" as the *more-different* (and anomalized) hijab gradually faded. Such a framing echoed across the field. It was, in Maha's words, a question of dilution: the hijab and the *muhajaba* needed to be diluted *in* Lebanese society because they were too different, too Other. It was this dilution, she explained, that formed the core of this thriving kaleidoscopic spectrum's emergence and structuring and resulting shifts in social experiences. Importantly, this rise and its specificities are surely also influenced by other factors from national and regional politics to economic and consumer turns and trends. Yet, for participants, *decreasing difference* with the modernized non-muhajaba woman was the key variable at play. In line with this and this book's objective in analyzing anti-Muslim racism, the remainder of this chapter will explore what this dilution is, to think through its implication in the racialization and inferiorization of the visibly Muslim. It remains for future work to further develop an understanding of this in its constitutive complexities and varied effects and lives.

Dilution as a Process: Hollowing Mummification and the Hegemony of the Modern Fashionable Hijab

In inquiring about what characterizes the spreading "new hijab" a number of features can here be summarized. The first was material. This included the extent of the body that was covered where the "modern hijab" revealed more of the wearer's body, especially in terms of the arms, the feet, and the neck. It also included cuts and colors, where it came in various "stylish" forms and shapes that were aligned with the latest trends—as contrasted to a "previous hijab" of standard cuts and plain colors. A third feature is change in the sense that hijab-wearing women did not wear the same dress but regularly renewed their attire in contrast to forms of Muslim dress that involve wearing a similar or identical dress daily. Fourthly, it meant the inclusion of "signée clothes" and designer marks to the hijab—or at least fakes of them if they were unaffordable. This included accessories from handbags to scarves. Here, the modern and fashionable hijabs were increasingly to be bought from the same shops and (middle- and upper-middle-class) markets that sell "regular clothes," participants explained, as the segregation in markets between a "Muslim" one and a standard Westernized one was gradually disappearing. Accordingly, this emerging hijab could involve a much heightened form of consumption and an alignment with the global fashion industry's main articulations in Lebanon. It was not, it must be noted, necessary for all these features to exist for a dress to count as "modern"—a combination of some often sufficed, albeit the more there were the more modern the dress was considered to be.

Tellingly, most participants who expressed an explicit rejection of the "new dress" and/or a choice to commit to more "unmodern" forms of Muslim dress explained that they tried to "integrate" components of the fashionable hijab as a tactic that could ameliorate their lived experiences. *Fashioning* their attire was a means through which visibly Muslim women could negotiate and contest their inferiorization as they establish their similarity, legitimacy, and rights in Lebanese society.

Salma stressed that, to understand the current "situation," one has to realize that the more the *muhajaba* "resembled" the "normal woman" the better she would "manage to live." This semblance, she explained, meant "not resembling the committed Muslim woman at all." In this sense, discrimination and exclusion could be alleviated by having the wearer of the Muslim dress distancing themselves from the Arabo-Muslim difference in excess. This includes a foregoing of what are commonly considered to be the jurisprudential conditions of the Muslim code and its requirements, signaling that the wearer is "not, strictly speaking, committed." Discussing this emerging hijab, a lower-class Sunni participant from a focus group in Saida and an older lower-class Shia participant living in a town in the Lebanese south explained,

> It's become the short and tight thing and all that. Plus, we need to realise it's a scarf on the head but with tight pants, showing legs, tight clothes. You look and you find no difference between the hijab-wearing and the non-hijab-wearing except for that [head] covering. Sometimes you have one hijabi and one not wearing hijab, you find that the dress of the non-hijab is more modest than the hijab! (Focus group, Saida)

> Many people wear a really horrible hijab. The other day, I saw this woman wearing these super tight clothes revealing everything and I felt so hurt and ashamed. I felt like I wanted to take off the piece of cloth she had on her head. (Nisrine)

The Saida focus group participant here expressed a burden and a pain: in Lebanon, the proliferating hijab was made to resemble "normal" dress by being made to lose its "Muslim identity." The "new" changed hijab was accordingly experienced as an assault where a language of loss and harm echoed throughout the field.

> There are types, we call it the *"mode"* hijab. The *"mode"* hijab is itself now differentiating, becoming degrees and levels. In one level there is coverage with some [attempt at] attraction, and then another level tighter and not non-baggy clothes, and then the next level ... a *vusson* [tights] ... It's catastrophic. Wearing black in *Ashura* [mourning commemoration of the prophet's grandson] but it [the dress] shows and describes [your body]. It's just physical head covering, nothing more or less. We are in a world, the world of internet, with high divorce rates, degraded movies, porn. (Tala)

For Tala, an older Shia social worker living in Dahieh, the *"mode* hijab" (*mode* being her word rather than a translation) was continuously differentiating to become more and more distanced from what she described as the "proper and legitimate hijab" that she categorized as Muslim in both social identity and Islamic jurisprudence. Covering the body in a socially identifiably Muslim manner that is in line with specific Islamic religious standards and conceptualizations of modesty and virtue as well as Muslim customs and habits was specifically what this emerging hijab was meant to be undoing. In this sense, the required dilution for improved lived experiences necessitated a specific kind of semblance to the non-hijab-wearing woman, the age, and its "soul" where the Muslim was abjected.

Tala's arguments echoed across the Lebanese geography and the various divides of class, age, education, and sect. Most tellingly, they were expressed by most participants who themselves wore what might be classified as "modern" and "fashionable" hijabs—a large number (if not majority) of this project's overall participants. Throughout, such participants expressed ambivalence, discomfort, and unease toward their own form of dress and a "wish" to reach a more "complete" hijab in the future:

> This looks beautiful, what I wear. I know it's not perfect, from an Islamic point of view, but it's not like I am not wearing a hijab at all and it would be, it would just

be super difficult to live and do what I do in a different kind of hijab. It would be just too difficult. (Noura, Beirut)

Noura made these statements with a significant tone of pain. From losing their jobs to exposing themselves to inferiorizing stereotypes and to paralyzing their mobility within Lebanon, the consumer fashionable hijab emerged as increasingly needed, even inescapable, under the hegemony of anti-Muslim racism. Salam, Shia and living in Beirut, and Shaza, who is Sunni and from the north and living in Beirut, explained,

> It's no secret that this fashion hijab, including what I wear, let's be honest, is not very proper, from an Islamic point of view. But I'm realistic, and I know what I can and cannot do. It hurts sometimes, like you have moments when you feel you just wish you could be wearing something different. When my parents came back from Hajj [pilgrimage to Mecca], I really felt that. But it is what it is. Maybe one day, you never know. (Shaza)
>
> It's not the end, you know, I'm still young. I wear this now, but I'm sure one day I will wear a better hijab. But now, it's not possible, God knows and understands, it's just not possible for me and my life. (Salma)

In the Tripoli focus group, comprised of participants wearing various forms of both "modern" and "non-modern" dress, a series of explanations from all participants around the "necessity" of wearing particular "modern" forms of dress to avoid discrimination and secure employment despite this not being considered as "really Muslim" ended with silence—a silence of deep wounding and exhaustion. One participant who wore what would be considered as modern hijab explained that she had tried to wear more "committed forms of dress," but found it made it impossible "to live and move in this society." Arriving at the conclusion that "God wants me to be able to live and move, definitely," she changed her form of dress even though she "loved it." As a consequence of this being a *needed dilution*, the changes required were unambiguously in the direction of resembling what participants termed "normal Lebanese woman" understood as middle class, secularized or performing secularity, Westernized, and modernized. There was, participants stressed, no other direction change could take. *Life* and being able to *live* were words that occurred and recurred in these explanations.

In colonization, especially in the colonization of culture and religion, there has long been a process whereby "the customs of the colonized people, their traditions, their myths," as Fanon had explained, were deemed unfit and were pushed into being cleansed "by a dose of Christian values" (Singh 2007: 346). With anti-Muslim racism, the situation is mostly similar: Muslim religious practice was deemed unfit and required, for its cleansing, a dose of secular modernity (Maldonado-Torres 2008), which meant a ceding of what are considered as the dress's physical and material Muslim identity and characteristics. As Asad (2003) explains, the secular is not the withdrawal of the religious and what remains thereof but rather the Eurocentric sovereign's power of governing religion and the religious to be regulated in line with a specific modern order that controls life and being. In this respect, the secular must be understood in its entanglement with modernity and its anti-Muslim articulations. As Mahmood (2009: 837) frames it, the secular is "the rearticulation of religion in a manner that is commensurate with modern sensibilities and modes of governance" where the Muslim constructed as the non-modern is powerfully erased. Through this secularizing dose, Muslim dress too would further resemble "normal" dress with its aesthetics and sensibilities.

The kaleidoscope of the Muslim dress was, therefore, far from the result of natural and innate diversification or developments or an organic benign cultural movement. A reaction to rampant discrimination and assault and driven by the pressure of improved lived experiences, it was an artificially invented and constructed spectrum emerging in deep entanglement with racialization with a clear wounding orientation away from the Muslim and constructing a Western-modern secular space/place; thus its experience as assaulting and wounding across the field and participants' rejection of its growing hegemony. In other words, modernity's artificial and enforced kaleidoscopic spectrum was a hierarchy: it was structured by modernity's hierarchy of the human coded by the religious practice's dose of secularity. Mobility, rights, and privileges depended on it.

Similar movements have been recorded across the West. Almila (2014), for example, explores how hijab-wearing women negotiated their belief in Muslim dress—constructed as "discredited stigma"—in pursuing a sense of comfort when in the public sphere (Almila 2014: 111). Almila (2014) explores the complexity of this negotiation, and its failure, and records how a change in the style of dress and hijab worn was mobilized "to control others' reactions through less conspicuous dress styles," where "inconspicuousness was framed in terms of colours (avoiding black), a particular style ('Western') and the season" (Almila 2014: 216). In this analysis, space emerged as a crucial factor that conditioned what women wear. Explaining that hijab-wearing women change their dress depending on the neighborhood where they are, her participants are offered as agentic architects of the modern sphere. Koura (2018) arrives at similar findings in the context of the United States where, she explains, her excluded hijab-wearing participants chose to change their dress in an attempt at (incomplete) similarity to their environment: shifting to pants and shirts, for example. For Koura (2018), as for Almila (2014), such movements are framed as "positive" and commendable strategies through which women agentively resist their exclusion and co-create the space they inhabit.

Speaking of the colonized, Fanon explained, "insofar as he conceives of European culture as a means of stripping himself of his race, he becomes alienated" (Fanon 2008: 224). While it was difficult for the Black man to dose his material Black skin with physical "whiteness," the nature of the hijab as a site of racialization meant that this stripping could begin with the dress, at the level of the material. And so were many participants, experiencing and expressing a deep alienation—as this and the following chapter will continue to explore.

While not negating the agency and creativity Almila (2014) and Koura (2018) highlight, my argument here is that this movement resembling the European is subject to the structure of anti-Muslim racism: wounding, power-laden, colonized. This is far from an argument that there is a "Muslim dress" that is essentialized, monolithic, invariant. Rather, the Muslim dress is surely and necessarily dynamic, alive, and variable and it is key that it remains so away from exclusionary or predetermined forms and dogmas. This is, further, not an argument to erase the agency of women living under intolerable conditions. It is rather an argument that emerges thinking alongside such women—it is their argument. It is, specifically, an argument that Muslim dress's dynamism and life are being aborted by the specific alienations and enforcements of Eurocentric modernity/coloniality and its Islamophobia.

Alongside Muslim dress's movement to resemble European wear, a movement to change what participants considered to be the hijab-wearing woman's Muslim behavior and conduct was also experienced. Here, acceptance into the mainstream appeared dependent on the hijab-wearing woman adapting to the norms, habits, and social customs of Westernized, secularized, and Eurocentrically cosmopolitan "mainstream Lebanese society." Fading into the social landscape to become dissimilar at the material level of appearance was not sufficient. One had to declare themselves modern and not-so-Muslim in conduct. In this sense, being allowed to ascend on the *hierarchy of being* required performing the habits of those at the top as well as resembling them in physical appearance. Such was what Nelly, a young Lebanese Shia *muhajaba* who appeared on a Christian-affiliated Lebanese media station (one of the first-ever hijab-wearing women on such media platforms), specified: the *muhajaba* that can be allowed on television was the one mainstream society felt "looks a bit like us, in the way she dresses and acts and all that." From a specific form of Lebanese Arabic accent and the mixing of Arabic with English and French to codes of physical conduct and to manners of bodily comportment, Nelly explained she not only needed to wear a different hijab but also needed to perform a different habitus. This, I came to find, was a norm:

> **Reem:** He [employer] accepted to give her [my daughter] the job, he saw her in a hijab, he told her that religious rituals ... like you might have a meeting and there is alcohol on the table, you would sit. You can't say no. She said ok.
> **Madawi:** She was forced.
> **Reem:** Forced, yes, she accepted. So this is a part of what's happening. She accepted. She has to go to places, I tell her "look away, don't look." (Reem and Madawi)

Reem's young Sunni engineer daughter joined the interview after being called over the phone by her mother to "share her experiences." She wears a "modern" form of the hijab and had a story that resembled many stories I encountered in the field. She was offered employment at a Christian-owned engineering company in a Christian-majority region after many months of waiting, following up, and persisting. Her "very modern elegant" hijab was key in the possibility of such an employment—one that she and her mother described should have been guaranteed given her qualifications and professional profile but "was stalled as the company appeared hesitant." After many delays, before being offered the job, she was invited to meet the company's manager where she was explicitly asked to consent to the norms and habits of the employing institution—to the "non-Muslim" lifestyle. She could not, it was made clear, "practice Islam" while on the job or make any "special request" based on her religion. Accepting, she entered a space to perform a mode of being that was, in the words of her mother, "deeply hurting" at both the individual level and that of the family. Reem went on to explain that the daughter, who was constantly scrutinized, often complained of a sense of being examined in her personal behavior where coworkers and supervisors sought "to find a mistake and then hold it against [her]." Her daughter interjected that the incidents were far more often than she complained to her mother, wanting to spare her "the headache and pain."

The situation of the visibly Muslim woman held significant semblances to Fanon's Black man who was pushed by his society into a situation where he had to constantly "furnish proofs of his whiteness to others and above all to himself" (Fanon 2008: 215). For participants, this meant they had to pass "tests" of their modernity, or of their "light Islam," as they had to completely avoid any association that would declare them too Arabo-Muslim different, too belated, too excessive. Fanon (2008: 112) declared, "I subjected myself to an objective examination, I discovered my blackness." Many hijab-wearing women subjecting themselves to objective examination were well aware of their *hijabiness* and the dominant structures of anti-Muslim racism. Yet, they continued to subject themselves to such a necessary examination as they lived as policed, surveilled, and controlled subjects of Eurocentric modernity/coloniality in Lebanon. Indeed, in a movement with great parallels to migration regimes, the hijab-wearing woman was assessed, tested, and profiled to be deemed either fit or unfit, to be denied rights (De Genova 2016, 2017; Mayblin 2017). In a world where "the colonized subject is always presumed guilty" (Fanon 2001: 16) such was no easy feat and itself produced wounds that were meant to become scars as the hijab-wearing woman ascended on the hierarchy of Lebanese society. Such a reality, Fanon (2001) explained, produces an inferiority complex that, in turn, leads to neurosis.

Maryam told and complained of experiences across social spheres where she was expected, because she "didn't wear *shar'e* or something," to be "lax with Islamic rules." From shaking hands with foreign men to prayer and to forms of recreation, she was constantly called to practices that breached her identity and faith, which many believed she would be willing to undertake. The result, she said, was "disturbing," "exhausting," and "infuriating." Yet, it was common as the hijab-wearing woman in more "modernized" dress was expected to perform secularity and Eurocentric modernity. Indeed, in many interviews, participants explained how an aggressive set of social norms dictating acceptable and unacceptable practices of the modern hijab-wearing woman were set in place. Conduct socially considered to be "very religiously committed" was unacceptable and, most powerfully, when women who are wearing the "modern" forms of the dress choose such conduct they were reprimanded and ostracized:

> For sure [different forms of the hijab are different]! Because the look, for example, the *jilbab* [long uniform dress] is different from me. The *jilbab* wearing [woman], it's impossible for someone to put their hand out to shake her hand. But I got into a situation and a fight with someone actually because he put his hand out and I said, "Sorry, I don't" so he said: "Put your hand on your chest!" and yelled and stuff like that and then started saying "You work in [names

humanitarian organization], how do you even hold a patient?" and things like that. (Focus group, Saida)

This young lower-class Sunni participant then further explained the situation had arisen because her dress did not "give off that idea" of someone who is "fully committed"—and that these were common occurrences. As she was wearing a more modern form of the hijab she was eventually expected to be "less-Muslim." She was expected to have been more liberated, more adapted. She had proven, she felt, that she was unbefitting of the assumption he had made of her and of her inclusion in a civil society humanitarian organization, of being permitted to ascend on the *hierarchy of the human*.

Including changing both dress and associated behavior, Muslim women in Euro-America have sought to be perceived as more "moderate" and more "modern" as they changed conduct in order to gain social acceptance (see, for example, data from Almila 2014; Koura 2018). A quite similar mechanism was unfolding in Lebanon where the hijab-wearing woman needed to tone down her social form through both shape and conduct as a means of evidencing her modernity, her dissociation from the Arabo-Muslim difference in excess in response to rampant anti-Muslim racism. Anti-Muslim racism in Lebanon, therefore, functioned similarly to anti-Muslim racism in the West as the hijab across the Global North and South was being pushed to resemble the European (either at "home" or in white settler colonies such as the United States and Canada) to dilute into coloniality's "mainstream" in an erasure of Otherness. Dilution, ultimately, appears to refer to an ongoing effort under a homogenizing impetus inherited from Eurocentric empire that required the erasure of the Muslim *difference* to enter modern *"whiteness"* (see Singh 2007).

> I feel it [the shape of the hijab] is definitely changing in that it's now more like [western] fashion, you know? It's like if you look at Instagram, there are these hijabi bloggers everywhere and there's this term *hijabis* everywhere and then … now you have people who design for hijabis … designers that call themselves, who design for hijabis, a lot of people are now … Loosening it. (Nibal)

Continuing her narration of the "way things are now," Nibal, a young lower-class Sunni participant from the north of Lebanon, extensively spoke of the role played by social media as well as other media forms in "bombarding" the *muhajaba* with hijabi models, fashion, and trends to create wants and desires. The result of this, Maya, who is a young Shia upper-class participant, strongly complained, was "a lot of time and effort and interest" as the *muhajaba* herself "was changed." Explaining that she had gone through "a phase like that" herself, she quickly asserted that she "fought it" and "stopped" because "that's not who I want to be." Salma, a young middle-class Shia from the south of Lebanon, similarly argued that, for her, the hijab was meant to "Islamically" work toward "stopping materialism from you." Instead, and given the dominant modernist Westernizing consumer culture, wearing the hijab was rather forcing the *muhajaba* to spend extra time "shopping for an acceptable attire" and becoming "obsessed" with how she looked. Indeed, many participants complained that the "hijab culture [has become] toxic" and loaded with "competition" to prove who wore the more expensive, more stylish, and more attractive clothing as Muslim women needed to spend significant time, effort, and money in pursuing such distinction and modernity. In this respect, a consumerist culture and set of interests and occupations was deeply entwined with this fashionable hijab's emergence and workings. With the commodification of the hijab the *muhajaba* is invented as a consumer: capital was key as consumption and marketization emerged as an important tool in negotiating Islamophobia, claiming "modernity," and erasing Otherness.

The required dilution did not cease at the shape, at the sign, but rather permeated the content, the signified, and produced the acceptable hijab with its predefined conduct and ethos: it was dilution aggressing Muslim subjectivity as well as what constituted Muslim codes and identity for participants. Wearing the more modern hijab, the supposedly modern *muhajaba* was required to be, and was made to be, what participants understood as a less-Muslim subject. Soha, a young lower-class Shia living on the outskirts of Beirut, formulated this as being the creation of a hijab and a hijab-wearing woman that "had the looks of what might look like a semblance of a hijab, but was not a hijab or a *muhajaba* at all." As Tala, an older Shia social worker, explained, "They're emptying the hijab, inside out, they're hollowing it." Diluted and emptied out, the remainder was "a piece of cloth on the head," Maha argued, where mainstream Lebanese society "might not [even] think she is *muhajaba* if she is in a turban. They might think it is normal, fashion or something." Eventually, what was unfolding in Lebanon appeared to be no other than the old European policy of "subsume, dilute, and assimilate all particulars under the hegemony of a single particularity" (Grosfoguel 2012a: 95).

Fanon (1994b) theorized "mummification." He explained,

> The setting up of the colonial system does not of itself bring about the death of the native culture. Historic observation reveals, on the contrary, that the aim sought is rather a continued agony than a total disappearance of the pre-existing

culture. This culture, once living and open to the future, becomes closed, fixed in the colonial status, caught in the yoke of oppression. Both present and mummified, it testifies against its members. It defines them in fact without appeal. (Fanon 1994b: 34)

In this sense, mummification can be understood as a process of colonization that creates the practices of the colonized along a different image, along an image that would render them an alterity at coloniality's service. Discussing institutions, Fanon (1994b) explains that this creation of mummified institutions meant "the setting up of archaic, inert institutions, functioning under the oppressor's supervision and patterned like a caricature of formerly fertile institutions" (Fanon 1994b: 34). Shariati (2011) similarly outlines,

> In summary, in this swamp, colonisation was struggling to consolidate, maintain and extend its roots to the depths of the society of Eastern nations, their thoughts and their tastes, by reversing their cultural and historical values as well as their moral and religious personality by way of a caricature preceding their erasure. (Shariati 2011: 45, own translation)

Accordingly, I propose mummification occurring at the level of religious practice and emerging from within the structure and experience of anti-Muslim racism closing and foreclosing religious practice and forcing it into agony. I further contend that anti-Muslim racism in Lebanon functions through the creation of mummified caricatured practices. This mummification, I advance, unfolded through a process of "emptying out" as a systematic movement enforcing coloniality's order by materially changing the practice into a specific Eurocentric direction and negating the Muslim identity, subjectivity, and conduct meant to accompany it—a reaction to anti-Muslim racism moving to erase the "Muslim subject."

Shariati (2011), discussing imperialism and the processes through which modernization pursues its assault on native cultures, proposed the concept of the "emptying of the self" whereby "cultural imperialism" pursued a systematic attempt at destroying the habits, traditions, and practices of the colonized. Fanon (1994b: 13) had similarly employed the concept in his objection to the colonialist push erasing the Arab when he writes, "Well, don't you have the impression that you are emptying him of his substance?" In line with this, I suggest a conceptualization of this emptying as a process where the practices of the colonized themselves, who are made to "endure," are fractured away from their iconography, symbolism, meaning, role, and impact. Emptying is, therefore, the technique of mummifying, as it has long been, working in anti-Muslim racism as it had long worked in colonization.

Eventually, the dilution Maha, a young Sunni participant from Beirut, for example, referred to was the disappearance and fading of the hijab into a semblance of colonized mainstream society through its emptying mummification into a proclaimed "modern fashion hijab" under rampant anti-Muslim racism. Diluted and emptied out, this hijab that "did not resemble itself" in "shape or in content" was inconsequential: it was not Arab anymore but European-like, it was not Muslim anymore but secular-like. It was not it anymore, but a colonized being that had little effect, even performed Europe without ever being it, without ever becoming it: a shadow version of a soulless self. Such was how participants experienced the colonial emptying of the colonized's practice: emptied and mummified was the modern fashionable hijab's darker side emerging in entwinement with the hijab-wearing woman's racialization and assault.

Alongside this mummified hijab a different form of hijab constructed and imagined as "committed" and "unmodern" continued to exist. Here, an additional movement unfolded. As the mummified hijab-wearing woman was expected to be less-Muslim, less "committed," and less religious, the committed hijab-wearing woman was expected to be Muslim and religious in an augmented and amplified manner. Hijab-wearing women refusing to dilute into the colonizer's shape and practice, as explored above, are expected to be an ideal complete Muslim subject and the infallible idol in their lives' various spheres in a movement that compounds social expectations of them and places them under constant scrutiny for an unrealistic always already failed religious, Muslim, and ethical demeanor:

> The sister not wearing a abaya, whose hijab is sporty, like regular, the same as everyone else [who is not wearing a hijab] … you feel that the religious requirements are low, they don't wait for great things, they don't expect them. The one wearing *shar'e*, you feel they expect more. The one in the abaya, they require the maximum. As I said, she needs to be carrying the *Tahrir* [Islamic jurisprudence book] in her head and walking in the street. [It is] that much. Like my husband's family call me *shaikha*. That reflects what is demanded [of me]. So you feel if someone makes a mistake and she is wearing the lowest level of the hijab, there is no problem, it is normal. The mistake that comes out of the one wearing *shar'e*, there is something there. If the one in the abaya makes a mistake, like that's really huge, and it's on everyone [all abaya-wearing women]. (Fatima)

Shaikha is a female conjugation of the word *sheikh*, standardly used to refer to a male religious scholar in Lebanon. For Fatima, a middle-aged Shia who is herself an activist living in Beirut's Shia southern suburb, by choosing to wear the *abaya*, she was situated as a religious scholar with the expectations of being a religious expert and a representative of Islam anticipated to be, she clarified, versed in Islamic rulings, philosophy, and history, among others. This included, I was told, an expectation of the complete ethical subject: in terms of temperament, respect toward others, material and nonmaterial "purity," and myriad traits taken to be those of the idealized ethical being. The result of this was, participants argued, the burdening of the "committed" form of the hijab with a heavy weight that, in most instances, was doomed to failure.

Povinelli (2002) had identified a "cunning of recognition" imposed on indigenous populations forced into an "impossible standard" of an imagined authentic indigenous culture in her study of Australian "multiculturalism." In this mechanism, by enforcing this impossible standard, the colonized subject would be forced to collapse under "impossible desires: to be this impossible object," consequently subjugating this authenticity to the politics of the colonized present (Povinelli 2002: 6). This cunningness, Povinelli (2002) concludes, renders multiculturalism a mechanism of the colonial order's reproduction. A similar mechanism, I contend, is unfolding in Lebanon: burdening the *muhajabas* with a weight under which they were doomed to collapse as they were forced to perform an impossible imagined authenticity under colonial structures of anti-Muslim racism pursuing their own recognition as *different*.

In this sense, anti-Muslim coloniality in Lebanon worked through a double mechanism. The first, and more prominent one, was the push à la Fanon (2008) where the racialized dwelled under the gaze of the colonizer in pursuit of necessary recognition. The second, on the other hand, was one where a specific segment of the racialized—comprising those who were deemed to, in their practice, refuse this gaze—were forced into the gaze of an imagined idealized proclaimed authentic culture of their own to collapse under an impossible weight.

As women under a sexist patriarchal structure and in the Fanonian zone of nonbeing, a zone where "class, gender and sexual oppression as lived by the 'Non-Being Other' are aggravated due to the joint articulation of such oppressions with racial oppression" (Grosfoguel 2016: 14), the compounded strain from entangling markers of subjugation unfolding through this movement emerged as most agonizing, most wounding. Soha, a young lower-class Shia who wore such a dress, lamented,

> It's a terrible thing [wearing the abaya]. It's like being on a mission all the time, through behaviour and actions. It's like the infallible Imam whose actions are

law. It's not right for it to be this way, but that's how society treats it. And if one [abaya-wearing woman] makes a mistake, everyone [abaya wearing] gets attacked. (Soha)

By doing this, the *muhajaba* in the abaya (or any other more non-modern dress such as the niqab, as the following section will explore) was being deliberately overburdened in a process designed to exhaust her into self-dilution, self-erasure, as the practice was being made impossible. It was, in this sense, a process where the abaya or niqab-wearing woman functioned as a case in point to others: as cautionary signaling of the dangers ensuing from choosing a dress that was *different*, that was *too* Muslim.

Nisrine, an older Shia woman living in the south of Lebanon, is a social activist and a religious preacher in the community who does not wear the abaya. Explaining that she would have "loved to," she said that the abaya is "perceived as more perfect" and "too much of a responsibility" for her, something she "cannot live up to." Further, it was surrounded by "gossip and taboos." Tala told of how "if you ride with a bus or taxi driver, you hear all the talking there": that "[the] abaya-wearing woman she rides with me [driver] and then gets somewhere and takes it [the abaya] off," that they were "no good," and that "people should know what they were really like, beneath it [the abaya]." It was, in this sense, a "difficult, difficult choice." Forced into an impossibility, such was the unavoidable outcome. Ultimately, this movement worked, it appeared, where the *muhajaba* in such a hijab is preemptively created as an image of unbearable idealized conduct to abort the "more-Muslim" form of the dress and produce those wearing it as always already a failure.

In line with this, the mistake of such a *muhajaba* could never be pardoned as she was not framed as an individual whose errors—understood in Lebanon as strictly "Islamic" or otherwise—relate to their own self. Forced into an impossible display of authenticity, this *muhajaba* was treated as a representative and a reflection of the religious community, even of Islam as a religion. The dynamics at work, in this sense, echo those of Western anti-Muslim racist discourses where violence by those racialized as white is individualized, pathologized, and excused as a discrete constrained error while violence by Muslims is rendered symptomatic of the wider religion's inherent ailments (Boulila 2019; Patel 2017). Needing to move away from such a position, participants accounted for how they were pushed into more modern forms of Muslim dress: ones that dilute and mummify their practice.

Eventually, it became clear that anti-Muslim racism in Lebanon did not require the removal, prohibition, and/or outright complete rejection of any piece of clothing covering Muslim women's hair. Rather, a specific diluted form, emptied and mummified, itself was rendered a site of an erasure stemming from two positions, two enforced gazes. In other words, the emergence of a specific and dictated emergent hijab considered as a modernized fashionable dress was powerfully implicated in erasing the Muslim while being constituted by the Muslim's very erasure. In the following section, I will continue exploring this modern dress's effects and its role in reproducing the anti-Muslim racism that underwrites it.

The Mummified Hijab's Implication in Reproducing and Legitimizing Anti-Muslim Racialization

As noted in previous sections, participants affirmed that the modern fashionable forms of the hijab were exponentially increasing in Lebanon. In this respect, Maya explained that they have not only become common within the "religious community" but were also the only ones, as "not-so-different" hijabs, that were making progress into mainstream Lebanese society. Nelly, the young Shia media presenter participant, explained that her "light hijab" allowed her to use the media industry's simple financial need, dictated by capital, through external (gulf) funding she had obtained and make a breakthrough. In retelling this, her explanation arrived at its conclusion: "we [the TV station] can have the *muhajaba*. But this *muhajaba* looks a bit like us, in the way she dresses and acts and all that." Nelly's dress was "not very Muslim," she said, hence her ability to succeed. Through her diluted dress, a dress of much "elegance and apparel," the modern fashionable hijab-wearing woman could resemble the modern/secular/Christian, distance herself from its Other and be relatively allowed into the space of mainstream society.[4]

Nelly further stressed that this dilution was exclusive: it was the necessary condition through which the Muslim *muhajaba* could "advance." Indeed, the more the modern and fashionable hijab spread, the more required it became:

> There's a problem, and I'm going to tell you this, if you watch the news, go to a company, you might [now] find *muhajabas*, but which *muhajabas*? [wearing] Make-up, wearing the latest trends, very elegant, me as a female I have that urge to look at them. So they're there as propaganda. … Why do they impose so many conditions on their dress? And their behaviour? (Farida)

> [If the hijab-wearing woman] wants to blend into a certain atmosphere, or [if] she wants to get a certain job or something, you find she decreases her hijab a bit. She has to, in our day. She just has to. (Nibal)

Explaining that this dilution had become a necessity exacerbated by a "dispensability" greatly evocative of neoliberal capital market logic where "if she [the *muhajaba*] doesn't, they'll simply go for someone else," Nibal, who is a young lower-class Sunni participant, lamented the enforced situation and the reality of "their [certain hijab-wearing women's] readiness" to comply, placing all other *muhajabas* in a "difficult" situation.

Soha, of similar age and social class but Shia, was quick to affirm the impossibility of an abaya-wearing woman "making it into the Lebanese state" when reflecting around the image of Inaya Ezzeddine, the first Shia hijab-wearing woman in Lebanese politics (and government):

> People were really happy that a *muhajaba* made it to the state and got that far. It was really widely spoken of. But, like, if she was wearing a abaya, of course it wouldn't have been possible. (Soha)

Soha's retelling immediately slipped into a qualifier: the joy experienced at this "breakthrough" of a hijab-wearing woman entering Lebanese politics was mixed with sorrow as "everyone knew" that she only succeeded in a specific kind of hijab and that had she been wearing a different kind, she would not have obtained such a position. Indeed, she explained, everyone knew that she could not choose to "move" into other "more visibly Muslim" forms of the hijab if she wanted to. Further, Soha explained, this modern image pressured hijab-wearing women as the "old" hijab was increasingly "forgotten."[5] In this sense, I would argue, a feeling of increased alienation was established where the "very presentable" hijab in Lebanese politics, for example, dwelled as a constant reminder of the (only) kind of hijab that could be worn if the hijab-wearing woman wants to lessen her assault, and the (many) kinds of hijab that could not be worn.[6] Exerting great psychological pressure and harm, wounding those hijab-wearing women who don't and many of those who do, this emerging fashionable hijab was accordingly reproducing the inferiorizing racialization of women committed to forms of dress deemed "non-modern." With the presence of this hijab, the "contrast" between the "non-modern" hijab and "normal" wear was being further accentuated, further affirmed in the eyes of wider society. This emergent condition meant that hijab-wearing women dwell under an added burden to self-dilute in a self-perpetuating loop. While not negating the achievement participants spoke of, and while acknowledging its significance and worth for their lived experience, I am here developing the arguments of the previous section to stress that this very breakthrough was implicated in the reproduction of anti-Muslim racialization and racism. In this, participants explained how they have come to increasingly see, to "sense," the Muslim in their dress as a multilayered compounding problem, and the "modernity" and "fashion" they could/should introduce into their dress as the increasingly inevitable "solution":

> For example, the full true hijab, the abaya with jilbab, we won't wear it, we don't want to commit ... people might look at us as terrorists, so no, we won't commit to it. So we would want to be more modern. This is playing a big role influencing [what we wear], being fashionable. We have that [way of wearing it]. (Bana)

This risk of being perceived as a terrorist, Bana, a young lower-class university student from the north of Lebanon, explicitly confirmed, existed within the Muslim community just as it did outside of it (see Bayrakli and Hafez 2018). This anti-Muslim fear of the excess, I was told, permeated the Lebanese space:

> And even Islamic institutions, they fear the niqab-wearing women. They have long conversations with them to know the reason of the niqab. They want to know it's from them, and not a commitment to any extremist group. This is emerging, [especially] with ISIS ... they wonder why she would wear it, it raises questions, why wear this specifically. (Farida)

> You might see it, the niqab in Lebanon, God help her. That complete hijab is seen as terrorism. Even me, if I object to some of these things [secular Lebanese cultural practices], they immediately call me ISIS. It's happened so many times. (Maha)

Farida, who is a middle-aged lower-class Sunni, lamented the degree to which Islamophobia had established its reality. The unequal presence of the modern forms of the hijab's role became further evidenced: if the hijab was a practice of faith that could be met in a "normal" form of dress the choice of an "extreme" shape was necessarily deemed as cause for concern and alarm. Indeed, many participants explained that people constantly used a discourse of "why this [non-modern] hijab when you have that modern hijab as an option."

Accordingly, this modern form of the hijab is constitutive of a non-modern hijab's construction, inferiorization, and stigmatization in a manner highly similar to the invention of good (secularized, Westernized) Muslims as opposed to bad Muslims (see Maira 2009). Good Muslims were invited to join, required to join, the battle against bad Muslims, to exorcise Islam (Mamdani 2004) as this mechanism was internalized by many hijab-wearing women.

The appearance of this dress, it can be argued from participants' position, co-constitutes the complete abjection of the so-called non-modern forms of the hijab, such as the niqab in wider Lebanese society, beyond being a "synthesis" of modernity and Islam as suggested in the literature—for example, as Deeb and Harb (2013) on Beirut, Abaza (2006) on Cairo, and Houston (2016) on Istanbul argue. Consistently circumscribing the zone of being's qualities and the zone of nonbeing's characteristics, this was ultimately productive of the gazes discussed in the previous section, and underwriting of the experiences discussed in the previous chapters.

In this sense, Inaya Ezzeddine, for example, is an instance of the Lebanese state displaying a dweller of nonbeing adjoining its border as an act of anti-Muslim racism's hegemony where Lebanese politics "assimilates" this specific form of the hijab to subsume it under coloniality and further establish the anomalization of the more-Muslim: a disciplinary move to demonstrate what kinds of hijab in their Arabo-Muslim excess will not be tolerated as the possibility and the conditions of toleration—rather than acceptance—under the hegemony of coloniality's racialization and anti-Muslim hate are established. In this, colonizing recognition unfolds "through the production of colonised subjects" (Balaton-Chrimes and Stead 2017: 8).

Nelly, in a similar vein, is the instance of the same process in Lebanese media and cultural scene where a television appearance reproduces a specific normativity and chosen ideal, thereby reaffirming the anomaly of the abject difference further sedimented in the so-called non-modern hijab. This mummified hijab is a colonized being that reproduces an inferiority and stands as a powerful symbol declaring what the superior is and what the inferior was and remains. Thus, I assert, there is a crucial component in the mixed feelings of joy and sorrow among participants who themselves expressed a wounded double-consciousness.

There is, additionally, a further movement: fieldwork indicated that this modern European-like hijab further functions to socially legitimize the discrimination against its opposite while it allows mainstream society to proclaim itself as increasingly inclusive and accepting. Here, as participants explained, the few places where modern fashionable hijabs are allowed to dwell celebrate themselves as beacons of acceptance and render any accusation against their exclusionary practices unimaginable. They are not excluding of Muslim dress but are rather the pioneers of its acceptance challenging Lebanese mainstream society's outright rejection and discrimination. Pioneers of inclusion could not be racist xenophobes even if they were; under modernity and by *only* accepting the "modern hijab," reproducing the complete rejection of other forms of Muslim dress and further enshrining their colonial difference, legitimizing their ostracization, and perpetuating the ensuing wound.

In the presence of this "alternative," of this form of Muslim dress that could relatively blend with a "modern society," the complete ostracization of the conservative hijab, therefore, was becoming justified and legitimized: the presence of the European-like hijab in (relative) proximity to the zone of being could increasingly *respectfully* anomalize other forms of the hijab deep into the zone of nonbeing. The ultimate result is the complete inability of hijab-wearing women who refuse to "modernize" and lessen the "Muslimness" of their dress to accuse or claim, her complete subalternity, the impossibility of her position.

What remains of the hijab, therefore, remains as a testament of what must be defeated and what must be born. In this sense, it is a reminder that must always remain, which serves and creates, which erases in its existence, in its proliferation, as structures of anti-Muslim oppression become concealed in a move greatly similar to that of assimilationist postracial and "anti-racialist" claims (see Ahmed 2012; Lentin 2011).

While fashionable hijabs have been recorded to reproduce exclusions among hijab-wearing women within Muslim communities (see, e.g., Robinson 2015) an analysis of the modern fashionable hijab's power effect within wider society especially in the Arab-majority world has yet to be developed. Starting this conversation, these insights highlight the need for further research in this area: research that centers anti-Muslim coloniality and the processes this chapter has attempted to make visible.

Before closing, a final realization must be made explicit. Describing the condition of the "Black," Fanon (2008) writes,

> The Negro's behavior makes him akin to an obsessive neurotic type, or, if one prefers, he puts himself into a complete situational neurosis. In the man of color there is a constant effort to run away from his own individuality, to annihilate his own presence. (Fanon 2008: 43)

In this explanation, it is useful to draw out two key characteristics of the colonized. The first is an obsessive effort where the colonized must consistently, fanatically, strive and labor to be recognized. The second is that of a movement away from his individuality toward an erasure of his own self. And so it was with the Lebanese *muhajaba*, as this chapter has made visible. These characteristics, Fanon (2008) explains, are ultimately structured by the oppressed people's condition as pursuing whiteness yet being, as a "Black person," inherently incapable of attaining it. This cycle, he goes on to affirm, is at the core of the "Negro's neurosis." The point to be made here is that despite the movements alluded to throughout this chapter, the impossibility of whiteness persisted for the modern fashionable hijab as, ultimately, even the most modernized hijab never grants equal entry into Lebanese society—in those space where entry is granted at all. While this must be nuanced, and while it applied to different extents depending on a number of variables including those discussed in Chapter 4, I here contend that the Muslim *muhajaba* is never admitted into the zone of being as an equal but is rather allowed to climb the hierarchy within the zone of nonbeing, reproducing the oppression on which the very existence of the zone stands. Participants from across the sectarian, age, and class divides asserted,

> Even if the girl is hijabi presentable, neat, chic, nice looking and all, but no, that's it. [If she is] hijabi [she] is looked at as closed. [She remains] different from someone who has done her hair and has it loose. That [will always be] the more prestigious [state]. (Maryam)
>
> If you go to Christian regions, even if you're modern and wearing tight clothes and all that, you'd still feel a [different] *thing*. (Iman focus group)
>
> Eventually if one has a turban and one a hijab like me, they are both not represented [in the state]. As long as there is a piece of cloth on the head, she won't be represented. (Marah)

Nelly indeed explains this when she describes her experiences at the TV station and across related spaces; from her interactions with coworkers to her perception even by security guards as "something *waw*, a scarecrow." Indeed, it is worth noting that Nelly has since decided to remove the hijab, stating that it was not something she felt she could continue to identify with on her social media page.

Writing about the Black man arriving in France, Fanon (2008: xxi) explains his dilemma as one where he strives to become white: "confronted by the dilemma turn white or disappear." To do this, much has to change in the Black man, from his language and mode of speech to his bodily comportment and norms. The hijab-wearing woman expressed a very similar dilemma: turn modern or disappear. Yet, the Fanonian Black man faced an impossibility of whiteness. This, I hold, was not only due to material or biological inevitability. A score of anti-colonial thinkers have realized the "impossibility of assimilation" and equality among the colonizer and the colonized where "assimilation/ integration essentially means two things: first, that by it the white man means 'be like me'; second, that the white man is convinced that the black man can never be as good as he is" (Singh 2007: 345). The situation of the hijab-wearing woman is no different. In striving for acceptance and an improvement of her lived experiences through a particular and exclusive articulation of fashioning and modernizing Muslim dress the dress was diluted as its Muslim identity and traits were gradually forgone. Yet, the *muhajaba*, any *muhajaba*, can never be the same, can never be an equal. She is, rather, left in a diluted hollowed mummified caricatured dress to live her inferiorization, to create and constitute the racialization and inferiorization explored in the previous chapters. Anti-Muslim racism, it ultimately appeared, *cunningly* reproduced itself.[7] Ultimately, I contend that participants' rejection of the modern fashionable hijab cannot be reduced to a "conservatism" or, even worse, "fundamentalism" but rather must be understood in relation to this form of dress's colonizing workings. In this, this rejection could be fostering the hijab's dynamism and plurality on different terms—terms that seem to harbor both patriarchal components as well as anti-colonial ones as they grate against any simplistic accounts and analyses of lived experiences.

Conclusion

There are various forms of Muslim dress; these forms are perceived differently and, most importantly, they are positioned hierarchically as they are entangled with a system of avowals and disavowals. Under the weight of Islamophobic Eurocentric modernity/coloniality, Muslim women in Lebanon were pushed to wear a dress considered to be "modern" where modern was understood as meaning "less-Muslim." Under constant scrutiny and perpetually threatened, this dress proliferating in Lebanese society emerged as increasingly hegemonic as well as wounding and assaulting. The kaleidoscopic spectrum of Muslim dress in Lebanon can consequently be said to be a colonized one. Examining this colonized spectrum, this chapter has argued that it is deeply implicated in erasing the Muslim at the levels of both material appearance as well as conduct and social practice as well as in reproducing the racializing inferiorization of the visibly Muslim woman. With this, hijab-wearing women are to cede to the Islamophobic order by being present as an emblem of the hierarchy of the human upon which the *muhajaba* is to be positioned as she is both alienated and defined without appeal as a threatening belated difference. Further, by testifying against the more "conservative Muslim" in rendering her an extreme excess, this mummified hijab functioned to pressure hijab-wearing women into self-dilution as those who refused were increasingly exhausted and anomalized and a justification of racist exclusion was produced.

The literature on Muslim dress identifies a specific and "new" form of the hijab with a Eurocentric orientation emerging as valorized across the Muslim-majority and Arab-majority worlds within the larger "resurgence of Islam" of the past decades. This chapter's arguments raise the question of what kind of "hijab" is "resurging" and invites an exploration of the reproductions involved and the hegemonies affirmed through such a resurgence—a questioning of its structuring engine. With this, one can begin to problematize the assumption claiming that the hijab stigma has receded in the Global South to an extent where the dress has been normalized and the claim that "in a majority Muslim context, a particular item of Islamic dress such as the veil is not a contested issue and therefore is not questioned" (Wagner et al. 2012: 532).

The arguments presented here do not imply a normative judgment or value statement regarding the presence or practice of the "modern" or "fashionable" hijabs. Similarly, this chapter's argument is far from being an affirmation or call for a practice of a so-called imagined "traditional" form of the hijab. Rather, this chapter's argument is to deconstruct and critique the very presence of the categories of traditional, modern, and fashion and to argue that their presence and functioning unfolds within Islamophobia and modernity/coloniality. Examining the dynamics, rather than the "shapes," the argument is that the living dynamic life of Muslim dress is colonized and forced into specific categories in a process that is deeply implicated in the production and reproduction of Islamophobic coloniality. It is an argument for the liberation of Muslim dress to live its plurality and dynamism while the ultimate normative judgment to be made remains for Muslim women themselves to make.[8]

6

From *Difaʿ* to Delinking: Anti-Muslim Racism and the Reproduction of Modernity/Coloniality

Throughout fieldwork, participants consistently argued to (re)claim the legitimacy of the hijab in both subtle and not-so-subtle ways through what appeared to be mastered narratives comprising a variety of different elements, reasonings, and discourses. Often, these interventions were unprompted, especially as the dress was not challenged within conversations and as I never asked questions or raised issues that called forth such argumentation—neither intentionally nor explicitly at least. This chapter argues that this negotiation, what participants referred to as *difaʿ* in Arabic, is itself largely structured by coloniality and, consequently, is implicated in the reproduction of the modern/colonial order and its anti-Muslim racism. In the second section of the chapter, I turn to explore what might be a more delinked movement recognized during fieldwork as I identify the hijab's role in alternative forms of being in the world, Islamophobia's epistemic workings, and modernity/coloniality's erasures.

Difaʿ under Coloniality

Offering an elaborate engagement with the question of legitimization and "resistance" against the anti-hijab movement, Akbulut (2011) identifies two main discourses circulating among Turkish women. The first claims the need for civic forms of activism, through NGOs, demonstrations, and rallies. The second argues that this activism will not secure the right to wear the headscarf and that Muslim women should, instead, combat the exclusion of pious Muslim women through "developing themselves" at the levels of education and careers (Akbulut 2011). Other scholars have argued that Muslim dress is standardly justified through discourses of desexualizing the body, combating commercialization, resisting material consumerist culture, and an affirmation of identity. Here, the literature points to the centrality of a modern human rights–based discourse as claims vis-à-vis the state are made (Ahmed 2014; Ahmed-Ghosh 2015; DeCoursey 2017). Based on this scholarship, one can identify the unfolding of resistance and negotiation through specific modern discourses, from within a specific grammar. Across fieldwork, similar dynamics could be identified.

In Lebanon, participants referred to their need to defend, and defended, their hijab with discourses of universality and Christianity, of secularism, of science, and of anti-patriarchy. Often, this was referred to as a *duty* to resist their inferiorization. *Difa'* is an Arabic word meaning defense. It generally connotes a form of action that is taken as a reaction to a particular attack or assault, and is often used to refer to military defense against military aggression. Further, it has held associations with the defense of religion and the religious community, both militarily and non-militarily, in Lebanon over the past few decades in particular. Its usage to defend the hijab can therefore be quite telling. The following subsections will explore the formulation of and drawing on these discourses in the quest to resist colonizing anti-Muslim racism.

It must be noted here that this presentation emerges from conversations in a research setting. While the interlocutor was often myself, I hold that these trends are significantly representative of standard and common conversations circulating in Lebanese society today. This is based both on interviews where participants identified these as reflective of conversations they have in their daily lives and wider observations in the Lebanese field before, during, and after formal fieldwork. Yet, ultimately, this does not mean that the entirety of the relevant discourses, or a fully developed conceptualization of them, is presented here. It surely does not mean that all conversations relevant to these questions are captured in this analysis. Rather, I will focus on what I managed to think and collate to draw out a sketch in pursuit of this book's questions and opening up this conversation to be continued with future work.

A Parochial Universality

Participants across the field argued that the hijab could not be encompassed under the mark of a culturally specific Arab or Muslim object in the contemporary world. Instead, their dress was said to be a particular manifestation of a universal urge "beyond differences." As Shia participants in a focus group in Dahieh, and Naila, a young upper-class Shia, specified,

A1: I would like to point a note that this [the hijab] is not a Muslim concept. This is a concept of the mind and logic ...

A3: I see this heavily related to *fitra* [nature]. God made it in the human *fitra* [nature]: modesty. And this is something we do: we either develop it or it dies out. Otherwise, it is a question, chastity for any girl, is from *fitra* [nature], when there are the right conditions and pedagogy, the girl will accept the dress with all enthusiasm because it is part of her *fitra* [nature]. That is the deal.
[Group approval by nodding and affirmative words]
[Markaz focus group]
The hijab didn't start with Islam, and it is modesty ... Now the hijab might not be the typical person covering their hair. It could be any modesty. In other religions, they don't wear this, but they wear an equivalent to the hijab, so that would be the hijab for them ... The hijab didn't come up yesterday, it has its roots, which go back long before Islam. (Naila)

The hijab was henceforth rendered a *concept* that manifests the same core differently in different geographies, religions, cultural settings, and times. It was, in this sense, redefined as a question of a proclaimed "human morality," away from the stigma of Muslim and Arab as one form or material articulation of a set of "values in all communities, for all groups and religions," as Tala, an older lower-class Shia participant, elucidated. The hijab was no longer a signifier for the specific signified of Muslim dress but was rather the signifier of any form of dress that manifests particular drives in the self of the wearer as in wider society. The result was a remarkable "inclusive" definition of the hijab, as one among many, all to be accepted.

This "universality," as expressed in the quotes above and as echoed in many others, was also presented as having a clear basis: it was rooted in the "mind and logic." Further, in a most striking move, one participant (in the Abbesiye focus group in south Lebanon) specifically traced this to ancient Greece and claimed that dress that "covers" was a "thing of civilization": civility, plainly associated with Greece, required covering as it drew the human away from the (uncovered, naked) animal—as a number of other participants similarly argued. The group of young, middle-aged, and older Shia women from the south met this with great approval and affirmed that the hijab was a "normal and natural" component of "civilization." In other words, the claim was that the hijab was the expression of an innate human urge toward civilization, and that this urge and this expression were "reasonable" and "logical." Here, participants appeared to be drawing on the Western liberal (exclusionary) notion of universalism and civilization and its roots in ancient Greek order, ultimately arguing for the "inclusion" of the hijab in a Eurocentric universalism where ancient Greece was rendered as the starting point of human development and progress (see Heit 2006; Shohat and Stam 1994: chapter 2).

The hijab was further presented as a phenomenon of particular relevance and prominence "across all religions." Insisting that the hijab was "something which had to do with people who want to be close to God," a key focus was on rendering the hijab a nexus of meeting for the "various religions of the world," as Nelly, a young Shia participant, said.

It was particularly noteworthy how, in developing these arguments, Christian beliefs and practices held a central position.[1] Participants here claimed that had Christians been practicing their religion "no one would be able to distinguish us from each other, she would be hijab-wearing too," as Sara, a middle-class Sunni, put it. With Christians, it was not only the same universalized core or concept but the hijab was also the same material manifestation. Bayan, an older Shia lower-class woman, argued,

> [Lebanese] Christians are completely different. [They have a] different culture and different everything. But the hijab, they wear a hijab too, for them they can't enter a church without a hijab, but the practice is lax and no one watches over this. But it feels like it's a different country for Christians. (Bayan)

In thinking through this, I better understood participants repeatedly urging others to realize that many of their behaviors are "not for religious [Muslim] reasons, not necessarily" (Salma).

It is important to note that the claim was rarely about the hijab having been historically practiced by Christians. Rather, the claim consistently focused on the fact that the hijab still *is* practiced. Here, participants powerfully preempted any claim that their practice resembled that of historical Christianity, already countering their construction as a belatedness. In doing this, both Christian nuns and "laywomen" on Sunday mass and on religious occasions, especially in rural regions, were offered as key demonstrative examples. Eventually, it appeared that participants were developing a carefully thought out argument of overlap and resemblance with Christians who, *still*, wear the hijab. Such moves are of clear and evident direct relevance to the (colonial) Islamophobic invention of difference within Lebanon. They were clearly conscious of their racializing construction including modernity's narratives of linear time and progress as well as Lebanon's specific formation. Participants' *difaʿ* appeared quite elaborate as it reflected a deep understanding of Islamophobia in Lebanon and the hijab-wearing woman's assault.

While El Guindi (1981), for example, had long argued that the "veil" of the Muslim is different from the "veil" of the Christian nun where the Muslim dress does not entail the seclusion of women from worldly life and sexuality, for example, participants advocated in the reverse while, simultaneously, advocating for the entry into worldly life and sexuality, for example:

> If [the Christian nun] has pretty hair or something, she would be showing beauty [by showing her hair]. They would summarise it as all wanting to be the same. That I do not want to appear as a woman. Amongst women! In the covenant they are all sisters, all sisters, this is a concept of the mind [logic], of *sitr* [modesty] and chastity. We apply it in Islam [in the hijab].
>
> A4: Lady Mary peace be upon her how is she portrayed? Always with her head covered! (Makaz focus group 2)
>
> … for Christians, our lady Mary peace be upon her was covered, there isn't one image of her not covered. Even when they enter the church. It's not just a Muslim thing. It wasn't us Islam that came up with it. To the contrary! It's everyone! (Marah)

Through these quotes from Marah, a young Sunni middle-class participant and a focus group with Shia participants, Christianity seems to be an example holding sufficient legitimacy to claim universality. Explaining how Christians practiced and valued the headscarf, participants found it easy to move to an argument of *everyone* practicing the hijab, at least "everyone civilised that is," as Ghada, an older lower-class Shia woman living in the south, specified. In other words, the Christian was not (only) the relevant example but was a key nexus, a logical basis, upon which the claim for the universal could be made. If Fanon's Black man could never become white, hijab-wearing women were claiming the hijab to be universal—Christian, modern.

With this, I was told, the objection to the hijab could not be legitimately made and the hijab could no longer be perceived as a threat. It could, further, no longer be classified as different, as inferior, as uncivil, or as backward. In this, an (alternative) Lebanese identity, a collective Lebanese identity drawing on Islam and Christianity as oneness and on a universal normative "civility," appeared to be proposed.

Ultimately, the claim to universality here was a specific claim to the "mind" and "logic" over *experience* and the *lived*, to a Greek-based civility, to a semblance of Christianity: It was a "universal narrative" that was centered in imagined Europe (see Mignolo 2012). Decolonial scholars have long insisted that modernity/coloniality is a lens structuring the social world (including the epistemic and the lived) through the transformation of (provincial) knowledge and modes of being into *universal* ones, a transformation that is essentially obscured by its normalization in Western hegemonic civilizational discourses (Grosfoguel 2002, 2013; Mignolo 2012, 2018; Mignolo and Walsh 2018). There lay the conditions rendering this move possible as well as useful in contemporary Lebanon.

While this was allowing participants to ease their stigmatizing marker it involved a movement toward recognition, even assimilation, through a claim of commonality and semblance. Assimilation can here be understood, as defined by Shariati (2006), as the movement of the colonized to "distance oneself from all personal and social or national characteristics in order to identify with the [colonizing] other to overcome one's inferiority and enjoy the feeling of honour and superiority sensed in the [colonizing] other" (Shariati 2006: 3). It was, accordingly, not only a movement toward something but also a movement away from something: a movement away from the Muslim.

Surely useful in advancing their cause, both given the nature of anti-Muslim racism's order as well as the standard imagined identity of Lebanon and the positions of many interlocutors they engaged, the point I wish to make here is that this maneuver was not claiming the Muslim (or the Arab) on its own terms but rather seeking space for the hijab through the Christian, the "civilized," the "universal." In other words, this strategy of *difa'* was not asserting or reclaiming the label of the Arab or the Muslim but was rather maneuvering around that label of inferiority to retrieve (only) the wearing of the hijab dissociated from the larger set of beliefs, practices, and formations of which it was a part. Within this, the hijab was being reduced into a common cultural artifact that floated with little identity, outside of power, with no power.

I would contend here that this maneuver was not threatening anti-Muslim racism or redressing it. Indeed, it could be argued to be complicit in the reproduction of anti-Muslim racism as it was complicit in the reproduction of coloniality as a wider order. From anthropocentrism to the construction of barbarians and savages, participants' arguments powerfully embraced a modernity/coloniality epistemic space and worked from within it, thereby reproducing its categories, hierarchies, and constructs—leaving its disavowed in its disavowal, its delegitimized in its illegitimacy. This *difa'* tells of itself implicated in the reproduction of wider colonial structures beyond the coloniality of dress.

It was colonization of epistemologies with an inability to escape the language, categories, and thinking of Eurocentric liberalism, the man of the Greek demos.

Accordingly, while the presence and emergence of the hijab might be claimed a sign of the ostensible failure of the Muslim's erasure in Lebanon, the data grates against this and suggests that the subsumption of *difaʿ* into colonial liberal language demonstrates the success of the project of epistemological colonization, even its colonizing reproduction by that which is claimed to be its antithesis. Many hijab-wearing women were perhaps, after all, "*modern* Muslim women."

I must stress here that my interest is not in the content of the claims being advanced by participants. Nor am I pursuing a normative judgment of these pursuits. Rather, I am seeking an exploration of the effects of participants' form of *difaʿ*, the meaning of the act, and its power implications, as I attempt to analyze what it reveals regarding the conditions under which they dwell, regarding anti-Muslim racism's processes of erasure. In this, my argument is that the mode of negotiation adopted in claiming the hijab as universal where Christianity holds a central position does not claim the legitimacy of the Muslim, dwells under the coloniality of epistemologies and knowledge, and is implicated in the reproduction of coloniality's wider hegemony. This does not render such attempts illegitimate. That would be a needed conversation that remains for Muslim women themselves to have.

A Parochial Secularism

Throughout the field, participants insisted that both secularism in Lebanon and, concurrently, the country's Christian identity were key in structuring their marginalization and exclusion.[2] Participants accordingly explained how the secular in Lebanon was experienced as an assaulting apparatus where the hijab is met with "no respect," a flagrant "unfair" violation "of rights," and as a key component in the structure of power pushing for the Muslim's erasure, as Nourhan, a young Shia participant from Dahieh, objected. Naila similarly explained,

> When I first went to work, and then, sorry, but it's at the border of Dahieh, [where] my work [is], these people had some seriously weird ideas. I would get surprised: are there people who still think this way? They think the hijab should not even exist, especially the secular atheists. I am dressed like this, consider I am just wearing this, apologies it's bothering you so much Mr secular. But I am dressed like this! If you remember that thing last year with the AUB professor. Like just stop. That simple. It's like being so bothered by a dotted shirt. Stop. This is something personal between the wearer and God only ... It's just that! (Naila)

In making her argument, Naila, a young upper-class Shia, was objecting to the "secular rejection" of her dress by claiming it a private matter, the equivalent of a "dotted shirt," and something that should be unproblematic. In the previous section, I presented the attempt to draw out the hijab as a not-only-Islamic practice in the pursuit of a legitimization of the non-Christian dress. In the pursuit of this same legitimization of the religious, that is, non-secular, dress, participants seemed to perform a similar move: secularizing the hijab. In doing this, participants did not reject secularism or attempt to reclaim a different form of social order whereby they can practice their dress. Rather, they seemed to accept the secular as they argued for a deproblematization of the hijab under it. As Maha, a young Sunni participant, exclaimed,

> Mind you, I understand it [secularism] as accepting everyone, that is how I understand it and see [it]. That someone wants to speak secularism, they should accept the Muslim and the Christian and the Jew, each in his own particular things. That is how I understand it, and that is how I am secular. But they understand it differently, that we [practicing Muslim women] are breaking secularism in Lebanon. Says who? (Maha)

The English word itself, the French word of Laïcité, or, at times, the Arabic translation of 'Ilmani were used while arguing that a secular order did not necessitate the current state of exclusions. In inquiring about specificities, or about how they defined the term, answers consistently revolved around a separation between religion and state, religion and politics, and/or religion and "public life." Secularism was, it appeared, the depoliticization of religion, its privatization, and its removal from the helm of public effect. This was, I was told, the state where the plural of beliefs and belongings can coexist without either one infringing on the other. Secularism could therefore be offered as the guarantee of equality, rights, and a proper citizen–state interaction: as the means through which Lebanon's religious plurality could function and thrive. Nadine, a young Sunni from Beirut, and Nelly, a young Shia, explained,

> [Lebanon] is trying to go towards secularism, now you have a very big generation in Lebanon, my age and less, like from 35 and less, people going not to communism but to secularism and secularism does not contradict with religion. It has become part of you. Today you can be secular and go to the mosque and pray. What stops you? Secular in terms of rights of the state, of citizen, of equality and all that. But I want to be religious, go to the mosque and pray. (Nelly)

> Like, secular people should be accepting of all people, like that is the secular ideal … But the secular in Lebanon is someone who fights religion, not someone who accepts it and wants it separate from the state, someone who fights it. (Nadine)

Ultimately, the claim was that the secular did not contradict with the hijab nor with the wider Muslim practices that were often assaulted and rejected in Lebanon. Such practices should not be problematized under a secular state where religion is depoliticized and privatized. In making this argument, some participants—although not all of them—stated that they agreed with secularism's broad postulates and that they believed that religion should only be practiced privately, "between the person and their God." Yet, they said, "What can I do with this hijab? It's just the way the hijab is, I have to wear it, it doesn't work for it to be done in the home. That shouldn't be such a big problem, though, should it?!" (Maha). In this, the hijab's public nature and its presence in the social world were presented as necessities, realities, which the *muhajaba* who wished to commit to her Muslim religious jurisprudence lived under.

Much of the participants' conceptualization and discourse was, based on the manner in which these arguments were formulated and in which secularism was defined, heavily structured by a Eurocentric enlightenment-based debate around religion and its place in a democratic social order (see Asad 2003; Mahmood 2015; Maldonado-Torres 2008).[3] Importantly, this echoed findings across Euro-America where "the primary framework influencing their attempts to legitimise, justify and defend the hijab is an Enlightenment one, which stresses the free, rational choice of an individual" (Almila 2014: 241). In France, hijab-wearing women have been found to justify their choice through discourses of "emancipation and achievement of individual autonomy" and "laïque republican rationality" (Rootham 2015: 984). In Lebanon, secularism was key as French Laïcité, from Lebanon's colonizer, loomed large.

In France as in Lebanon this was evidently not the secularism practiced across mainstream society and state. Ghada, an older Shia lower-class *muhajaba*, was one participant who explicitly addressed the discrepancy: a distinction between an imagined ideal form of secularism to the secularism exercised was needed as she explained that secular people in Lebanon are not really "democratic," "accepting," or "welcoming" of others but rather have a "problem with religion" (without mentioning Islam) and want its "removal." Therefore, a clear separation between the ideal and the practice was established, as Ghada then drew on that ideal to argue for the redefined secularism outlined above.

Many participants raised the case of France, where similar exclusionary applications of secularism unfolded, as a key example of "bad secularism." Sara, who is a young middle-class Sunni, elaborated,

> Like for example, the example of France. Because you had something which was focused on having all the state be secular or liberal the hijabi was no longer

allowed, like being on the beach. This is their own perception of what is secular. They invented something ... they defined the secular. But look at someone else and they would tell you that liberal and secular means that the person has the right to do what they want and the hijabi can be secular for them. So for me, this is what I follow more. (Sara)

This act of condemning the French secular and of claiming it illegitimate might be taken to be an instance of the colonized speaking back. Yet, as I examined the few cases where such acts of speaking back were found two key assumptions appeared uncontested. The first was that the "good secularism" Muslim women were advancing itself originated in Europe. Here, the claim was that of surprise that Europe was practicing "bad secularism": as secularism "is Europe's ... they should be accepting," as Fadia, an older lower-class Sunni, objected. In other words, the assumption was that this was a model "discovered" in and by Europe, albeit currently ill-applied in *some* European countries. The second assumption was that Europe had, despite its bad secularism as applied to Islam, reached an advanced stage in that "good secularism" in managing other forms of difference. While political circumstances, many participants claimed, rendered the Muslim a subject of "bad secularism," "good secularism" was common across the West and was evidenced by, for example, the "various pluralities" found in what participants referred to as Europe's capitals. Further, many participants claimed that secularism was also the "only way" globally with the advent of globalization and communication where "secularism allows everyone to co-exist." Secularism seemed, at least for many participants, to be the ultimate, inevitable, European global horizon. The act of speaking back revealed itself as an act of speaking from within coloniality's epistemic territory.

When I asked participants if they were making this argument because they felt this was the best option they had to change the status quo in Lebanon, or if it was their belief, most affirmed that such was their belief. A few, on the other hand, stated that they would have preferred a "religious state" (rarely saying Muslim) had it been possible but, given Lebanon's "situation," a "secular state" was the only "realistic option." This was further explained with the inability of expressing any alternative in mainstream society. A Sunni schoolteacher-participant lamented,

If I say I want a Muslim state, then people will go mad in mainstream society and they will start calling me names ... like backward, crazy ... things like that. You can't say this in Lebanon, in Beirut for example, you can't even think it. (Iman focus group)

Evidently, the claim that a Muslim alternative to the secular was an option existed outside of the realm of intelligibility in mainstream Lebanese society. The possibility that it would provide for non-Muslims was even more inconceivable, it appeared. The Muslim's, and religion's, epistemic and sociopolitical inferiorization eventually went unchallenged, even reproduced, as the secular was presented as the necessary inevitable horizon. In this sense, the Muslim was here not claimed, was unclaimable, as anti-Muslim racism went unchallenged and appeared rampant well beyond Muslim dress and different material practices.

Maldonado-Torres (2014b) has argued that, with its narrative since the seventeenth century, Eurocentric modernity has identified humanity with "being secular bourgeois" where Christianity looms in the background (also see Maldonado-Torres 2008; Mignolo 2009b).[4] Within it, "secularism, individualism, and racism" emerge as entangling forces rendering humanity a question of "degrees" and foregrounding racialization and assault (Maldonado-Torres 2017: 131; Tlostanova 2014). In line with this, I contend that the acceptance and reproduction of the secular as horizon is not challenging anti-Muslim racism but is rather implicated in the reproduction of wider modernity/coloniality where the Muslim remained disavowed.

This was, therefore, the perceived inevitability of the (European, parochial) secular and the attempt to salvage a singular element of a now-fragmented Muslim practice so as to render it enunciable, imaginable, under the modern. Yet, as Fanon had made quite clear, "culture must be lived, and cannot be fragmented. It cannot be had piecemeal" (Fanon 1994a: 41). In this sense, by making room for their Muslim practice dissociated from its epistemological and ontological wider order and situated under a secular regime, participants' attempt might offer advances toward salvaging the surface materiality of the dress but appears incapable of advancing its continued existence as an element within a non-Western "culture" and, indeed, a non-Western cosmology. It was not, eventually, the claiming of the term so as to allow *their being* to exist under a world of anti-Muslim coloniality.

The argument I wish to make here is that by adopting the secular as a term and by accepting its European claimed postulates and framing, from privatizing religion to depoliticizing it and from its European origins to its global coming, and aware that the secular can only be a part of a larger structure that includes, for example, the liberal, and, ultimately, the wider Eurocentric modern/colonial, participants were implicated in the reproduction of the structure underpinning their exclusion and were, eventually, contributing to the reproduction of coloniality and its anti-Muslim racism.

The colonized, I felt, could not speak as, ultimately, their very acts of *difaʿ* not only radically paralyzed but also reaffirmed coloniality and left its anti-Muslim racism unscathed: from the offered and accepted secular, to reproducing Europe as both center and horizon, to leaving the disavowal of the non-European Muslim as firm as ever. In defending the possibility of the singular hijab, the wider structure of anti-Muslim coloniality was being sustained.

Modern Science

During an interview midway through fieldwork, I was offered a most intriguing piece of knowledge: the hijab is attacked for being "unhealthy." Although captivating, I did not at first give this much attention. Yet, as the project progressed, it appeared that a particular line of argumentation against the hijab in Lebanese society was its health risks: by covering the hair and so much of the body, the woman was preventing her body from exposure to sunlight, damaging both skin and hair, even putting her immune system at risk. The hijab was not accepted, this argument went on, because it had "scientifically proven" health risks. Here, it appeared that details of how sunlight was essential for a healthy body, about vitamins, about the influence of cloth on the skin, among other arguments, were central to the hijab's expulsion.

Nisrine, an older Shia woman living in a village to the south of Lebanon, for example, told me how people constantly talk about the hijab's "according to them scientific bad influence on the head" and how it is claimed to "cause headaches and migraines" as it puts pressure on the brain to argue for the banality of such claims and to say that if a health concern emerged then the kind of hijab that is being worn can be changed without having to give up the entire dress. Indeed, interviewees seemed to want to bring forth these arguments to swiftly present their *difaʿ*, their counterarguments. In the Saida focus group with young and older Sunni participants I was told,

> S2: And many [people] say that the hijab causes hair fall and things like that. For your information, hair fall does not, it does not, happen because of the hijab! To begin with, you are not hijab-wearing 24 hours. This is one. And two, the sun rays, it is harmful more than useful. Modern science has proven that hair fall is due to a loss of vitamin D, and iron. You can get this from supplements, you can get sun inside your home. They keep talking like this. But no! the hijab is keeping your hair from external factors, like pollution and the like. So even medically, the hijab is preserving you.

S4: Absolutely! It's [the sun] destroying the hair!
[verbal agreement]
Me: And these debates happen in society?
S3: Yes, of course, all the time. And there are disagreements, and people fight and stop talking to you. They don't like advice. (Saida NGO focus group)
And this whole thing about the need for sunlight and all that medical thing, it's just them using medicine. The hijab has scientifically medically proven benefits! (Reem)

It was, henceforth, not only that the hijab was not harmful but that it was proven by "modern science" to be "preserving" as Reem, an older lower-class Sunni, and many others objected. Ironically, it was presented as preserving against the pollution so-called modern science and technology had brought about—although no participant made this connection. While for Nisrine, the results of "modern science" were unquestionable, and a change in the kind of hijab could be required, for Reem, "modern science" proved the hijab's worth. Throughout, participants stressed that they were themselves building on "modern science" and "experiments" (words used by many participants across the project) evidencing the dress's health advantages.

To refute this health risk, the *muhajaba* appealed to "scientifically proven" health benefits rendering the counterargument not about the nature or terms of the claim but about its content. While these comments need to be contextualized as refutations of specific arguments against the hijab present in Lebanon today, I contend that the entry of the health question into the debate about the hijab, and the terms on which it did with the figuring of the word "modern" and with a dominant presumption of a very specific sort of empiricist knowledge inquiry, is indicative of the hegemony of a Eurocentric power discourse. Indeed, "modern science" appeared as a form of unquestionable truth to which any individual must yield: the only way to refute an argument based on this science was to draw on the same science with counterevidence. In parallel, the illegitimacy of other discourses to contest that of modern science, that is, the silence, resounded.

Indeed, even when discussing other facets of *difa'* and counterargumentation, the discourse of modern science made it into the conversation. The following is an example:

[A student in a class] goes up and says: "Oh … we … I … I think the reason for backwardness is the hijab they wear." I looked around the class and realised I was

> the only *muhajaba*. I was a sophomore and it was a senior class … I [later] spoke and said that if we give this comparison, I can simply give you an Arab country and a non-Arab country, the hijab is in both and we have different results, this means that, by science and experiment, that the hijab is not the factor [of backwardness]. (Shirine)

Shirine, who is a young Shia from the south of Lebanon, went on to explain that visible progress in countries where the hijab was practiced was scientific and technological progress where "nanotechnology" and "stem cell research" were key examples presented for measuring "human advancement." This comparison, she said, was in reference to Iran, contrasting its claimed "progress" to that of "backward … Arab countries." The result was the clear acceptance of the Arab as backward and the clear separation between the hijab and Arab culture. The result, I would say, was (again) the disavowal of the Arab while "science and experiment" are instantiated as the supreme legitimate mode of making an argument. In either case, in resisting this argument against the hijab, the *muhajaba* was once again speaking from within modernity/coloniality's epistemic space where, as Asad (1993: 49) had long explained, "religion is indeed now optional in a way that science is not."

Especially aware that the discourses of science have long been foundational for Europe's claim of superiority (see Saliba 2007; Sonn 2001) and that the question of science has long been that "of the commercialization of nature and of food and the assault to human health in the name of science with the purpose of capital accumulation" for coloniality's reproduction (Mignolo 2007: 160) where "secular science" plays a foundational role for modernity (Mignolo 2018) I hold that participants' negotiation was producing and reproducing the structures of coloniality, well beyond the coloniality of the hijab, in the very kind of *difaʿ* they made.

I am here making an argument about the coloniality of the way the discourse of modern science entered the debate around Islamophobia in Lebanon. This, it is important to stress, is informed by a larger discussion around the entanglement of modern science and coloniality and the dichotomy between Western "science" and non-Western forms of knowledge: "what is science, and how this standard account of science seems to represent a colonized (i.e., globalized) conception of science that is Western, modern, and secular" (Boisselle 2016: 1; Ideland 2018; Mercier 2013).[5] This, nevertheless, invites a wider discussion beyond the scope of this chapter and book focused on Islamophobia in Lebanon and its reproduction.

Anti-Patriarchy

The questions of feminism, women's emancipation, and patriarchy were rarely absent from any interviews and focus groups. Given the role of Westernized liberal feminism in the anti-hijab assault across the globe (Brayson 2019; Hancock 2015; Moruzzi 1994) and the key characteristics of Lebanese society this did not come as a surprise. Before exploring how participants engaged this question of women's empowerment in arguing for their dress, I must reiterate that my attempt here is to explore and reflect not on the substantive content of the arguments being made but on what they reveal in regard to the hegemonic structures of Lebanese life and, consequently, anti-Muslim racism and wider modernity/coloniality of which it is a part.

For participants, the hijab worked for "a true Muslim community" in which men and women were said to be equal outside the home and exist as "sexual beings" within it:

> If the hijab's main purpose was simplistically to cover the women up, it would simply be that God asks her to stay at home. You have that idea, that the woman is meant to be at home. But these are completely opposite ideas! Because the basis of the hijab is to push the woman towards society, so that she can be engaged with [society] as a human being, only. When I reach society ... when the woman is not sexualised in society ... Sexuality is an internal differentiation within the family, but should not go beyond that. In the community, this margin is mutual between the men and women and whoever is more competent is worthy of being in a position or a responsibility, whatever it is ... this is what the hijab is about. (Shirine)

> I cannot demand the hijab without there being modesty. And even Islamically if I go and look, this modesty is so central and it's not just for women. And the Quran isn't like this. In so many places, it addresses the men with this [modesty] before the women ... And there's this big misunderstanding about the hijab, that it's differentiating [between men and women]. That the woman has to do everything and the man doesn't have to do anything. But no, he can't do whatever he wants. And I don't like to use this word, but sometimes one feels one has to because there is this patriarchal element in the cultural discourse we produce. That the man wants to limit the woman but does not want to limit himself, so you get the male scholar telling the woman "yes it's you, it's your fault, you are the devil, you are all that," but he doesn't, he keeps everything allowed for him. No, it's not like that. In our *hadith* [narration from the Prophet and his household], in our tradition, it's not like that. Even in *fikh [Islamic jurisprudence]*, and the rulings. (Zahraa)

Zahraa, an older Shia resident of Dahieh, then went into a lengthy exploration of Quranic texts and examples from Islamic jurisprudence to showcase how both the "hijab's core" and its "general application," from modesty to the construction of the self, applied to both men and women. The simple difference of "a little bit" of added clothing on the basis of gender and women's added "seductive potential" put in place to desexualize the public sphere and allow her to be engaged as "an equal human being" does not change that and render the dress a tool for women's subjugation, she argued.

In what might be considered a more radical move, a number of participants explicitly claimed that the hijab was not a form of dress specific to women. In a focus group with Shia participants in Dahieh, I was told,

> And this dress, covering the head, is not special to women. If you look at Jewish people, in the temple, or any religious group ... it's like something which has something to do with religious people, with a relationship to God. I don't know why. You must search, I am not the researcher. They wear, above their clothing, which is already [covering], and before Islam and after Islam, there was wide clothing too, so this piece above the clothing was worn, like to cover a part of the head and face and the hips to somewhere and then it evolved and became a design with a abaya like this with a button and all that. There is no difference, it is the cover with different names ... Like the *sheikh* [Islamic scholar] always covers his head! (Markaz 2 focus group)

In this explanation, which was met with great approval from everyone in the focus group, the participant expressed many of what I had termed the universalizing trends and their consequences in her depiction of the hijab: from it being something "any religious group" exercises to it being deproblematized "clothing to cover" and a core that manifests itself in multiple manners. Yet, very interestingly, she included gender: citing the example of Jewish men, of the Muslim sheikh/scholar, and of Arab forms of dress where covering the head for men is the norm. Strengthening the argument by drawing on Muslim jurisprudential rulings that specify that it is highly recommended for men to cover their head in many instances, such as during prayer, she later claimed the hijab has been misread because of patriarchy and "because of the west [now]." In other words, many participants argued that the strict gendering of the hijab was misplaced, and that society's patriarchy is "un-Islamic."

The absence of a discussion around men's dress, and the normalization of men adopting Western dress were clear instances of misogynist patriarchy and male privilege in Lebanon. In building and elaborating on this, a number of participants lamented how "Islam is misunderstood" and taken to be a patriarchal religion. Rejecting this reading of Islam, participants offered their "belief system" as one where patriarchy is rather combated and a strict gender hierarchy is untenable. Maryam, a middle-aged upper-class Sunni from Beirut, confirmed,

> For us, as Muslims, the Muslim woman can do anything and everything. She can do all activities. She can work, she can drive, raise her kids, take and bring and do everything while she is *muhajaba*. God did not say become *muhajaba* and sit at home and do nothing! (Maryam)
>
> There were Muslim women who have long participated in war, no one told them to sit at home! (Iman focus group)

In addition to this, examples from Muslim countries around the world today were mentioned. Here, Iran consistently figured, as did a number of South Asian countries including Malaysia. No Arab country did. The Iman focus group discussion went on to discuss how people in Lebanon are "unwilling" to explore "the possibility" that Islam isn't patriarchal where these discussions are "simply not happening"—that they simply can't happen. In line with this, the hijab conceptualized as a Muslim dress with a clear aim of "women's empowerment" and presented as thus was "not something people [in Lebanon] were willing to listen to," as Fatima, the project's middle-aged Shia activist from Dahieh, asserted. The idea that Islam, or Muslim practice, would actually be and work for the empowerment of women including in the contemporary world, I was told, was nonsensical, laughable, in mainstream Lebanese society. Such affirmations of the Muslim, in other words, were impossible as well as futile in negotiating and resisting anti-Muslim racism.

Regardless of this conceptualization and presentation, or perhaps despite of it, participants continuously affirmed that one of the key factors "working against the hijab" in Lebanese society was its claimed patriarchal nature where changing the stigma of Islam's patriarchy was impossible, regardless of what participants had to argue. I am not here interested in evaluating this conceptualization, or in engaging its claim of being anti-patriarchy. Participants presented this as the anti-patriarchy they pursued. I am here mainly interested in the fact that this could not be voiced nor heard in "mainstream Lebanese society."

Incapable of proclaiming the hijab as this tool of liberation they perceived, participants explained they rarely raise or discuss these issues within Lebanese society and their lived experiences. Rather, in arguing against the hijab as patriarchy, they focus on "debunking and showing" the current order's patriarchy where, as they said, what is being presented as liberation through rejecting the hijab actually had a darker side and held women's objectification within it. In other words, in making their counterargument against the claim that the hijab is a patriarchal form of dress designed to subjugate women, they reverted the accusation to claim that the "attacks against the hijab" were actually attacks meant to disempower "women and render them sexual objects for the pleasure of men" (Nisrine).

As serious judgments were passed on those who choose to "parade their bodies for men's sexual gratification" in Lebanon participants declared themselves the (already) liberated ones. With examples ranging from how much time such women had to spend "on the mirror" to the psychological pressure of "pleasing men," the hijab was accordingly offered as potential relief in the consumerist society of Lebanon and source of empowerment for the woman to actively counter her "objectification" under the current conditions of subjugation, without delving into the "Muslim ordering" they believed in. Nada, a Beiruti Sunni, explained,

> Our society is a materialistic society, and unfortunately, the biggest seller is the woman's body. Every man who does not hire a *muhajaba*, wants a front, a toy, to receive people. (Nada)

It appeared that, eventually, it is not fathomable for mainstream Lebanese society, loaded with modern patriarchy and misogyny, for emancipation or liberation to come from a Muslim position. In a time and space of hegemonic coloniality, the only "progress" could come from a Eurocentric futurity. While participants held a belief and an argumentation that redeemed the Muslim and pushed for its avowal, this avowal was unenunciable, unintelligible, unspeakable, and hijab-wearing women resorted to a critique of the current model without being able to openly offer what they perceived to be an alternative.

Carving out a position they presented as rooted in Islam, participants were here not accepting Islam's disavowal but rather harbored and expressed beliefs and views that clearly articulated their rejection of this disavowal. In this *difa'*, negotiation meant an attack and a critique of the current status quo—but could go little beyond critique. This critique itself is structured by the fact that this disavowal was being combated by attributing to it a position that European representation also claims as modern European with slogans of anti-patriarchy and feminist emancipation co-opted by sexist misogynistic Eurocentric modernity/coloniality (Brayson 2019). It must be understood as enunciable under such a hegemony. The fact such discourses echoed and were common across the West is in this respect particularly noteworthy. This nevertheless harbored a mostly unspoken avowal of the Muslim. Participants' claims held the potential of shifting Eurocentric assumptions—but seldom did. Although much of what participants expressed could not be spoken, it could be listened to. For the remainder of this chapter, I will attempt to push this listening to begin sketching a delinked conceptualization of the hijab beyond Islamophobia's confines as it emerged during fieldwork, further illustrating the stakes of extant anti-Muslim racism and the practice's very potential in resisting the erasure of the Muslim.

Reframed: The Hijab and Being Otherwise

Based on the way the hijab was presented in the field, when I inquired about its role and when I did not, in the way it was spoken of, the language used to refer to it, and the experiences narrated with it, the hijab emerged as a practice used by participants in a process of self-forming a Muslim subject attuned to Islam's "ideal figures." Accordingly, I came to realize that a "delinked" conceptualization of the hijab could exist. While fully constructing such a conceptualization is beyond the scope of this book, this section offers some preliminary insights into the transformation of Muslim dress itself into a potential site of Islamophobia's resistance and negotiation. Doing this, it further highlights the meaning of Muslim dress for its wearer and the stakes of its erasure. Important to note here is that this exploration is informed by Asad (1993) in conceptualizing the bodily practice of Muslim dress as ritual and Mahmood's (2012b) theorization of ritual as *performative*. For Mahmood (2012a), the mosque and the practices of the Muslim women alongside whom she worked are a place/space to approximate the exemplary model of the *Muslim pious self* where people's *telos* is the achievement and harnessing of one's rational and emotional capacities (which are not seen as contradictory or unrelated in contrast to hegemonic Cartesian dualisms). It is through practices such as prayer, therefore, that the self is oriented, constituted, and constructed; that it is trained, formed, and forged as part of a larger Islamic model of being in the world. Crucial to realize is that Islam and the Muslim subject discussed here, and throughout this chapter and book, are not essentialized, ahistorical, or self-contained. Rather, these are contextual signifiers—contested and with no clear boundaries—working within a specific set of discursive traditions and conditions.

As participants narrated experiences from their daily lives, the hijab was presented not as an object that is only worn in obedience to a particular religious scripture, to gain particular social advantages, or to become identifiable as belonging to a particular religion and sect. The hijab was not limited to being a religious duty, obligation, which needed to be heeded for one to avoid the wrath of God, or of society, for example. While not attempting to make a statement as to *why* hijab-wearing women wear the hijab (a statement with a kaleidoscope of possible answers) I would argue that key and central in participants' understanding of the hijab is it being a tool through which the moral Muslim self ordained by Muslim religious belief is developed and acquired. In this sense, the idea of practicing the hijab was the idea of "living it" and allowing it to imbue one's daily life and to shape one's mode of being in the world in pursuing "Islam." As something that is worn on a daily basis, embodied and constantly felt in its materiality, participants explained, it formed a potent tool through which the self can be "molded":

> Like, let us ask: what is the hijab? What does it mean? It's not me covering my hair, or covering my body, wearing it and nothing [of my body] is showing and that is the hijab. No. Not at all like that. Even in our *hadith [sayings of the Prophet]*, or models, how they represented it ... it does not stop at the body, there is a way to it, criteria, the way I speak ... the way I interact ... there, my voice ... And here you get levels, how much you can improve, the upward you go ... how much you can get that in all your dimensions. That is it. The hijab encompasses all these things. Even with yourself, your environment, your kids. You can widen it as much as you want, get to the bigger circle. What is the perfect hijab? That is what you reach. On the outside, it is the *abaya*, but then you get the inside where you need to start with. How much have you let the hijab influence you? How has it influenced you? [Islamic] Jurisprudence is there to control your behaviour so that you can reach a purpose. God is wise and we are born for a reason, and this reason is different from one person to another. There is the general reason and then a reason for each person. So in reality what is your role and what is mine? (Fatima)

Speaking of the dress, Fatima took very little time to delve into the question of our existence's very reason. It was a material object that is meant to "influence you" so that you achieve "your reason," "your role." It was an "encompassing" practice that was meant to express itself in the way one sits, speaks, and interacts, as examples. It was something that was to be lived inside your home and outside of it, when alone and when in the presence of others, when wearing it and when not wearing it. In the pursuit of the "perfect hijab," defined as a state of both the material dress and the inner self (sometimes referred to by participants as the "inner hijab"), the wearer was someone placing herself under the influence of the worn. Through it, Islam could be enacted and its erasure could be resisted, participants expressed.[6] The *muhajaba* no longer perceived herself as a *muhajaba* only when she is wearing the hijab. She was *always* a *muhajaba*:

> The hijab becomes who you are, your identity. Always. (Nada)
>
> [you are *muhajaba*] Even in the private gatherings which are between sisters [where the hijab is not worn]. Me as a *muhajaba*, who understands the meaning of the hijab, the nature of it, the purpose of it as being the preservation of society and its modesty, this modesty goes with me wherever I go, not just where there are others ... So if I want to be really understanding what the hijab is, committed to all its conditions, that it exhibits my identity, that I am someone committed, Muslim, Shia, I know this hijab has led me to having chastity and modesty [and] this will be my behaviour [everywhere]. (Markaz focus group 2)
>
> For me, [to be a *muhajaba*] I should be getting up, even on morning prayer, praying, never missing that. I don't do this all this much. For me yes, the *muhajaba*, to be honest, should be like this. Even my mother, I wanted to become a *muhajaba* before, but she didn't let me because she used to say: I want to see you praying on time and then think about this [wearing the hijab], and take your time and don't act hastily. For her, I had to reach the spiritual before the appearance. But it's also the other way around: it really encourages and helps the person to reach the spiritual. Both are fine. There is no rule ... So these things, practices, I can improve. And the hijab, it can really teach you, a lot. I felt I matured like 5 years [after I started wearing it]. (Sara)

While the hijab aimed at "the preservation of society" and its betterment, it simultaneously aimed at the "preservation" of the wearer herself and her betterment. In this sense, the argument I am making here alongside participants is not a negation of the hijab's various possible roles: from creating the public sphere as a "Muslim space" to allowing the woman to perform a "calling to Islam" through dress and pursue the "modesty of the community," among others mentioned by both participants and the literature on Muslim dress. Further, it is not an attempt to define these roles, or claim that there is a set of homogeneous roles that participants agreed to. It is also surely not an attempt to negate the various ways through which the Muslim dress is implicated in the reproduction of patriarchy, misogyny, and gendered oppressions. Rather, it is to say that another role of *forming the Muslim* thrives alongside these dimensions.[7]

As a method of learning, as a "teacher," the hijab was engaged in a sort of dialectical relationship with the "complete Muslim subject." In other words, the hijab was an element to gain the qualities, traits, and characteristics that Islam has ordained as it was a space where these qualities, traits, and characteristics exhibit themselves and affirm their presence. It was not merely an exteriority that declares or expresses an interiority but rather an exteriority that plays a role in forming the interiority. In this sense, the hijab was a sort of self-addressed speech act: an instance of performativity where the wearing of the dress can be thought of as an act of naming oneself a *muhajaba*, enacting oneself a *muhajaba*. It was, ultimately, enacting oneself as different from the (Eurocentric) modern subject.

It was here that I came to understand why the hijab was not only a dress: the traits it sought were to become "a permanent feature of a person's character," in the sense of the practice being "a teleological process" that is "aimed at making moral behavior a nondeliberative aspect of one's disposition" (Mahmood 2012a: 135–6). It was, ultimately, the formation of what Mahmood (2012a) termed an "Aristotelian habitus." As a daily act, oriented, it was a powerful exercise yielded by participants that entered into the pursuit of a Muslim civilizational model. One cannot but wonder and reflect on the absence of such a practice for Muslim men, and the gendered inequalities at play—complex and multifaceted inequalities that remain for future work to examine and develop.

The Hijab's Muslim *Telos*

It is important to reflect on the *telos* of this act: the "Islamic improvement and growth" of the wearer, in "all dimensions." Inquiring about the specificities of these dimensions and how they come to be lived, I received a variety of answers that can be, at the risk of reductionism, collected under the title of becoming a "Muslim moral person" where morality exhibits itself in *all* aspects of one's life:

> She can make use of it [the hijab] to learn. I am a person who before wearing the abaya, my parents were telling me to postpone it. I wore it at sixteen and they said that I should wait till I finish high school, to have grown more, got more awareness, they really focused on that idea of awareness, and that I needed to have more traits [to wear it]. But I insisted and really wanted it. Anyway, I did wear it and then it added things to my personality. I wasn't aware of things, didn't realise them, and then I did [wear it] and started developing them. Like what? Like my self-confidence. I still don't know the link, but it really gave me

huge self-confidence. Even my relationship with others changed. There are many traits it added to me. (Markaz focus group 2)

The group later went to discuss how, and where, this Islamic "chastity and modesty" were to exhibit themselves. Examples included how one speaks to neighbors and those "at work," how one selflessly gives their time for social and political activism, as well as who one chooses as friends, companions, and even spouse:

> This hijab, if I am to benefit from it, knowing that I have chastity and have modesty, this must be embodied in every position, in every gathering anywhere, in all my behaviour, wherever I am. (Markaz focus group 2)
>
> Like as someone who is too humorous, laughs all the time … I am a joyful person, but the hijab balances it, makes me poised. It's not a dress, it's like something which teaches you. It's more than a dress. It's a code of conduct. (Nourhan)

Both Nourhan, a young Shia participant from Dahieh, and an older Shia participant from a focus group in Dahieh concurred. It did not have a code of conduct; it could be the Muslim code of conduct. The hijab was not a material object that reminded you to be poised, to be balanced. The hijab could be the object that balances you, makes you poised (given certain conditions, as explored below). The hijab was an object to be engaged, as a tool of knowledge, through which a particular set of behaviors is to be developed and acquired. Engulfing both ritual practices as well as social ones the hijab covered both the "religious" and the social, the political and the economic. Its scope ranged from being spiritual and non-materialistic to being wise and reflexive, including "political worldviews" and one's "belonging." From not sitting at a table where there is alcohol and not entering a nightclub or a casino to not speaking about others behind their backs and not throwing garbage on the street, it is very difficult to delineate, based on this project's data, what participants presented as the Muslim hijab's code of conduct. This code of conduct could not be understood, it appeared, through exclusionary, categorical, confined, or identitarian definitions of what Islam or the Muslim are or what they can be.

In this sense, I was told that the hijab was a means toward the formation of a Muslim ethical self and, crucially I would say, that this ethical self is the self that, as an ethical self, goes to work, to the marketplace, votes, and participates in political rallies. In this sense, the formulation of ethics I encountered drew great resonance with that which Mahmood (2012a) had drawn out as "the careful scrutiny one applies to one's daily actions in order to shape oneself to live in accordance with a particular model of behavior" (Mahmood 2012a: 187) with, perhaps, a more expansive scope, given participants' insistence on both "formal" and "informal" direct political participation as part of their ethical conduct. In other words, while participants affirmed that their dress was a means for the achievement of what might be termed Muslim ethical qualities, these qualities must not mistakenly be thought of as belonging to a sphere separated from the daily, the economic, or the political. Ultimately, the dress revealed itself as a pedagogical exercise across aspects of one's life. The Abbesiye focus group participants living in the Lebanese South were unequivocal:

> W4: And it's not just about behaviour. Even the spiritual, to speak of the spiritual, at the level of the spiritual it changes the girl in a weird way. Me, now, if I want to speak to some guy on WhatsApp really late at night and I think that I am a hijab-wearing, how can I do that? These small details ... if I want to like something [on social media], I think I am a *muhajaba*, how can I do that?
> W3: It really disciplines.
> W4: Small details, but of course we think them small but they are much bigger and have a very strong influence. It is *wikar* and *wikaya* [dignity and preservation] for the woman [who wears it].
> W5: Even the way one speaks. It's not the same at home.
> W3: There is more poise, the way one interacts.
> W4: It makes us be more patient with one another. I am a bit like that. If someone contradicts me or disagrees with me, I get agitated and would want to jump, but when I am wearing the hijab, it stops me. When you're wearing a hijab, it makes you more alert.
> W2: It really stops the person [from doing those things].
> [agreement] (Abbesiye focus group)

Saying "it's not the same at home" one must realize that what the focus group participant meant, as she later explained, was that she "wish[ed] that it was," that she was working toward it being, but that she was "not there yet." In this sense, while the hijab was already exerting significant influence over her conduct "outside," this conduct has not yet been fully *internalized*. She considered herself in the making, in the becoming.

This was, therefore, a performative transformative act that required accumulation, sedimentation, to enact that which it names. With practice, with time, with effort, these traits, whatever they are, become a part of you and the hijab elevates, progresses, to develop other traits, "higher" traits, within you. The practice was, therefore, a clear illustration of how bodily behavior "endows the self with certain kinds of capacities that provide the substance from which the world is acted upon" (Mahmood 2012a: 27).

The hijab could consequently be said to be an object with two distinct entwined dimensions: it was oriented toward one's self, to form one's self, as it was oriented toward society: to form the social sphere.[8] Further still, the hijab did more, as Shirine, a young Shia from the south of Lebanon, clarified:

> There are traits it [the hijab] develops. The hijab needs to be a means ... like prayer. A way of building up your potential to control, to endure. It teaches you deep philosophies. But people don't think of it like that. They think if you are hijab-wearing, you should be there already. But it's your way of getting there! They say if you are hijab-wearing and doing this [bad thing], then the hijab is not doing what it's meant to do for you. (Shirine)
>
> Knowledge, more piety. The hijab can do 20 things, but it depends on how you approach it and that is what it will do to you. (Mona)

The hijab offered Muslims "knowledge," taught "deep philosophies." Mona, who is young and from the north, explained that the hijab unequivocally "moves you" toward a "much larger whole" where you are no longer an individual but rather part of "something bigger." While Shirine agreed that some of these traits, such as developing one's "potential to control, to endure," are linked to the particular experiences of assault a *muhajaba* goes through in Lebanon, she insisted that such was not the whole story and that there was a "deeper dimension" having to do with the meaning one finds in belonging to Islam that allows this to unfold.

The hijab, I would say, was contributing toward the formation of the *muhajaba*'s non-Eurocentric episteme despite coloniality. It was, consequently, producing a hybrid, wounded, fractured episteme between coloniality and its Other as I conclude this chapter with. Before moving on, a note is worth making explicit: thinking of the hijab as an object that pushes the *muhajaba* to commit in obedience to the social gaze as not to be accused, as might be suggested, would be misplaced. The hijab for participants is not, or at least should not be, a social performance. Yet, in a performative reading of the hijab, such a performance is not deemed illegitimate. Rather, such a performance can be the starting point, as participants in a focus group in Dahieh explained:

Researcher: Is this [commitment to the hijab's code of conduct] because I don't want people to talk about the abaya? Or to talk about the people who wear it?

> A4: This can be a reason, but it is not the main reason for me. I don't know, but on the personal level, I feel it is simply not befitting [in itself] to break it. As a way of sitting, as a hijab-wearing woman, wearing a abaya, you are meant to sit in a particular way. I see another way as not befitting. But even if I did not see it this way and saw no problem in it, another main reason I would take into consideration is "does this thing influence the reputation of the hijabi?" Because we hear a lot of this. But really I don't do it because I don't accept it.
>
> A2: Agreed agreed.
>
> A1: It starts like that [for others], it is not wrong, but it starts like that and then it becomes [more]. (Markaz focus group 2)

In this sense, the wearing of the hijab could be an act that was "not so much as manifestations of their will but more as actions that produce the will in its particularity," where "the pious subject does not precede the performance of normative virtues but is enacted through the performance" (Mahmood 2012a: 162).

Yet, this performative act was far from unconditional and its success far from guaranteed. While any iteration always holds the possibility of failure, three conditions particularly stood out for participants. The first and most important of these was intentionality: anyone forced to wear the hijab, anyone not doing it out of will, is not, could not be, a *muhajaba*. This was said to be because one cannot learn if they do not want to learn and embrace the exercise. The second is consciousness: anyone who does not know what the hijab means, and does not realize what the hijab is meant to do in one's life, cannot be a true *muhajaba*. In this sense, a perceived increase in "awareness" in Lebanon, mainly brought about through the spread in religious classes and religious activism, was key. The third was perseverance. This was particularly important in a society where the hijab was unwelcome, but it was also claimed to be important even had the society been welcoming of the dress. Here, participants stressed that becoming a true *muhajaba* was no easy feat but was, rather, one that required huge labor and much determination in the pursuit of a cumulative self-formation. It was only with time, patience, and insistent hard work on one's character that the hijab can manifest itself throughout one's life. Participants at the AUB focus group, young, Sunni, and upper middle class or upper class, and Nisrine, an older Shia woman from the south of Lebanon, concurred,

> So back to the reference point question, what is this girl's idea on the hijab and why is she wearing it? If it's a religious reason, it would be a reminder all

the time. you are doing this for God, how can you do this [thing]? Or, [asking herself] is this right or wrong? But if it's culture, or she was asked to at home, it becomes nothing. Just a dress code of her culture. And if she is forced, it will be suffocating and have a counter-reaction. so it depends. Like prayer, if you pray just because you're used to it from being a kid, and you don't understand or feel what it is as a relationship and speaking to God, if it's just a casual cultural behaviour, it won't do anything. But when it's not like that, it will make all [the] difference. (AUB focus group)

The hijab definitely plays a role shaping her personality and who she is, who she becomes. But there is one condition: she must have knowledge and be wearing it out of awareness. It will take a lot of hard work, and a lot of determination for her to make it. It is not easy, not here [in Lebanon]. (Nisrine)

The hijab was something that must be "respected," that could be "offended," that could be "tarnished," that one can develop a "relationship to," and that, most importantly, one "learns from." Just like any teacher, if one is to follow Muslim ethics as I was told, one must heed it, obey it, and engage it. For many participants, the dress was about the "entire lifestyle" and the "very being" of who the person was, rather than being about a limited set of religious behaviors with a clearly circumscribed sphere. It was, participants explained, about being a "true Muslim" with the hijab an element of "that entire system."

Importantly, this conceptualization of participants' labor does not delve back into an autonomous liberal subject but rather adopts "a model of agency that is far more sophisticated than that of the strategical, calculating subject that constructs its own reasons," where "agency ensues not from sovereign subjects, but from trained and disciplined bodies" (Baerveldt 2015). In other words, resistant agency, "a capacity for action that historically specific relations of subordination enable and create" (Mahmood 2001a: 203), exists without simplistically and categorically belonging "to the women themselves, but is a product of the historically contingent discursive traditions in which they are located" (Jacobsen 2011; Mahmood 2012a: 32). Through this Muslim discursive tradition, the *doing* of the Muslim dress turns it into habitus and renders it rooted in the character—what Mahmood (2012a) refers to as *Malaka*—an Arabic term encompassing such engrained habits in the self that become a constitutive part of it and its dwelling in the world. Thus, a Muslim subject is made to be.

In this sense, and based on the above, the hijab could act as a tool of delinking against modern colonial subjectivity allowing the wearer to inscribe herself in a different field, to move away and beyond modernity's subject and to fashion herself, her subjectivity, her habitus, her dispositions, in line with a different cosmology, with a different code of conduct, and a dwelling in the border. It is, consequently, an act that enacts the Muslim subject and pushes for the establishment of a different social order. Crucial in this respect is the relationship to ancestrality, which I will explore before closing this chapter.

Muslim Ancestrality

While my purpose here, the lack of space, the nature of the data, and my own positionality mean there is much beyond the scope of this book to be explored in regard to the hijab as a practice and the dynamics of such a performative act in Lebanon, one point raised in the field is of particular relevance: that of Muslim ancestrality. It is useful to note here that participants often left this topic to the end of discussions, only expanding and explaining when I asked follow-up questions.

In the hijab as practice, a clear presence of Islam's key figures, the prophet and the members of his household (*Ahl lbayt*, in Arabic), were presented as pivotal. Often offered as the *telos* reached, they were deeply entwined with the hijab. Both as representatives of this *telos* and its actualization, participants spoke of their dress as a practice that connected the wearer to Islam's key figures. Leen, a middle-aged Sunni participant from the north, and a niqabi Sunni participant living in Saida explained,

> This is the first thing, to become like *Ahl lbayt* peace be upon them. To respect how they were, to love and to do like they did. The hijab is behaviour plus dress. You can expect ethics. Like the *muhajaba* must always have, like manners in speech, poise, to know how to answer, the way she looks, there are many things. Like Islam's ethics. One must, as much as he can, know Islam's ethics ... There are things you get ... then you have to go and apply them, with people. (Leen)

> And it's the same thing with the niqab. To give you a personal experience, when I first wore the niqab, I wore it out of love. I loved it, it was an emotional thing. This was seven years ago. I had the knowledge and knew this is the dress of the prophet's wife; peace be upon them. (Saida focus group)

Clearly presenting the hijab as something that "teaches by doing" rather than by "learning," Leen placed this act of doing in direct emulation of *Ahl lbayt*. Central to this process of teaching were learning "respect," "love," and what to "do," in sync with *Ahl lbayt*. The hijab was, accordingly, the material object allowing the wearer to establish, preserve, and "live" a "link" to these model Muslim selves.

In this sense, the hijab brought the "past" into the "present": "this is *Ahl lbayt* peace be upon them, right here ... If you ask me ... it [the hijab] is sacred for it," Tala, an older lower-class Shia, declared. As Tala explained, it ultimately "allowed" the women not to fall into oblivious forgetfulness as to "who they belonged to and who they needed to be." It was, further, a means of building and expanding on the relationship with these individuals: if one commits to the dress, if one respects it and heeds it, then one is bound to develop their relationship with these individuals, an identification with these individuals. That, in turn, will develop one's *similarity* to them.

Through this relationship, I was told, one belongs and becomes Muslim. Through this relationship, one learns and develops to resemble Islam. In other words, it was by bringing these figures into the present, and by placing what many participants claimed as their embodiment onto one's own body, that both a relationship is developed and built upon to *become*, as a middle-aged lower-class Sunni participant expressed,

> Oh, this idea [of the relationship to the Prophet and his household]! How present it is [sighs] ... for me, it wasn't there all that much at first. But after I wore it [the hijab] and committed to it, and I started loving everything which linked me to the prophet peace be upon him and God. So that idea really grew with me. It grows with the person. But did we have this awareness? No. Before, no. (Farida)

Similarly to the "traits" that the hijab develops, this "relationship" and "link" to ancestrality were themselves developed by the hijab: it was an element of the *muhajaba*'s growth. The link was performed, enacted, brought into being, by being *muhajaba*:

H: They [*Ahl lbayt*] are the whole role [in the hijab].
Me: How do they play a role?
H: Through influence, when someone is touched by them, by how they were, their purity, what she [the prophet's granddaughter] went through and kept her hijab, not like lost control, stayed strong. Not like ... when we keep hearing their stories, their ethics, their knowledge and how much they knew, not like a *muhajaba* that doesn't know anything, in everything they are on top, education, socially, economically, you're touched, the girl is touched and the woman. And you have to do like them. It's not like you can do and cannot do. You have to. Because they are the perfection. That is how a woman should be. It's not that she can be *muhajaba* and doesn't know, or *muhajaba*

and sitting at home. What they do, she should be. Their personality most importantly, their knowledge. (Hanin)

Jumping between economic wealth and political steadfastness, Hanin, a middle-aged lower-class Shia, was referring to the incident of Karbala: the slaughtering of the prophet's grandson and his family members in 680 CE. After that incident, the prophet's granddaughter, Sayyeda Zainab, took center stage to become one of the Muslim community's key figures. As a political leader and a public figure, as well as an "idol in worship," her image echoed throughout the field (particularly, but not only, in interviews with Shia participants, and particularly in identification with the abaya) as the ultimate subject, the complete *telos*. Zahraa, an older Shia resident of Dahieh, and a Shia participant in a focus group in Dahieh, confirmed,

> The outer hijab is not sufficient. It is required, but there is something more important that we must work on. The abaya is this thing, the perfect dress, the Sayedas' [Zainab] dress, peace be upon her, so I must stick to all the ethics, all the manners, all the details. There are things, the abaya is not a black piece I wear and that is it ... It's not a duty, it is more perfect and this must come with ethical perfection, and behavioural perfection, and understanding and knowledge for me to stick to this. (Zahraa)

> Linking the hijab to the household takes it out of the mind and makes it emotional. Like besides the logical thing of understanding what it is [the hijab] and why it's important, if she links it to them she would have that emotional relationship. We would be covering both the mind and the heart like this. (Markaz focus group 3)

In a relationship that required both a conviction in "the mind" and a relationship at the level of the emotional, the role of *Ahl lbayt* in the hijab's performativity was unmissable. The reference was to the insufficiency of a theoretical conviction in achieving the perfect hijab. There was, rather, a need to have an emotional connection to human figures, idols, where the emotional and the "logical" complete one another. It was through this that the hijab could become the tool and the object.

Mahmood (2009) had explained that the "Muslim's relationship to Mohammad is predicated not so much upon a communicative or representational model as an assimilative one," where a "labour of love" was necessary to shape one's self in that image (Mahmood 2009: 847). Echoing this, and expanding it to include figures from various religious traditions, participants eventually drew out a line of "perfect individuals" (rather than communities) to be presented as the history: the Muslim ancestrality the *muhajaba* sought to be a continuation of.

There is a clear separation between this ancestrality and "history": the hijab was not to be retrieved from Lebanese or regional history. Further, the hijab was not to be retrieved from a past "society" or era in any geography. It was, rather, to be retrieved from specific persons who participants describe as "transcending time." Perhaps similar to what Deeb (2006) had titled "authentication," a concept of time, very unlike that of modernity, was at play. It was a time where there was no linearity between past, present, and future and where there were specific subjects who represent "completeness," to be connected to, scattered beyond what modernity termed past, present, and future.

Eurocentric modernity seeks to erase "the past, turns the future into the teleology of progress and holds the present to be the only site of the real" (Vázquez 2009: 3). Based on the above, I would argue that, for the *muhajaba*, a different concept of temporality was at work where the past was not degraded and where the future aimed at the subject's reformation in an image in the "past," an image that is not "past." Indeed, where *Ahl lbayt* were "real," the *muhajaba* ascribed to a real that transcended Eurocentric modernity's temporal logic, even delinked from it. In such a system, the Eurocentric obsession with futurity becomes untenable. In such a system, the subject holds different relationalities and acts upon them for an alternative becoming.[9] In this sense, the hijab allowed its wearer a resistance and negotiation of Eurocentric modernity itself as it was powerfully working against anti-Muslim hate—particularly its internalized dimensions. No parallel dress existed for Muslim men. While patriarchy and misogyny were the key forces working here as Muslim women were wounded and burdened, it is interesting to note that this absence of a parallel dress offering Muslim men in Lebanon much privilege was also one that deprives them and denies them of decolonial possibilities.

While coloniality has long attempted to delegitimize this link, the hijab has stood the "test of time," resisting erasure and allowing hijab-wearing women "never to forget," allowing the subaltern to "link" with their past, their memory, to aspire to living their past in their future. I cannot pursue a larger exploration of the concept of time that can be learnt from the *muhajaba* engagement with her dress in this book, and much remains to be explored around this Muslim ancestrality and its workings and possibilities. Indeed, many questions remain and the shifting of Islamophobic modernity's temporality is but one illustrative example of the delinking potential harbored within the non-Western practice.

Within the West, the hijab could not be read beyond it being a symbol. As Baldi (2017a) identified, the hijab could only be a "sign of" and this does not only "not take into consideration the plurality of meanings and practices of veiling and the historical and cultural context within which the will and certain practices and desires develop, but it also imposes a specific semiotic ideology on different cultures" (Baldi 2017a: 36). Under such an imposition, it was not by claiming it as more than it could be claimed as legitimate: this pedagogic role of the hijab rarely if ever figured in participants' *difa'*. Rather, participants were left to accept their dress, in the arguments for legitimization, as a fixed symbol to then argue for what that symbolism was as they sought to create space for its existence. Much was remaining unsaid as absences and silences resounded under Islamophobic modernity/coloniality.

Conclusion

Subjected to marking, exclusion, and discrimination, subjected to coloniality's Islamophobic erasure, Lebanese hijab-wearing women pursued *difa'*. Their negotiation revolved around subduing the hijab's Arab and Muslim identity, a parochial universalizing and de-Islamizing, a redefining under a naturalized privatizing and depoliticizing Eurocentric secularism, and a drawing on "modern science." Arguing for the legitimacy of their mode of being, they pushed for its conceptualization as a tool against hegemonic patriarchy and objectification. Analyzing this *difa'*, I have contended that it is implicated in the disavowal of the Muslim and the Arab as it worked from within the colonial epistemic framework, even reproduced wider Islamophobic Eurocentric modernity.

Yet, there was more to participants' Muslim practice as it emerged as a tool through which a Muslim subject could be pursued. This (gendered) dimension of Muslim dress dwelled in the background, further affirming coloniality's aggressive hegemony and pursuit of Islamophobic silencing. Presenting and engaging the material garment as a pedagogical exercise in a Muslim civilization model, participants offered a conceptualization of the hijab that would render it a tool of resistance, a tool of delinking, to construct the ideal Muslim subject's self and connect it to its Muslim ancestrality. Shifting Eurocentric modernity's linear time, shifting its *telos*, shifting its episteme and its norms, the hijab was a means through which the *muhajaba* could still be, outside, beyond, at the border of Eurocentric modernity. Accordingly, a key stake of anti-Muslim racism's assault on the Muslim hijab was in rendering the Muslim subject impossible materially as well as epistemically—erased, invisibilized, unenunciable.

As I wrote this chapter, my reflections were dominated by one idea: it did not make sense. Its two sections were incoherent, dissonant. How can the same fieldwork, conducted in the same place at the same time with the same people and by the same researcher, produce data, often from the same participants, where the hijab is claimed a simple "dotted shirt" as well as an all-encompassing self-forming exercise in a Muslim model? How can this same researcher, how can the same people, claim their *telos* as perfected all-encompassing Muslim moral subjects and, at the same time, express a commitment to European secularism and its so-called privatization of "religion"? Indeed, how can the same participant, in the same interview, insist on science, futurity, a secular horizon, and a Eurocentric universalism, while claiming her dress an exercise in the pursuit of a semblance to Muslim ancestrality and a Muslim ordering of the world?

Such was not incoherence. Such was the state of double-consciousness, of a wounded self, of a self dwelling in the border of modernity. Such was the lived experience beyond Western binaries, beyond neat categories, and beyond linear narratives. With a deeply wounded habitus, with a deep colonial wound, participants were both deeply colonized and deeply different. The world today is touched by coloniality. Yet, its inhabitants cannot be fully subsumed under it: an outside of modernity continues to exist where Europe's others continue to be. Indeed, modernity/coloniality is an aggressive machine that is constantly resisted, subverted, and eluded in various ways across the globe. Yet, modernity, more than five hundred years in the making, is a machine that has touched the whole globe. Hence, those who have resisted, and continue to resist and refuse it do not do so without being touched by it. In other words, there is no pure exterior to the condition of modernity/coloniality. Nevertheless, there is a border and in the border things can/are lived differently as the colonial difference persists, the otherness survives, resistance thrives. It is there that the *muhajaba* dwells.

Conclusion

Fanon identified a core element of the Black man's predicament: "For some time there has been much talk about the Negro. A little too much. The Negro would like to be dropped, so that he may regroup his forces, his authentic forces" (Fanon 2008: 186). This book has attempted not to talk about the hijab-wearing woman, as, like the Black man, there has been too much talk about her both within academia and outside of it. Rather, this book has attempted to listen to and voice the hijab-wearing woman's racialized lived experiences as a contribution toward the regrouping of her forces and, ultimately, the dismantlement of the wounding and destructive structures abjecting her into erasure. Concluding, this chapter begins with a brief summary of this pursuit to then discuss some key implications and questions around both Islamophobia and Arab-majority and Muslim-majority societies.

Map and Arguments

In this book's first chapter, I historicized Lebanon's colonial foundation as the basis of its Eurocentric imagination and multiple contemporary crises. Noting the absence of Muslim dress in the writing of Lebanese history I moved to a historicization of Muslim dress within the West Asia North Africa region of which Lebanon is a part. Based on this, I argued that the history of Muslim dress in the region is one of systematic aggression and erasure, particularly under colonial as well as postcolonial nation-state building.

In Chapter 3, I examined the construction of the hijab-wearing woman as a "social form" in Lebanon: a belated Arabo-Muslim difference in excess. There, I argued that the Muslim woman is invented at the intersection of postcolonial national imaginaries, global hegemonic Imperial Western secular–liberal discourses, patriarchy, sexism, and modern time to begin with an exclusion from citizenry and arrive at an exclusion from humanity. Accordingly, belatedness, difference in excess, and wounded habitus were advanced as key conceptual tools for the analysis of anti-Muslim racism while the visibly Muslim woman was argued to be a racialized subject of Eurocentric modernity/coloniality.

In Chapter 4, and building on this experienced racialization, I presented and analyzed what participants shared from their material lived experiences of anti-Muslim racism across social spheres. In the domestic sphere, the family was shown to be a site of erasure and aggression, under banners of protection and care, as the *muhajaba* is socialized into the illegitimacy of her stigmatized form of being. In the public sphere, a collectivist effort mobilizing myriad social actors functions to aggress and enforce subjugation "from below." In the work sphere, this aggression is further underlined as the *muhajaba* faces structural Islamophobia and is pushed into erasure. The state, additionally, was demonstrated as a space of assault, neutralized as a potential source of protection. In this scene, I argued that the market is the most prominent space of aggression, rather than the (neoliberal) state, as geography, the conservatism of the dress, and socioeconomic status entered as key variables in structuring the *muhajaba*'s racialized lived experiences. Throughout, Lebanon's imagined identity entwines with a global discourse of Eurocentric hegemony to enforce a colonizing uni-verse of being. In this respect, a series of micro-processes of Islamophobic erasure were identified. These include cumulative converging pressure through micro-aggressions, systematic vulnerabilizing, devaluing and impoverishing, spatializing difference, and the establishment of borders for cloistering within and beyond geography and institutional spaces.

In Chapter 5, I turned to explore the different forms of hijab present and practiced in the Lebanese space. Conceptualizing this as a kaleidoscopic spectrum structured around a measurable "modernity," I proposed that the different forms of the hijab dictate a different social experience based on the degree to which they have been diluted into mainstream Lebanese society. Dilution, I argued, is a process of erasure consisting of a hollowing mummification through an emptying-out where the practices of the colonized are systematically disrupted in both material shape and entangled effects and meanings. This, I contend, is the modern and fashionable hijab: a diluted dress and practice that distance itself from the Arabo-Muslim social form and advance a semblance to the imagined European under the colonizer's gaze. In parallel, I identified a second mechanism co-constitutive of this dilution's erasing effect: the establishment of an imagined idealized proclaimed authentic gaze forced upon those women who refuse to distance themselves from the Arabo-Muslim association. Under this gaze, I explained, the *muhajaba* is pushed into exhaustion to collapse and self-dilute as she is faced with the impossibility of an enforced Muslim authenticity.

Building on this, the chapter further explored the power effects of this diluted hijab's presence in the Lebanese space. This mainly involved a process of further anomalizing the "non-modern" hijab and underwriting its difference, legitimizing and justifying the Islamophobic exclusion of women in such forms of the hijab, and forcing the *muhajaba* into an augmented sense of alienation. These, I argued, are disciplinary moves establishing anti-Muslim racism's hegemony on the conditions of tolerance while offering a legitimatization of anti-Muslim racism. The diluted hijab, I concluded, is deeply implicated in the erasure of the Muslim and Islamophobia's reproduction. Closing this exploration, I maintained that this diluted colonized and colonizing hijab is, despite the improved social experience it might be said to offer, racialized and assaulted: the impossibility of whiteness persists.

In Chapter 6, I turned to explore the discourses of *difa'*—defense and negotiation—mobilized by hijab-wearing women to argue for their dress in Lebanese society. I began by identifying a parochial universalism seeped in "rationality," Europe, and Christianity and a discourse of a provincial secularism offered as a horizon that originates in Europe and that holds the potential to protect difference and ensure rights in a globalizing world. Broadening, privatizing, and individualizing the Muslim practice, I argued that these discourses are implicated in the disavowal of the Muslim and the Arab as they naturalize the parochial European as universal. Further, a discourse of "modern science" as undisputable truth was identified where questions of health, medicine, and even technology are central in the *muhajaba*'s reclaiming of her Muslim dress. Participants' negotiation further disavowed the Arab and the Muslim while implicated in the reproduction of coloniality well beyond the question of dress. In discussing patriarchy and resistance, participants explained how they perceive the hijab itself to be a tool of women's liberation in complex and multilayered ways. Yet, they also explained, this claim was not enunciable in mainstream Lebanese society. This, in turn, meant they were often limited to an argumentation objecting to the current model of Western neoliberal consumption as patriarchal subjugation. Consequently, I argued that coloniality largely controlled negotiation whereby its entwinement with Islamophobia became further evident. Further, I held that Islamophobia itself functions as a tool of coloniality's wider reproduction in Lebanon.

In the second section of Chapter 6, I turned to explore some elements of the hijab as a delinked practice laying outside of the concealing logic colonizing its analysis. There, I identified the hijab as a tool of self-formation wielded by participants to attain the complete moral Muslim subject they seek. Through this performative practice, a habitus of Islam is developed as a relationship to Muslim ancestrality is both nurtured and mobilized in pursuit of a Muslim *telos*. Reflecting on the discrepancy between the colonized negotiation identified and the evident *different* conceptualization present, I closed the chapter affirming that the dissonance between its two sections evidences the *muhajaba's* double-consciousness and wounded being. Based on this, I posited that anti-Muslim racism functions to erase this "Islamic" at the epistemic as well as at the material levels through its assault on the Muslim dress.

This book's key argument is that systematic and structural anti-Muslim racism is present and rampant in Lebanon with magnanimous wounding effects. Based on an analysis of this racism, from its formations to its control and reproduction, the book posits that it functions in deep entwinement with larger Eurocentric modernity/coloniality and, most importantly, its reproduction in both the erasure of the Muslim and the enforcement of the Eurocentric "modern." Through the experiences of its racialized and assaulted Muslim participants, it hopes that a better understanding of the modern/colonial condition may be pursued for its disruption, for its subversion, for its redress.

This book has sought to think alongside participants focusing on their oppression and its conditions. It has not sought, in any form, to establish a normative or value judgment about women's Muslim dress, nor an analysis of this dress and its meanings (particularly its contemporary *modern* patriarchal meanings) per se. It has not, in other words, had much to say about the hijab itself. Rather, it has sought to discuss the hijab's racialized being within modern Lebanon. In thinking around participants' anti-Muslim erasure with Muslim visibility and dress being a key site of this oppression, I remain deeply committed to an acknowledgment and centering of participants' own agentive being and relation to these processes. It is here important to reiterate that this is an agency that does not delve back into an autonomous liberal subject but rather adopts "a model of agency that is far more sophisticated than that of the strategical, calculating subject that constructs its own reasons," where "agency ensues not from sovereign subjects, but from trained and disciplined bodies" (Baerveldt 2015: 542). As noted in Chapter 5, agency, "a capacity for action that historically specific relations of subordination enable and create" (Allen 2007; Mahmood 2001a: 203), exists without simplistically and categorically belonging "to the women themselves, but is a product of the historically contingent discursive traditions in which they are located" (Jacobsen 2011; Mahmood 2012a: 32). Indeed, the world today is a world touched by coloniality but nevertheless a world whose inhabitants cannot be fully subsumed under it. It is a world where an outside of modernity continues to exist, where Europe's Others continue to be: modernity is not a totalizing machine; it is not an irresistible successful hegemon that faces no resistance or refusal. Yet, modernity, more than five hundred years in the making, is a machine that has touched the whole globe. There is no pure exterior to the condition of coloniality. Nevertheless, there is a (material as well as non-material) "borderland" where difference continues to exist as the colonial difference persists, the otherness survives, and resistance thrives. This book has argued that it is there that the *muhajaba* dwells, leaving it for future work to develop an understanding of this dwelling in its various entangling and intersecting complexities and layers. Accordingly, I contend that this book's focus on the experiences and conditions of subordination and oppression is essential, and that it paves the way for an analysis of the various forms of agentive being the colonized in Lebanon pursue and enact. Lebanon itself, ultimately, must not be reduced to an Islamophobic hegemony as it remains far more complex.

Rethinking Lebanon, the Region, and Anti-Muslim Racism

Lebanon

Sectarianism is the dominant lens through which Lebanon's various problems, contradictions, and instability are standardly presented and analyzed (Baytiyeh 2017; Cammett 2014; Gade 2017). In this framing, much of the hijab-wearing woman's lived experiences are, when acknowledged or seen, often reduced to sectarian tensions and intercommunal conflict. Yet, as explored throughout this book, the hijab-wearing woman's experiences are those of an Islamophobic aggression that cuts across various divides, including sectarian, religious, regional, and class. Within this, Westernized elites and Eurocentric modernity's "Others," including (practicing) Lebanese Muslims, are themselves deeply implicated while self-orientalism and self-hate are key. This makes clear how anti-Muslim racism in Lebanon cannot and must not be reduced to a question of Lebanon's sectarian conflict or be understood outside of global modernity/coloniality. Surely, this is not to deny the significant presence of sectarianism in Lebanon but rather to work against simplistic and reductionist understandings of the Lebanese condition. In this, sectarianism becomes one force working alongside and in entanglement with other forces, including anti-Muslim racialization. Accordingly, this book invites us to ask what a decolonial analysis of sectarianism can offer and how it would challenge current conceptualizations of the Lebanese sociopolitical order.

Islamophobia in Lebanon is certainly not limited to women or to the hijab. Despite the patriarchal absence of a parallel dress for Muslim men, long beards or Muslim rings and jewelry typically worn by practicing Muslim men among various sociocultural practices identified as Muslim are significant sites upon which anti-Muslim hate is exerted in the country. As Muslims are prevented from renting or buying homes in a number of "Christian regions," practices associated with Islam and common to both men and women, from praying during work hours to having an accent that connotes being from a Muslim community, are standardly assaulted across Lebanon. Indeed, widespread experiences of discrimination in education and employment as well as a dominant inferiorization as less cultured or less civilized and a tyrannical pursuit of a secularized and Westernized "good Muslim" for social recognition and capital permeate Lebanese life. Yet, it is possible to affirm that women's experiences of Islamophobia are more pronounced, often far more violent, than men's lived experiences of Islamophobia. The visibility of the hijab is key in this, albeit this gendering is far from being limited to this. In this respect, one of this book's main propositions is that Islamophobia in Lebanon is deeply gendered: this book's very focus on the hijab is the greatest attestation of this patriarchal gendering, of male privilege, and of modernity/coloniality's sexism.

Lebanon is a country where there are over 1.5 million non-"citizens" coinhabiting the geography with around 4 million "citizens." This book has not systematically engaged with this presence, nor its effects. From limiting participation to Lebanese women in a methodological move to sidelining an extensive incorporation of migrants and refugees' presence in an analytical move, the arguments drawn throughout this book do not address this major component structuring all of Lebanon's dwellers' daily lived experiences. Asking how this "refugee" presence, itself a majority-Muslim presence, impacts the *muhajaba's* and the Muslim's dwelling, therefore, becomes significant. Similarly, asking what effect the Syrian civil war, in particular, has had on the intensifying demonization of Islam and Muslims within Lebanon and how certain kinds of Muslim identity have come to be increasingly understood, performed, and countered further appears pertinent. In parallel, the need to (re)explore the lived experiences of other subalternized and racialized groups in Lebanon, including refugees deeply wounded and aggressed at the intersections of their non-Lebanese citizenship, refugee status, and multiple other compounding markers from sexuality to phenotype and "Islamicness," is raised.

On October 17, 2019, an overwhelming wave of mass demonstrations mobilized by severe economic grievances erupted across Lebanon. From unemployment and increasing poverty rates to insecurity and widespread oligarchic corruption, the Lebanese state had become unbearable. Indeed, following months of austerity with a collapsing economic system, this movement emerged as a cross-sectarian leaderless revolution protesting a largely Westernized capitalist ruling elite. It came to be known as Lebanon's October Revolution, or Movement. While this was a cross-sectarian diverse mobilization that, for example, welcomed refugees among its ranks in a major achievement within Lebanese politics, its delinking from colonial Western imaginaries of (economic) growth, "emancipation," nation-states, and "progress" remained ambivalent. Indeed, its embeddedness within narratives of Lebanese exceptionalism, its turning toward the "international community" (and France in particular) and global financial institutions such as the IMF and the World Bank, and its commitment to a pursuit of Eurocentric "development" left much to be wanted.

Since this aborted revolution, Lebanon has entered an unprecedented economic crisis: from massive currency devaluation to magnanimous inflation, mass unemployment, and ever-growing public debt (currently the third highest in the world). This has only been exacerbated by the Covid pandemic and growing global and regional instabilities. Often situated as a "national" crisis shaped by internal corruption, this crisis has invigorated a nostalgic romanticization of the era of the 1950s and 1960s. Often termed Lebanon's "golden age," this was a period when the country was steeply a Eurocentered, capitalist, and tourist project in the "orient" as "Switzerland of the East," with Beirut as "Paris of the East." In this respect, many calls out of the current crisis revolve around demands for a return to a beautiful era of Westernizing prosperity and abundance. Yet, this era was only made possible through various exclusions, inferiorizations, exploitations, and inequalities as the celebrated prosperity of the few only came to be through the mass exploitation and corruption-driven marginalization of various groups and geographies across the country—including much of Lebanon's Muslim populations and Muslim-majority geographies in the Lebanese south, the Bekaa, and the north. Further, it was an era that only came to be through larger global political alignments as well as regional socioeconomic conditions. What does it mean to romanticize, celebrate, and call for the return of a time that was oppressively characterized by Maronite superiority? For a time predicated and produced to the detriment and through the consumption of various othered groups across the country? For a time when Lebanon was celebrated as the Eurocentrically "civilizing beacon" of the Arab world? What inequalities and injustices does this require? What alignments does this calling necessitate? What violence does it make possible? What exclusions does it entail? Prior to this crisis, Felsch (2018) had noted a significant return of Christian (supremacist right-wing) nationalism in Lebanon. The current situation might very well have exacerbated this "return." This, in turn, is further confounded by the role in, and blaming of, Hezbollah and Lebanon's "involvement" in regional "Islamic" politics for the current crisis and the country falling out of favor with the United States and its proxies within large segments of the Lebanese population. The imaginary of the Lebanese and the possibilities for alternative futures consequently appear dim and slim. With worsening economic conditions and heightened precarity, and aware of the central role of the market and financial necessity in aggressing and erasing the Muslim, much indicates that Islamophobia in Lebanon will only continue to thrive and assault.

The West Asia North Africa Region

In Chapter 2, I argued that Lebanon is a colonial invention where the ongoing legacies of its history form it as a space of hegemonic and aggressive Eurocentric modernity. Given its particularities and historical formation, some might argue that the racialization and assault of hijab-wearing women is a "Lebanese" phenomenon with little relevance to other Arab-majority or Muslim-majority regions and spaces. I would contend that it is not. What this book has argued is that this is a modern/colonial phenomenon, and the modern/colonial certainly permeates the region. Indeed, as shown in Chapter 2, the assault against Muslim dress has long existed and wounded across West Asia North Africa over the past decades. Yet, this presence has not been understood as a form of racism as colonialism and postcolonial nation-state building seem to be conceptualized as specific historical periods where coloniality and its (anti-Muslim) racialization are absented. Informed by the anti-, post-, and decolonial theorizations drawn on and engaged throughout this book, I posit the need to rethink the anti-hijab and anti-Islam phenomenon of the past century across the region.

On another level, the anti-hijab movement in the region, also as shown in Chapter 2, is assumed to have abated: from Iran's "Islamic republic" to Egypt's social "repentance." Has this phase of postcolonial modernization as Westernization been surpassed across the region while Lebanon holds on to its colonial foundation? Here too, I would argue differently. Beyond thinking this anti-Muslim racism in terms of linear history—a deeply Eurocentric conceptualization—I would contend that it needs to be understood in complex and fluctuating terms: a phenomenon that ebbs and flows, that rises and settles, that mutates, that feigns retreat. Such a rethinking has already been paved for in previous chapters. For example, in light of the arguments presented around the "modern hijab" and the "fashionable hijab" in Chapter 5, a rethinking of the hijab's proclaimed resurgence becomes necessary, complexifying the very category of the modern hijab and the hijab-wearing woman and asking which hijab has resurged and how this resurgence functions in relation to the disavowal of the Muslim and its ultimate inferiorization and erasure. Further, even this resurgent hijab's tolerance was shown to be limited where the visibly Muslim woman persisted as a racialized Other. Here too, the question was of modernity/ coloniality, ongoing and persistent.

Indeed, much indicates that the aggression against visibly Muslim women persists across the Arab-majority and Muslim-majority worlds. In Egypt, for example, activist Manal Rostom began a large campaign in 2014 contesting what she described as rampant discrimination against hijab-wearing women in many sectors and spaces of the country. A Facebook group she started seeking to create a safe space of support for hijab-wearing women to connect and work together to face this discrimination now has over 1 million participants. Similarly, an elaborate discussion around the niqab at the American University of Cairo starting in 2015 arrived to a court ruling in 2020 upholding a ban on the niqab for academic staff members. In fact, throughout conversations with colleagues in Tunisia, Morocco, Jordan, and (pre-2011 as well as current) Syria, various and multiple forms and articulations of anti-Muslim racism were noted and identified. Crucially, this includes persistent anti-hijab discrimination and the construction of the ideal citizen as non-hijab-wearing, non-visibly Muslim. A stigma of practices identified as Muslim, such as declining to make physical skin contact with nonkin member of the opposite sex or refusing to partake in events where alcohol is served, were some other recurrent examples of anti-Muslim racism where narratives of "backwardness" and "uncivilized" prevailed. In much of the Gulf countries, a significant "white privilege" permeates, and a deep need for a "modernized Islam" has recently gained growing prominence. Indeed, a deep move to "privatize" Islam echoes across the Muslim-majority world as discourses of "emancipation" and "progress" dominate. Meanwhile, the demonization of so-called political Islam and its securitization and assault pervade as claiming Islam "political" becomes intolerable. Surely, these are complex and layered phenomena and require their own analysis and examination paying attention to the specific contingent forces structuring them within and across the various countries and the regions where they unfold. Nevertheless, I contend here that assaulting "modernization" is not historical but is rather ongoing in all its violence, in continuation with the colonial, as anti-Muslim racism floods the Arab-majority and Muslim-majority worlds. Just as a call to a Phoenician identity in Lebanon is made, a call to a Pharaonic one is made in Egypt. Lebanon is not an exception, nor is it an outlier. Aware of each space's particularities and specificities, away from simplistic or reductionist statements, and beyond homogenizing "grand theories" and categorical analyses, this book's invitation is to rethink the contemporary condition's inequalities in their historical and ongoing global connections. Accordingly, I posit here the need to rethink what is presumed to have ended, to look again and look differently. To center racialization and racism decolonially.

A key question is understanding how other variables either alleviate or worsen such lived experience of racialized being. A intersections/entanglements analysis is, in this respect, imperative. While class might be suggested to improve such experiences based on this book's discussions, for example, much is needed to speak of sexuality, of age, of ability, or of ethnicity. Crucially, what about color and phenotype? Here, questions of spatialization, of urbanizations, of states and state sovereignty, of identity and citizenship, and of borders and walls offer themselves as significant axis that further complexify and nuance racialized lived experiences. Relatedly, the omnipresent challenges of capital, neoliberalism, consumer societies and markets, and their foundational presence in anti-Muslim racism and the erasure of Eurocentric modernity's Others emerge as key avenues of examination and reflection. Indeed, how does anti-Muslim racism unfold within different national contexts across the region? What is the common denominator and where do these experiences diverge? What is the role of self-hate and self-orientalism within them? How do various groups—non-Muslims, migrants, "refugees"—understand and engage anti-Muslim racism? How do they understand and engage anti-Black racism in the region? Such work would be key for a better conceptualization of the hierarchy of markers and the articulation of the colonial difference in embodied lived experiences and could offer significant insights into racism including and beyond its anti-Muslim articulation. The need is hence to examine these and related questions across different moments and forms of modern racialized subjugation throughout the so-called Middle East North Africa region and beyond, without, of course, claiming that mechanisms and processes transcend all boundaries or function universally. Based on this, a better elaboration of an agenda for an anti-coloniality resistance in a deeply colonized region may be further advanced.

The relevance and value of such a rethinking is not only conceptual or theoretical. It is material and political: it would allow an engagement with the various struggles of different inferiorized and aggressed groups across the region and the world differently and, most importantly, *together*. In this respect, the struggle against Islamophobia would be inseparable from the struggle against anti-Black racism, anti-Semitism, and anti-Asian hate, to name a few relevant examples today. In this, such a rethinking would necessitate centering modernity/coloniality and its resistance across these various forms of assaulted lived experience, across spaces and places.

One might argue that such a framing of anti-Muslim discrimination as a form of racism further opens up the space for "rights-claiming": from national laws that would protect "freedoms" to international human rights that would offer a tool of policing anti-Muslim violations. Yet, from a decolonial position, such forms of resistance would be working from within the confines and episteme of Eurocentric modernity/coloniality, appealing to its apparatuses and institutions. Such forms of negotiation and resistance are bound to be implicated in its reproduction and structured by its discourses, not least about "rights," "freedom," and authority. Some might choose to adopt such paths and could make use of this book's arguments for this. Some might find no other choice. I would call here for a resistance beyond such institutions and structures whenever and wherever possible—beyond the postcolonial nation-state and its legal form and beyond the "international" institutions of Eurocentric modernity/coloniality.

Broader Anti-Muslim Racism Today

Anti-Muslim racism is on the rise across the globe. In the West, the hijab has become the grand symbol of an abject otherness as "the foil or negative mirror in which western constructions of identity and gender can be positively reflected" as the West fashions itself in opposition to its invented Muslim Other and conceals its own contradictions and patriarchy (Al-Saji 2010: 877; Meer 2022). In France, for example, the republic's political community has increasingly turned hysterical in a space where missionary-ism has long sought to "emancipate Muslims" from an ideologized and culturalized Islam where Islamophobia generally, and anti-hijab discourse particularly, has seen unprecedented escalations with the escalation of far-right twenty-first-century fascism. The hijab-wearing woman, therefore, finds herself the object of converging discourses for erasure where the dress's "criminalizing evidences the attachment of the colonial past to the present and future" (Brayson 2019: 62). Consequently, Islamophobia, misogyny, stereotypes, and nation-state projects increasingly entangle Muslim dress with gendered politics of race and whiteness for erasure across the Global North (Al-Saji 2010; Brayson 2019; Franks 2000; Mason-Bish and Zempi 2019; Massad 2015; Moosavi 2015; Zempi and Chakraborti 2014).

This anti-Muslim racism is far from being limited to the hijab. From moral panics around the construction of mosques to heated debates around Muslim names, cultural decline, and "replacement," Islamophobia is a complex multifaceted structure. Throughout, it carries its own violent manifestations. These include, for example, the New Zealand mosque's mass shootings in 2019, leaving over fifty-one dead and over forty injured. They also include the killing of a mother, father, daughter, and grandmother as a son was orphaned when a truck driver decided to run over the family for being Muslim in Canada in 2021. In the United States, much has been written on Islamophobia—as an industry, a practice, a policy, and a lived experience as Muslim Americans are surveilled, harassed, marginalized, and assaulted. In Bosnia, with a long history of genocide, mass murder, and "cleansing," the sands of anti-Muslim racism have begun shifting again with intersecting discourses of Muslim threat and difference. Permeating life from the cultural to the political and the everyday, anti-Muslim racism is a major force structuring the contemporary world across Euro-America and the Global North.

In the Global South, similar developments can be identified. In India, anti-Muslim racism has (re)emerged potent within a larger project of Hindutva nationalism. There too, Muslim dress and women's bodies have been subject to much assault and discrimination as Muslims are increasingly transformed into the intolerable Other. From online platforms offering Muslim women for "sale" to open calls to "kill Muslims" that pass uncommented on by authorities and to an escalating rhetoric rejecting the country's Muslims as a threat and a menace, anti-Muslim hate is very much alive in a state with over 200 million Muslims. In Myanmar, long-marginalized Muslim communities have faced intensifying aggression over the past years, including torture, arson, rape, and mass murder. Tellingly, in 2019, a statement by the Hungarian government after Orban's meeting with Myanmar's Nobel Peace Laureate Aung San Suu Kyi identified "growing Muslim populations" as one of the key common "challenges" across Europe and Southeast Asia. In China, Uyghur Muslims continue to be constructed as a national threat and pushed to assimilate across what has been described as "concentration camps." In multiple African spaces, various forms of violence against Muslims and Muslim practices have been recorded over the past years. In 2017, for example, two mosques were attacked and defiled in Cape Town in events that authorities labeled as adopting "Islamophobic methods."

These various incidents have been analyzed through various frames: nationalism, ethnic conflict, geopolitics, and security, to name a few. They have even been dismissed, or conceptualized as "reactions" to "Muslim terror" or "Muslim intolerability." Standardly, they are situated (exclusively) within their local settings, and analyzed accordingly. Yet, these instances are not separate or discreet. They must rather be understood in relation to both the historical and the global: in relation to violent modernity/coloniality and its exclusionary structures of erasure and assault and, most importantly, its reproduction.

In line with this, I am led to ask what other forms of erasure plague the globe today that go unregistered and unacknowledged? What other hates, self-hates, and internalized inferiorities ravage the Global South today? What forms of oppression and violence has the modern exclusionary logic birthed against Eurocentric modernity's various Others within and outside of empire's metropoles? How do these exclusions entangle, converge, and diverge? What conditions make these various forms of violence possible? What neurosis drives and feeds them? What processes continue to transform their perpetrators into monsters? Informed by Fanon's realization that "a former European colony decided to catch up with Europe. It succeeded so well that the United States of America became a monster, in which the taints, the sickness, and the inhumanity of Europe have grown to appalling dimensions" (Fanon, 2001, 313), I ask how successful is this Eurocentric modernity across today's postcolonial Global South and how do various forms of racialization, including anti-Muslim racism, allow us to understand this success and examine its "progress"?

As to this project's hijab-wearing participants, this book remains ambivalent. This is not because there is an essentialized category called "Muslim woman" and I do not fit within it. Nor is this because there is an absolute subaltern that cannot be voiced. Not even because it was being authored in the prosperity of the English South Downs and the Scottish capital city while Lebanon burned, witnessed a radical mobilization in which the *muhajaba* remained disavowed, and descended into further dependence, inequalities, and precarity. It is, rather, counterfeit because I have not lived, loved, hated, been weighed down, or been elevated by Muslim dress. I do not hold the scars I speak of. Nevertheless, it is a legitimate labor emerging from echoing pains and an insistent commonality advancing a subaltern cause, fostering radical empathy, building bridges across colonial wounds, to debunk the ultimate forgery of our time: modernity.

This project's most valuable politicization will eventually be in rendering coloniality's violent erasure and reproduction visible to advocate and develop means of delinking resistance and refusal by advancing a liberatory agenda "with respect to thinking, being, knowing, understanding, and living" as it "encourage[s] venues of re-existence"—of non-modern existence (Mignolo and Walsh 2018: 4). As Frantz Omar Fanon concluded in *The Wretched of the Earth*,

> For Europe, for ourselves, and for humanity, comrades, we must turn over a new leaf, we must work out new concepts, and try to set afoot a new [Hu]man.

Notes

Prologue

1 The term "Islamic" is used throughout this book as a translation of the word "Islami" in Arabic, meaning "of Islam" or "relating to Islam." This usage is therefore external to the debates on the distinction between the Muslim and the Islamic or any Eurocentric assumptions about "the Islamic."
2 This was a course run by Dr. Nazanin Shakaroni.

1 Introduction: Thinking Islamophobia Elsewhere and Otherwise

1 For a decolonized theorization of gender see Lugones (2010) and Wawzonek (2017).
2 This must not be taken to mean that these are things participants wanted to voice in the absolute, as the project and myself, among multiple other factors, surely influenced what they did and did not say, and what they chose to voice and what they chose to keep silenced, not do, and not say. Reiterating this is important as not to fall into an assumption that the data holds floating legitimacy, is complete, or is representative of any complete external reality.
3 For a good brief exploration of the concept of "civilization," refer to Briand, Dupont, and Longhi (2018).
4 By consequence, there is no room, with such a definition of modernity, for multiple modernities, alternative modernities, or hybrid forms of modernity (see Bhambra 2007; Mignolo and Escobar 2009). Rather, room for alternatives *to* modernity is made.
5 This is also found in some "modern" literature. Stephen Toulmin (1992), for example, locates the beginning of "modernity" with fifteenth-century humanists.
6 Georges Saliba (2007), a historian of the "Islamic civilization," has argued that the "discovery" of the Americas is the most significant event in the known history of humankind and one especially important for the Islamic world as it was a key factor in bringing about its "collapse." Focusing on question of trade and the shifting of the global trade balance, the impact on the silk road, and the loss of resources for "Eastern civilizations," he argues that an understanding of the modern condition must begin with the discovery of the Americas.

7 It must be noted here that this does not ignore the fact that colonialism in Africa began before the conquest of the Americas.
8 It must be noted here that the Christianity I refer to throughout is European white Christianity of Western Christendom as a political project transformed starting 1492 and turned into an identity, a locus of enunciation, a civilizational erasing power structure. See Mignolo (2009c) for an introduction of these transformations and Grosfoguel (2013) on Christendom as opposed to Christianity.
9 The works of Oyeronke Oyewumi (1997, 2011), Sylvia Marcos (2006), and Catherine Walsh (2016) are particularly insightful in this respect. For an excellent elaboration on much feminism's entanglement with secularism and coloniality, see Carrasco Miró (2020).

2 Historicization and Framing: Lebanon and Muslim Dress

1 A "confessional democracy" is a democratic system where political representation is proportionally divided and distributed across religious groups—"confessions."
2 The Druze are a socioreligious group found mainly in Lebanon and Syria. They have a complex social system and live in mostly separate communities. For these reasons, in addition to practical limitation of access and scope, there were no Druze participants in this project. For further information refer to Hazran (2009a, 2010).
3 The Maronite church is a church in communion with the Catholic church.
4 The "Patriarch" was, and still is, the head of the Maronite church. By virtue of this office, he exerts great political power. For a brief overview of the Maronite church's history see Tabar (2014).
5 Note that this is not a critique of legal pluralism under one state. For a discussion of legal pluralism, see Possamai et al. (2014: Part 3). It is a critique of the way it was applied and used by the French and the subsequent regimes in the country. Also, see Mahmood (2015) for a discussion of what a similar system did in Egypt.
6 A Phoenician identity was invoked, particularly by Lebanon's Christians, before, during, and after the Lebanese civil war. This was present in fields as varied as literary production, media, social movements, and formal politics. For an engaging exploration of this, see Zogheib (2014). For a historicization of this, see Kaufman (2001).
7 For the accord refer to http://al-bab.com/documents/taif-accord.
8 Samir Geagea was one of the very few warlords to face trial for the Lebanese civil war. He was later released and pardoned after the Al-Hariri assassination to become the head of a major Christian political party (Lebanese Forces).

9 In terms of demographics, the last official census was conducted in 1932, meaning that no precise information on the Lebanese constituency exists. Nevertheless, it is estimated that around one-third of the population today identify as Christians (from Catholics to Protestants) while the majority of the remaining population identify as Muslims (Sunni, Shia, Druze, and other), with some other minority groups (Faour 2007).

10 This is not an ascription to the meta-narrative of a binary divide revolving around religion but rather an acknowledgment of the divides, negotiated and nuanced as they may be, within the country (see Peri 2014).

11 In recent years, a certain Christian revival has been noted by the literature. See Felsch (2018).

12 Certainly, the two identities are not mutually exclusive but rather exist in a complex relationship that differs across sects, regions, age groups, and classes.

13 The fact that Zeineddine was Druze is certainly interesting. Nevertheless, exploring this is beyond both my field of work and this book.

14 On February 1, 2018, then Prime Minister Saad Al-Hariri publicly demanded all state institutions to "commit themselves to accepting the applications of citizens having the necessary conditions as specified in the law, including hijab-wearing women, and that the hijab not be a handicap in their taking-up of a public position, under the auspice of responsibility and accountability" (direct transcription). This came after debates regarding hijab-wearing women's entry to municipalities, internal security forces, and the Lebanese army had been taking place in the country for several years. Also, this came three months before the 2018 Lebanese elections.

15 These constructions are deeply woven with Christian, Eurocentric, and imperial categories and understandings of matters ranging from the idea of women itself to self-formation and purity. An exploration of this nevertheless remains beyond the scope of this book.

16 For an excellent reconstruction of the history of women and their social conditions in Egypt under Mamluk rule, refer to Fay (2012).

17 Also see here Chatterjee (1986).

18 See Kosba (2018) and Abdelkader (2018).

3 Racialization at the Intersection of the Local and the Global: From an Expulsion from Citizenry to Dehumanization

1 It must be particularly stressed that the various elements of this experience are interconnected and overlapping, often messy and the chapter in no way implies that these elements are separate, nor that they do not co-constitute one another.

2 It must be noted here that the Christianity referred to here is the civilizational project of European "white" Christianity, more accurately referred to as "Western Christendom."
3 Surely, much can be said here, particularly in relation to the questions of population control and, to some extent, even eugenics. Nevertheless, this is beyond my scope here and remains for another work.

4 Domestic, Public, Work, and State Spheres: Lived Anti-Muslim Racism and Its Workings

1 It is to be noted here that these findings further raise the question of patriarchy and sexism in their relation to coloniality and how they structure and unfold within the hijab-wearing woman's personal, familiar, marital, and other relations. Especially relevant in the domestic sphere, such an analysis is of great importance to understand all the spheres of the hijab-wearing woman's life. This remains for future work to explore and develop to arrive at a better understanding of how coloniality intersects with gender, patriarchy, and sexism in its erasure.
2 The comparison with "ghettos" and racial segregation promises great insights, for example, with the work of Wacquant (2008) and related literature specifically in terms of space and spatialization. Yet, a specific exploration of this is not possible within the space of this chapter.
3 This can surely be linked to the questions of ISIS, terrorism, and the production of Islam as terror. Yet, this therefore remains for another project to explore more fully. See Bayrakli and Hafez (2018), El Zahed (2019), Sayyid (2014), and Tyrer (2013) for relevant analysis and theorizations.
4 See Maasri (2016) on the role of tourism in the invention of the Lebanese postcolonial modern imaginary.
5 These insights invite an engagement with different strands of work critically exploring the modern condition. A key example here would be Lefebvre's (2000) classic thesis on modernity's "colonization" of the everyday through the state where space is commodified under specific power structures. Nevertheless, such an engagement remains beyond the scope of this book.
6 For a more in-depth examination of the Lebanese banking sector's role in anti-Muslim racism in Lebanon, see Kassem (2022b).
7 It is worth noting that Islamic banks in 2012 (latest date for which reliable data could be found) held assets standing at less than 1 percent of the Lebanese banking market (Jouni 2012). There is nothing to indicate that they have grown since.

5 A Kaleidoscopic Spectrum of Muslim Dress and the Reproduction of Anti-Muslim Racism

1 The chapter will also not be pursuing an exploration of the reasons, motivations, or underlying rationales for which Muslim women practice Muslim dress in different ways and forms. Such reasons are complex and multiple, beyond the scope and objective of this work and project.
2 The movement differentiating the hijab is, ultimately, influenced by a large intricate number of variables that will remain unexplored given the limitations of this chapter and the data.
3 Terminology here was at times complexified and even contested by some participants in relation to various specific and different forms of Muslim dress, and this analysis should not be understood to suggest a monolithic reading of how these signifiers are understood across Lebanon. Rather, this analysis is meant to indicate the dominant trends encountered as it offers significant insights for the analysis of anti-Muslim racism in Lebanon.
4 Once the show aired, Nelly left the channel and moved to a non-Lebanese (online) media network for what she termed "complicated reasons" that she did not elaborate on.
5 It must be noted here that what participants referred to as "old hijab" is a very recent construction that does not predate the Lebanese civil war of women's Muslim dress in Lebanon. Prior to this, there was little to no practice of a hijab in the sense currently present, and what little Muslim dress was practiced was significantly different from the one currently present. It is, in this sense, interesting that participants who were well aware of this history qualified the dress as the "old hijab."
6 While I did not interview Inaya Ezzeddine, and while these statements remain hypothetical especially given the nature of my fieldwork, I contend that their spread among participants suffices to indicate the trends I will argue for here.
7 It is important to explicitly note here that this analysis reveals how the different forms of the hijab function to produce different forms of hijab-wearing subjectivity and how this is greatly structured by the social expectations enforced under modernity/coloniality. In this respect, the bodies of women are here again found to be the sites of both the formation and the representation of the different levels of religiosity within the public and social realms. This understanding complexifies the analysis of the hijab as a performative act forming a specific form of subject by inquiring about the specific form of this hijab and evidencing how such performativity is dependent on multiple factors revolving around the social meaning attached to a specific form of dress in a given sociohistorical context. The centrality of lived experiences is here evidenced, and modernity's sexism

and patriarchy whereby these experiences are not paralleled for men is further showcased. See, in this vein, Baldi (2018) and Mahmood (2012a).
8 It must be stressed that the analysis presented here emerges from the experiences hijab-wearing participants shared and aligns with how they themselves experienced the dynamics this chapter has explored. Other hijab-wearing women, in Lebanon and beyond, might of course have different experiences, understandings, and analysis of the hijab's kaleidoscopic spectrum.

6 From *Difaʿ* to Delinking: Anti-Muslim Racism and the Reproduction of Modernity/Coloniality

1 While some interviewees did mention Jewish practices, this was always presented as "Christian and Jewish," never Jewish alone, and remained secondary, with no other religious system mentioned. The exploration of this, and the construction of a Judeo-Christian tradition and its entanglement with modernity as well as the wider question of "Abrahamic religions," is beyond my scope in this book. For an interesting exploration of the "Judeo-Christian" refer to Nathan and Topolski (2016).
2 A number of participants had explicitly stated that secularism in Lebanon is "Christian," giving examples of secular institutions observing the Christian calendar and Christian holidays (but not Muslim holidays). A fuller exploration of this, while extremely valuable, is beyond the scope of this book.
3 For an exploration of how the secular narrative is foundational for modernity/coloniality refer to Mignolo (2011c). Also refer to Yountae (2017), Maldonado-Torres (2008), and Carrasco Miró (2020) for a good exploration of the entanglement of the secular with coloniality and a theoretical framing and basis for secularism's colonial workings and effects. Also refer to Asad (2003) for a critical reflection around "the secular" and secularism and their entanglement with the modern and its institutions particularly in relation to Islam.
4 It must be reiterated here that the Christianity I refer to throughout this book is the European white Christianity of Western Christendom transformed starting 1492 and turned into an identity, a locus of enunciation, a civilizational erasing project. See Mignolo (2009c) for an introduction of these transformations.
5 Also see Volume 12 issue 4 of *Postcolonial Studies* journal: *Science, Colonialism, Postcolonialism*.
6 While this may be related to the invented enforced authenticity destroying the *muhajaba* discussed in Chapter 5, I will keep these distinct as participants kept them distinct and affirmed them as separate movements. Nevertheless, it is not difficult

to suggest their entwinement. Such an exploration nevertheless remains for another project.

7   It is useful here to distinguish between personality, identity, and subjectivity and to note that the dress clearly functioned across these levels. The distinction between identity and subjectivity adopted here relates to power whereby identity is understood as the outward projected dimension of the self that oscillates in relation to its Other while subjectivity is understood as both the internal/ized forces and dimensions of power and the complex agentive work of the person on these power structures for their hybrid constitution as bound and binding, but not subsuming, work. Refer to Allen (2002, 2007) on subjectivity and Treacher (2005) for a useful discussion on postcolonial subjectivity. For a decolonial analysis of subjectivity and identity, refer to Ndlovu-Gatsheni (2015). Importantly, it must be acknowledged that these questions of identity and subjectivity are themselves categories that are greatly dependent on, and productive of, the modern condition and that the dress's functioning at the levels of both identity and subjectivity highlights both the coloniality at play as well as the possibilities of resistance harbored within it. This discussion remains, nevertheless, beyond the scope of this book. For a relevant reading, see Zima (2015).

8   It is to be noted here that a distinction and a conversation can emerge here with Mahmood's (2012) analysis in regard to the (Western, secular) public–private separation and an internal–external distinction in such formative practices and their telos. This, nevertheless, remains for future work to explore.

9   This is not to claim that the Islamic tradition or that the hijab are the only forms of dress where a set of rules accompany the dress or where dress can perform such functions. To the contrary, such an understanding has existed, and continues to exist, in a multitude of places, including within Europe. Nevertheless, this is to claim that this understanding of clothing is not part of modernity's project, that it does not figure in how clothing is understood within Western modernity today, and that it here connects to a non-Western discursive tradition.

Bibliography

Abaza, M., 2006. *Changing Consumer Cultures of Modern Egypt: Cairo's Urban Reshaping*. Leiden: Brill.

Abdallah, G., 2003. "Lebanon's Political System: An Analysis of the Taif Accord." PhD, University of Houston, Texas.

Abdelhadi, E., 2019. "The Hijab and Muslim Women's Employment in the United States." *Research in Social Stratification and Mobility* 61: 26–37. https://doi.org/10.1016/j.rssm.2019.01.006.

Abdelkader, D., 2018. "Old Wine in New Bottles: Secularism and Islamophobia in Egypt." In E. Bayrakli and F. Hafez (eds.), *Islamophobia in Muslim Majority Societies*. London: Routledge, pp. 125–36.

Abdul-Latif, R., and L. Serpe, 2010. The Status of the Women in the Middle East and North Africa: A Grassroots Research and Advocacy Approach: Preliminary Findings from Surveys in Lebanon and Morocco. Presented at the WAPOR conference. Chicago.

Abidor, P., 2012. "The Shiites of Lebanon under Ottoman Rule 1516–1788 (Review)." *Journal of Shi'a Islamic Studies* 5(4): 505–10. https://doi.org/10.1353/isl.2012.0061.

Abisaab, R. J., 2015. "Sayyid Musa al-Sadr, the Lebanese State, and the Left." *Journal of Shi'a Islamic Studies* 8(2): 131–57. https://doi.org/10.1353/isl.2015.0003.

Abisaab, R. J., and M. Abisaab, 2014. *The Shi'ites of Lebanon: Modernism, Communism, and Hizbullah's Islamists*. Syracuse, NY: Syracuse University Press.

Abou Ammo, R., 2012. *Onsoriya Loubnaniya Bilibas Elmani*. Beirut: Al-Akhbar.

Adu-Ampong, E. A., and E. A. Adams, 2020. "'But You Are also Ghanaian, You Should Know': Negotiating the Insider–Outsider Research Positionality in the Fieldwork Encounter." *Qualitative Inquiry* 26(6): 583–92. https://doi.org/10.1177/1077800419846532.

Afshar, H., 2008. "Can I See Your Hair? Choice, Agency and Attitudes: The Dilemma of Faith and Feminism for Muslim Women Who Cover." *Ethnic and Racial Studies* 31(2): 411–27. https://doi.org/10.1080/01419870701710930.

Aguilar, L. H., 2018. *Governing Muslims and Islam in Contemporary Germany: Race, Time, and the German Islam Conference*. Leiden: Brill.

Ahern, K. J., 1999. "Ten Tips for Reflexive Bracketing." *Qualitative Health Research* 9(3): 407–11. https://doi.org/10.1177/104973239900900309.

Ahmad, N., 2001. Colonisation and Hijab: A Case Study of Egypt and India (MPhil). Scotland: University of Glasgow (United Kingdom).

Ahmed, L., 1993. *Women and Gender in Islam: Historical Roots of a Modern Debate*, new ed. New Haven, CT: Yale University Press.

Ahmed, L., 2014. *A Quiet Revolution: The Veil's Resurgence, from the Middle East to America*. New Haven, CT: Yale University Press.

Ahmed, S., 2006. *Queer Phenomenology: Orientations, Objects, Others*. Durham, NC: Duke University Press Books.

Ahmed, S., 2012. *On Being Included: Racism and Diversity in Institutional Life*. Durham, NC: Duke University Press.

Ahmed-Ghosh, H., 2015. *Contesting Feminisms: Gender and Islam in Asia*. Albany, NY: SUNY Press.

Ajami, F., 1987. *The Vanished Imam: Musa al Sadr and the Shia of Lebanon*. Ithaca, NY: Cornell University Press.

Akbulut, S., 2011. Banning Headscarves and Muslim Women's Subjectivity in Turkey (PhD), University of Washington.

Al-Ali, N., 2000. *Secularism, Gender and the State in the Middle East: The Egyptian Women's Movement*. Cambridge: Cambridge University Press.

Allen, Chris. 2020. *Reconfiguring Islamophobia a Radical Rethinking of a Contested Concept*. 1st ed. Cham: Springer International Publishing.

Aljouhari, A., 2007. Ramziyat alhijab: Mafahim wa Dalalat. Beirut: Markaz Dirasat Alwehda Alarabiya.

Allain, K. A., 2014. "'What Happens in the Room Stays in the Room': Conducting Research with Young Men in the Canadian Hockey League." *Qualitative Research in Sport, Exercise and Health* 6(2): 205–19. https://doi.org/10.1080/2159676X.2013.796486.

Allen, A., 2002. "Power, Subjectivity, and Agency: Between Arendt and Foucault." *International Journal of Philosophical Studies* 10: 131–49. https://doi.org/10.1080/09672550210121432.

Allen, A., 2007. *The Politics of Our Selves: Power, Autonomy, and Gender in Contemporary Critical Theory*. New York: Columbia University Press.

Allen, C., 2015. "'People Hate You because of the Way You Dress': Understanding the Invisible Experiences of Veiled British Muslim Women Victims of Islamophobia." *International Review of Victimology* 21(3): 287–301. https://doi.org/10.1177/0269758015591677.

Allen, Christopher. 2010. *Islamophobia*. Farnham, Surrey: Ashgate.

Almayyali, N. M. J., 2011. *Al-fikr Al-Siyasi ind Al-Sayyed Mohammad Hussein Fadlallah*. Markaz Ibn Idris Alhilli liltanmiya alfokhiya wal thakafiya.

Almila, A.-M., 2014. Hijab as Dress: Muslim Women's Clothing Strategies in Contemporary Finland (PhD). University of Aberdeen (United Kingdom), Scotland.

Al-Qasimi, N., 2010. "Immodest Modesty Accommodating Dissent and the Abaya-as-Fashion in the Arab Gulf States." *Journal of Middle East Women's Studies* 6(1): 46–74. https://doi.org/10.2979/MEW.2010.6.1.46.

Al-Saji, A., 2010. "The Racialization of Muslim Veils: A Philosophical Analysis." *Philosophy & Social Criticism* 36(8): 875–902. https://doi.org/10.1177/0191453710375589.

Amin, C. M., 2002. *The Making of the Modern Iranian Woman: Gender, State Policy, and Popular Culture, 1865–1946*, 1st ed. Gainesville: University Press of Florida.

Anderson, B. R. O., 1991. *Imagined Communities: Reflections on the Origin and Spread of Nationalism*. London: Verso.

Ansems de Vries, L., L. M. Coleman, D. Rosenow, M. Tazzioli, and R. Vázquez, 2017. "Collective Discussion: Fracturing Politics (Or, How to Avoid the Tacit Reproduction of Modern/Colonial Ontologies in Critical Thought)." *International Political Sociology* 11(1): 90–108. https://doi.org/10.1093/ips/olw028.

Anthias, F., and N. Yuval-Davis, 1989. *Woman-Nation-State*. New York: Palgrave Macmillan. https://doi.org/10.1007/978-1-349-19865-8.

Asad, T., 1983. "Anthropological Conceptions of Religion: Reflections on Geertz." *Man* 18(2): 237–59. https://doi.org/10.2307/2801433.

Asad, T. 1986. *The Idea of an Anthropology of Islam*. Washington, DC: Center for Contemporary Arab Studies, Georgetown University.

Asad, T., 1993. *Genealogies of Religion: Discipline and Reasons of Power in Christianity and Islam*. Baltimore, MD: Johns Hopkins University Press.

Asad, T., 2003. *Formations of the Secular: Christianity, Islam, Modernity*. Stanford, CA: Stanford University Press.

Assaad, R., and F. Roudi-Fahimi, 2007. "Youth in the Middle East and North Africa: Demographic Opportunity or Challenge?" Population Reference Bureau, Washington, DC.

Assi, A., and J. Worrall, 2015. "Stable Instability: The Syrian Conflict and the Postponement of the 2013 Lebanese Parliamentary Elections." *Third World Quarterly* 36(10): 1944–67. https://doi.org/10.1080/01436597.2015.1071661.

Auerbach, J., 2017. Islam, Secularism and Cultural Conflict: How University Students in Turkey Negotiate Collective Identities across Places (PhD). New York University, New York.

Awan, Imran, and Irene Zempi. *The Routledge International Handbook of Islamophobia*. Taylor and Francis, 2019.

Azam, H., 2018. "Islamic Feminism between Islam and Islamophobia." *Journal of Middle East Women's Studies* 14(1): 124–8.

Baerveldt, C., 2015. "The Veil and the Search for the Self: From Identity Politics to Cultural Expression." *Culture & Psychology* 21(4): 532–45. https://doi.org/10.1177/1354067X15606861.

Bakali, Naved. 2016. *Islamophobia Understanding Anti-Muslim Racism through the Lived Experiences of Muslim Youth*. Rotterdam: Sense.

Balaton-Chrimes, S., and V. Stead, 2017. "Recognition, Power and Coloniality." *Postcolonial Studies* 20(1): 1–17. doi: 10.1080/13688790.2017.1355875.

Baldi, G., 2016. "Liberal Paradoxes: Women's Body, Religious Expression, and Gender Equality in a Secular Age." *AG About Gender—Rivista internazionale di studi di genere* 5(10): 166–85. https://doi.org/10.15167/2279-5057/ag.2016.5.10.327.

Baldi, G., 2017a. "'Burqa Avenger': Law and Religious Practices in Secular Space." *Law Critique* 29(1): 31–56. https://doi.org/10.1007/s10978-017-9208-5.

Baldi, G., 2017b. "'Visible Others': A Reading of the European Obsession with the Female Veil." *Sociology and Anthropology* 5(8): 677–87. https://doi.org/10.13189/sa.2017.050812.

Baldi, G., 2017c. What the Veil Reveals: A Critique of Religious and Secular Debate over the Headscarf (PhD). Birkbeck University of London, England.

Baron, B., 1989. "Unveiling in Early Twentieth Century Egypt: Practical and Symbolic Considerations." *Middle Eastern Studies* 25(3): 370–86.

Barras, A., 2010. "Contemporary Laïcité: Setting the Terms of a New Social Contract? The Slow Exclusion of Women Wearing Headscarves." *Totalitarian Movements and Political Religions* 11(2): 229–48. https://doi.org/10.1080/14690764.2010.511457.

Baubérot, J., 2008. "La Commission Stasi: Entre Laïcité Républicaine et Multiculturelle." *Historical Reflections / Réflexions Historiques* 34(3): 7–20.

Baumann, H. 2017. *Citizen Hariri: Lebanon's Neo-Liberal Reconstruction*, 1st ed. Oxford: Oxford University Press.

Baylouny, A. M., 2013. "Hizbullah's Women: Internal Transformation in a Social Movement and Militia." In J. Beinin and F. Vairel (eds.), *Social Movements, Mobilization, and Contestation in the Middle East and North Africa*. Stanford, CA: Stanford University Press, pp. 163–80.

Bayrakli, E., and F. Hafez (eds.), 2018. *Islamophobia in Muslim Majority Societies*, 1st ed. New York: Routledge.

Baytiyeh, H., 2017. "Has the Educational System in Lebanon Contributed to the Growing Sectarian Divisions?" *Education and Urban Society* 49(5): 546–59. https://doi.org/10.1177/0013124516645163.

Bazian, H., 2018. "'Religion-Building' and Foreign Policy." In E. Bayrakli and F. Hafez (eds.), *Islamophobia in Muslim Majority Societies*. London: Routledge, pp. 21–44.

Belzile, J. A., and G. Oberg, 2012. "Where to Begin? Grappling with How to Use Participant Interaction in Focus Group Design." *Qualitative Research* 12(4): 459–72. https://doi.org/10.1177/1468794111433089.

Benhabib, S., 2010. "The Return of Political Theology: The Scarf Affair in Comparative Constitutional Perspective in France, Germany and Turkey." *Philosophy & Social Criticism* 36(3–4): 451–71. https://doi.org/10.1177/0191453709358546.

Beydoun, K. A., 2008. "laïcité, Liberalism, and the Headscarf." *Journal of Islamic Law and Culture* 10(2): 191–215. https://doi.org/10.1080/15288170802285439.

Bhabha, H. K., 2004. *The Location of Culture*. London: Routledge.

Bhambra, G. K., 2007. *Rethinking Modernity: Postcolonialism and the Sociological Imagination*. Basingstoke: Palgrave Macmillan.

Bhambra, G. K., 2014. "Postcolonial and Decolonial Dialogues." *Postcolonial Studies* 17(2): 115–21. https://doi.org/10.1080/13688790.2014.966414.

Bi, S., 2018. "Panopticons, Power and Pleasure: Why the Hijab Is Not a Problem." *Journal of Muslim Minority Affairs* 38(1): 139–41.

Bialecki, J., 2017. "'Religion' after Religion, 'Ritual' after Ritual." In S. Coleman and S. Hyatt (eds.), *The Routledge Companion to Contemporary Anthropology*. London: Routledge, pp. 183–200.

Blix, B. H., 2015. "'Something Decent to Wear': Performances of Being an Insider and an Outsider in Indigenous Research." *Qualitative Inquiry* 21: 175–83. https://doi.org/10.1177/1077800414542702.

Bogues, A., 2010. *Empire of Liberty: Power, Desire, and Freedom*. Chicago: UPNE.

Boisselle, L. N., 2016. "Decolonizing Science and Science Education in a Postcolonial Space (Trinidad, a Developing Caribbean Nation, Illustrates)." *SAGE Open* 6(1): 1–11. https://doi.org/10.1177/2158244016635257.

Boittin, J. A., C. Firpo, and E. M. Church, 2011. "Hierarchies of Race and Gender in the French Colonial Empire, 1914–1946." *Historical Reflections/Réflexions Historiques* 37(1): 60–90.

Boulila, S. C., 2019. *Race in Post-racial Europe: An Intersectional Analysis*. London: Pickering & Chatto.

Bourdieu, P., 1977. *Outline of a Theory of Practice*. Cambridge: Cambridge University Press.

Bourdieu, P., 1984. *Distinction: A Social Critique of the Judgement of Taste*. Cambridge, MA: Harvard University Press.

Bourdieu, P., 1999. "Understanding." In *The Weight of the World: Social Suffering in Contemporary Society*. Translated by Priscilla Parkhurst Ferguson. Cambridge: Polity, pp. 607–26.

Bouvier, G., 2016. "Discourse in Clothing: The Social Semiotics of Modesty and Chic in Hijab Fashion." *Gender and Language* 10(3): 364–85. https://doi.org/10.1558/genl.v10i3.32034.

Bovone, L., 2013. "Fashion, Identity and Social Actors." In A. M. Gonzalez and L. Bovone (eds.), *Identities through Fashion: A Multidisciplinary Approach*. Oxford: Berg, pp. 67–93.

Bowen, J. R., 2008. *Why the French Don't Like Headscarves: Islam, the State, and Public Space*. Princeton, NJ: Princeton University Press.

Boyatzis, R. E., 1998. *Transforming Qualitative Information: Thematic Analysis and Code Development*. Thousand Oaks, CA: Sage.

Bracke, S., 2008. "Conjugating the Modern/Religious, Conceptualizing Female Religious Agency: Contours of a 'Post-secular' Conjuncture." *Theory, Culture & Society* 25(6): 51–67. https://doi.org/10.1177/0263276408095544.

Brannen, J., 2007. "Working Qualitatively and Quantitatively." In C. Seale, J. F. Gubrium, G. Gobo, and D. Sliverman (eds.), *Qualitative Research Practice*. London: Sage, pp. 282–96.

Braun, V., and V. Clarke, 2019. "Reflecting on Reflexive Thematic Analysis." *Qualitative Research in Sport, Exercise and Health* 11(4): 589–97. https://doi.org/10.1080/2159676X.2019.1628806.

Bray-Collins, E., 2016. Sectarianism from Below: Youth Politics in Post-war Lebanon (PhD). University of Toronto (Canada), Canada.

Brayson, K., 2019. "Of Bodies and Burkinis: Institutional Islamophobia, Islamic Dress, and the Colonial Condition." *Journal of Law and Society* 46(1): 55–82.

Brenner, S., 1996. "Reconstructing Self and Society: Javanese Muslim Women and 'The Veil.'" *American Ethnologist* 23(4): 673–97.

Briand, M., F. Dupont, and V. Longhi, 2018. La « civilisation »: critiques épistémologique et historique. Cahiers « Mondes anciens ». Histoire et anthropologie des mondes anciens, 11. https://doi.org/10.4000/mondesanciens.2173.

Brown, W., 2009. *Regulating Aversion: Tolerance in the Age of Identity and Empire*. Princeton, NJ: Princeton University Press.

Brown, W., 2015. *Undoing the Demos: Neoliberalism's Stealth Revolution*. New York: Zone Books.

Bruck, G. vom, 2008. "Naturalising, Neutralising Women's Bodies: The 'Headscarf Affair' and the Politics of Representation." *Identities* 15(1): 51–79. https://doi.org/10.1080/10702890701801791.

Bullock, K. H., 1999. The Politics of the Veil (PhD). University of Toronto (Canada), Canada.

Burawoy, M., 2009. *The Extended Case Method: Four Countries, Four Decades, Four Great Transformations, and One Theoretical Tradition*. Berkeley: University of California Press.

Butler, J., 2006. *Gender Trouble*, 1st ed. New York: Routledge.

Cammett, M. 2014. *Compassionate Communalism : Welfare and Sectarianism in Lebanon / Melani Cammett*. Ithaca, New York: Cornell University Press.

Cammett, M., and S. Issar, 2010. "Bricks and Mortar Clientelism: Sectarianism and the Logics of Welfare Allocation in Lebanon." *World Politics* 62(3): 381–421.

Carrasco Miró, G., 2020. "Encountering the Colonial: Religion in Feminism and the Coloniality of Secularism." *Feminist Theory* 21(1): 91–109. https://doi.org/10.1177/1464700119859763.

Carter, J., 2003. *Ethnicity, Exclusion and the Workplace*. London: Palgrave Macmillan. https://doi.org/10.1057/9780230005822_1.

Césaire, A., 2000. *Discourse on Colonialism*, new ed. New York: Monthly Review Press.

Chaib, K., 2010. "Femmes, musulmanes, libanaises du Sud: revendiquer une place par l'islam." *Revue des mondes musulmans et de la Méditerranée* 128. https://doi.org/10.4000/remmm.6848.

Chakraborti, N., and I. Zempi, 2012. "The Veil under Attack: Gendered Dimensions of Islamophobic Victimization." *International Review of Victimology* 18(3): 269–84. https://doi.org/10.1177/0269758012446983.

Chalabi, T., 2006. *The Shi'is of Jabal 'Amil and the New Lebanon*. New York: Palgrave Macmillan.

Chalcraft, J. T., 2009. *The Invisible Cage: Syrian Migrant Workers in Lebanon*. Stanford, CA: Stanford University Press.

Chatterjee, P., 1986. *Nationalist Thought and the Colonial World: A Derivative Discourse?* London: Zed Books.

Chehabi, H. E., 1993. "Staging the Emperor's New Clothes: Dress Codes and Nation-Building under Reza Shah." *Iranian Studies* 26(3/4): 209–29.

Chenail, R., 2011. "Interviewing the Investigator: Strategies for Addressing Instrumentation and Researcher Bias Concerns in Qualitative Research." *Qualitative Report* 16(1): 255–62.

Chiit, B., 2012. *Al-abaad Al-tarikhiya wal tabakiya lisooud Al-harakat Al-Islamiya fi Loubnan*. Beirut: Al-thawra Al-daima.

Clayton, A., 1994. *The Wars of French Decolonization*. London: Longman.

Cleveland, M., M. Laroche, and R. Hallab, 2013. "Globalization, Culture, Religion, and Values: Comparing Consumption Patterns of Lebanese Muslims and Christians." *Journal of Business Research, Recent Advances in Globalization, Culture and Marketing Strategy* 66(8): 958–67. https://doi.org/10.1016/j.jbusres.2011.12.018.

Cole, J., 2012. "Review of Burning the Veil: The Algerian War and the Emancipation of Muslim Women." *Journal of Modern History* 84(1): 217–19. https://doi.org/10.1086/663150.

Connell, R. W., 2007. *Southern Theory: Social Science and the Global Dynamics of Knowledge*. Cambridge: Polity Press.

Cooke, M., 2010. *Nazira Zeineddine: A Pioneer of Islamic Feminism, Makers of the Muslim World*. Richmond: Oneworld.

Cotton, J., 2006. *Forced Feminism: Women, Hijab, and the One-Party State in Post-Colonial Tunisia*. Georgia: Digital Archive @ GSU.

Craciun, M., 2017. *Islam, Faith, and Fashion: The Islamic Fashion Industry in Turkey*. London: Bloomsbury.

Crenshaw, K., 1991. "Mapping the Margins, Intersectionality, Identity Politics and Violence against Women of Colour." *Stanford Law Review* 43(6): 1241–99.

Crosby, E., 2014. "Faux Feminism: France's Veil Ban as Orientalism." *Journal of International Women's Studies* 15(2): 46–60.

Croutier, A. L., 1989. *Harem: The World Behind the Veil*. New York: Abbeville Press.

Crow, R. E., 1962. "Religious Sectarianism in the Lebanese Political System." *Journal of Politics* 24(3): 489–520. https://doi.org/10.2307/2127704.

Cvengros, J. R., 1967. "Politics of modernization in Lebanon." MA. University of Wyoming, Wyoming.

Daher, A., 2015. "In the Wake of the Islamic State Threat: Repercussions on Sunni-Shi'i Competition in Lebanon." *Journal of Shi'a Islamic Studies* 8(2): 209–35. https://doi.org/10.1353/isl.2015.0009.

Daniel, J., 2017. "Building Sovereigns? The UN Peacekeeping and Strengthening the Authority of the State in Lebanon and Mali." *Global Change, Peace & Security* 29(3): 229–47. https://doi.org/10.1080/14781158.2017.1363172.

Darder, A., 2018. "Decolonizing Interpretive Research: Subaltern Sensibilities and the Politics of Voice." *Qualitative Research Journal* 18(2): 94–104. https://doi.org/10.1108/QRJ-D-17-00056.

Davis, B. D., 2011. "Lifting the Veil: France's New Crusade." *Boston College International and Comparative Law Review* 34(1): 117–45.

De Genova, N., 2016. "The European Question: Migration, Race, and Postcoloniality in Europe." *Social Text* 34(3): 75–102. https://doi.org/10.1215/01642472-3607588.

DeCoursey, C. A., 2017. "Attitudes of Professional Muslim Women in Saudi Arabia Regarding Wearing the Abaya." *Asian Culture and History* 9(2): 16. https://doi.org/10.5539/ach.v9n2p16.

Deeb, L., 2005. "From Mourning to Activism: Sayyedeh Zaynab, Lebanese Shii Women, and the Transformation of Ashura." In K. Scot Aghaie (ed.), *The Women of Karbala Ritual Performance and Symbolic Discourses in Modern Shi'i Islam*. Austin: University of Texas Press, pp. 241–67.

Deeb, L., 2006. *An Enchanted Modern: Gender and Public Piety in Shi'i Lebanon*. Princeton, NJ: Princeton University Press.

Deeb, L., 2009a. "Emulating and/or Embodying the Ideal: The Gendering of Temporal Frameworks and Islamic Role Models in Shi'i Lebanon." *American Ethnologist* 36(2): 242–57. https://doi.org/10.1111/j.1548-1425.2009.01133.x.

Deeb, L., 2009b. "Piety Politics and the Role of a Transnational Feminist Analysis." *Journal of the Royal Anthropological Institute* 15: S112–S126.

Deeb, L., and M. Harb, 2011. "Culture as History and Landscape: Hizbullah's Efforts to Shape an Islamic Milieu in Lebanon." *Arab Studies Journal* 19(1): 12–45.

Deeb, L., and M. Harb, 2013. *Leisurely Islam: Negotiating Geography and Morality in Shi'ite South Beirut*. Princeton, NJ: Princeton University Press.

Deeb, M., 1988. "Shia Movements in Lebanon: Their Formation, Ideology, Social Basis, and Links with Iran and Syria." *Third World Quarterly* 10(2): 683–98. https://doi.org/10.1080/01436598808420077.

Denzin, N. K., Y. S. Lincoln, and L. T. Smith, 2008. *Handbook of Critical and Indigenous Methodologies*. Thousand Oaks: Sage.

Dhanda, M., 2008. "What Does the Hatred/Fear of the Veil Hide?" *Ethnicity and Inequalities in Health and Social Care* 1(2): 52–7. https://doi.org/10.1108/17570980200800021.

Douglas, J., 2008. "Why I Watch What Not to Wear, Or, How Women Get in Gender Trouble." *Americana: The Journal of American Popular Culture, 1900 to Present* 7(1): 1–8.

Dussel, E. D., 2000. "Europe, Modernity and Eurocentrism." *Nepantla: Views from South* 1(3): 465–78.

Eddé, C., 2013. "La mobilisation « populaire » à Beyrouth à l'époque du mandat, le cas des boycotts des trams et de l'électricité." In N. Méouchy (ed.), *France, Syrie et Liban 1918-1946: Les Ambiguïtés et Les Dynamiques de La Relation Mandataire, Études Arabes, Médiévales et Modernes*. Beyrouth: Presses de l'Ifpo, pp. 349-75.

Edmunds, J., 2012. "The 'New' Barbarians: Governmentality, Securitization and Islam in Western Europe." *Cont Islam* 6(1): 67-84.

Edmunds, J., 2017. *Human Rights, Islam and the Failure of Cosmopolitanism*, 1st ed. Abingdon: Routledge.

Edwards, C., 2010. Structure, Cladding and the Detail: The Role of Textiles in the Associations between Identity, the Interior and Dress, 1860-1920." In Alla Myzelev, John Potvin (eds.), *Fashion, Interior Design, and the Contours of Modern Identity*. Surrey: Ashgate.

Egan, M., and P. Tabar, 2016. "Bourdieu in Beirut: Wasta, the State and Social Reproduction in Lebanon." *Middle East Critique* 25(3): 249-70. https://doi.org/10.1080/19436149.2016.1168662.

Eid, P., 2002. "Research Note: Post-Colonial Identity and Gender in the Arab World: The Case of the Hijab." *Atlantis: Critical Studies in Gender, Culture & Social Justice* 26(2): 39-51.

El-Enany, Nadine. *Bordering Britain: Law, Race and Empire*. 1st ed. Manchester: Manchester University Press, 2020.

El Guindi, F., 1981. "Veiling Infitah with Muslim Ethic: Egypt's Contemporary Islamic Movement." *Social Problems* 28(4): 465-85. https://doi.org/10.2307/800058.

El Guindi, F., 2000. *Veil: Modesty, Privacy and Resistance*. Oxford: Berg.

El Zahed, S. Y., 2019. "Internalized Islamophobia: The Discursive Construction of 'Islam' and 'Observant Muslims' in the Egyptian Public Discourse." PhD. University of California, Los Angeles.

El-Bassiouny, N., 2018. "The Hijabi Self: Authenticity and Transformation in the Hijab Fashion Phenomenon." *Journal of Islamic Marketing* 9(2): 296-304. https://doi.org/10.1108/JIMA-12-2016-0102.

El-Bizri, D., 2014. *L'ombre et son double: Femmes islamistes, libanaises et modernes, Cahiers du Cermoc (1991-2001)*. Beyrouth: Presses de l'Ifpo.

El-Khazen, F., 1991. *The Communal Pact of National Identities: The Making and Politics of the 1943 National Pact, Papers on Lebanon*. Oxford: Centre for Lebanese Studies.

Ellingson, L. L., 2017. *Embodiment in Qualitative Research*. New York: Routledge.

Elsässer, S., 2007. "Between Ideology and Pragmatism: Fatḥī Yakan's Theory of Islamic Activism." *Die Welt des Islams* 47(3/4): 376-402.

Escobar, A., 2007. "Worlds and Knowledges Otherwise." *Cultural Studies* 21(2-3): 179-210. https://doi: 10.1080/09502380601162506.

Esmeir, S., 2012. *Juridical Humanity: A Colonial History*. Stanford, CA: Stanford University Press.

Esseili, F., 2017. "A Sociolinguistic Profile of English in Lebanon." *World Englishes* 36(4): 684-704. https://doi.org/10.1111/weng.12262.

Eum, I., 2017. "Korea's Response to Islam and Islamophobia: Focusing on Veiled Muslim Women's Experiences." *Korea Observer; Seoul* 48(4): 825–49. http://dx.doi.org/10.29152/KOIKS.2017.48.4.825.

Ewing, K. P., 2000. "Legislating Religious Freedom: Muslim Challenges to the Relationship between 'Church' and 'State' in Germany and France." *Daedalus* 129(4): 31–54.

Ezekiel, J., 2006. "French Dressing: Race, Gender, and the Hijab Story." *Feminist Studies* 32(2): 256–78.

Fadlallah, H., 2014. *Hezbollah wa dawla fi Loubnan*. Beirut: Almatbouaat lil tawzi' wal nashr.

Falen, D. J., 2008. "The 'Other' Gender?: Reflections on Fieldwork in Benin." *Men and Masculinities* 11(2): 164–73. https://doi.org/10.1177/1097184X08315094.

Fanon, F., 1994a. *A Dying Colonialism*. New York: Grove Press.

Fanon, F., 1994b. *Toward the African Revolution*, new evergreen ed. New York: Grove Press.

Fanon, F., 2001. *The Wretched of the Earth*, new ed. London: Penguin Classics.

Fanon, F., 2008. *Black Skin, White Masks*, revised ed. London: Pluto Press.

Fanon, S., 1969. "Algeria Unveiled." In Carl Oglesby (ed.), *The New Left Reader*. New York: Grove Press, pp. 161–186l.

Faour, M. A., 2007. "Religion, Demography, and Politics in Lebanon." *Middle Eastern Studies* 43(6): 909–21. https://doi.org/10.1080/00263200701568279.

Farah, M. F., and L. E. Samad, 2014. "The Effects of Religion and Religiosity on Advertisement Assessment among Lebanese Consumers." *Journal of International Consumer Marketing* 26: 344–69. https://doi.org/10.1080/08961530.2014.919126.

Fay, M. A., 2012. *Elite Women and the Paradox of Seclusion in Eighteenth-Century Cairo*. Syracuse, NY: Syracuse University Press.

Federici, S., 2014. *Caliban and the Witch: Women, the Body and Primitive Accumulation*, 2nd revised ed. Brooklyn, NY: Autonomedia.

Felsch, M., 2018. "Christian Political Activism in Lebanon: A Revival of Religious Nationalism in Times of Arab Upheavals." *Studies in Ethnicity and Nationalism* 18(1): 19–37. https://doi.org/10.1111/sena.12262.

Firro, K. M., 2002. *Inventing Lebanon: Nationalism and the State under the Mandate*. London: I.B. Tauris.

Firro, K. M., 2006. "Ethnicizing the Shi'is in Mandatory Lebanon." *Middle Eastern Studies* 42(5): 741–59.

Fleischmann, E. L., 1998. "'Our Moslem Sisters': Women of Greater Syria in the Eyes of American Protestant Missionary Women." *Islam and Christian–Muslim Relations* 9(3): 307–23. https://doi.org/10.1080/09596419808721158.

Flick, U., 1992. "Triangulation Revisited: Strategy of Validation or Alternative?" *Journal for the Theory of Social Behaviour* 22(2): 175–97. https://doi.org/10.1111/j.1468-5914.1992.tb00215.x.

Fox, A. M., S. A. Alzwawi, and D. Refki, 2016. "Islamism, Secularism and the Woman Question in the Aftermath of the Arab Spring: Evidence from the Arab Barometer." *Politics and Governance* 4(4): 40–57.

Franks, M., 2000. "Crossing the Borders of Whiteness? White Muslim Women Who Wear the Hijab in Britain Today." *Ethnic and Racial Studies* 23(5): 917–29. https://doi.org/10.1080/01419870050110977.

Gade, T. 2017. "Limiting Violent Spillover in Civil Wars: The Paradoxes of Lebanese Sunni Jihadism, 2011–17." *Contemporary Arab Affairs* 10(2): 187–206.

Gair, S., 2012. "Feeling Their Stories: Contemplating Empathy, Insider/Outsider Positionings, and Enriching Qualitative Research." *Qualitative Health Research* 22(1): 134–43. https://doi.org/10.1177/1049732311420580.

Gessier, V., 2010. "Islamophobia: A French Specificity in Europe?" *Human Architecture: Journal of the Sociology of Self-Knowledge* 8(2): 39–46.

Geukjian, O., 2014. "Political Instability and Conflict after the Syrian Withdrawal from Lebanon." *Middle East Journal* 68(4): 521–45.

Ghani, A. A., 2011. "Asian Muslim Women's Fashion History." *Aquila*, May/June.

Ghumman, S., and L. Jackson, 2010. "The Downside of Religious Attire: The Muslim Headscarf and Expectations of Obtaining Employment." *Journal of Organizational Behavior* 31(1): 4–23.

Ghumman, S., and A. M. Ryan, 2013. "Not Welcome Here: Discrimination towards Women Who Wear the Muslim Headscarf." *Human Relations* 66(5): 671–98. https://doi.org/10.1177/0018726712469540.

Gökarıksel, B., 2012. "The Intimate Politics of Secularism and the Headscarf: The Mall, the Neighborhood, and the Public Square in Istanbul." *Gender, Place & Culture* 19(1): 1–20. https://doi.org/10.1080/0966369X.2011.633428.

Gökarıksel, B., and A. Secor, 2010. "Islamic-ness in the Life of a Commodity: Veiling-Fashion in Turkey." *Transactions of the Institute of British Geographers* 35(3): 313–33. https://doi.org/10.1111/j.1475-5661.2010.00384.x.

Göle, N., 1997. *The Forbidden Modern*. Ann Arbor: University of Michigan Press.

Grace, D., 2004. *The Woman in the Muslim Mask: Veiling and Identity in Postcolonial Literature*. London: Pluto Press.

Green, Todd H. 2015. D*The Fear of Islam an Introduction to Islamophobia in the West*. Minneapolis, MN: Fortress Press.

Gressgård, R., 2006. "The Veiled Muslim, the Anorexic and the Transsexual: What Do They Have in Common?" *European Journal of Women's Studies* 13(4): 325–41. https://doi.org/10.1177/1350506806068651.

Grosfoguel, R., 2002. "Colonial Difference, Geopolitics of Knowledge, and Global Coloniality in the Modern/Colonial Capitalist World-System." *Review (Fernand Braudel Center)* 25(3): 203–24.

Grosfoguel, R., 2010. "Epistemic Islamophobia and Colonial Social Sciences." *Human Architecture: Journal of the Sociology of Self-Knowledge* 8(2): 29–38.

Grosfoguel, R., 2011. "Decolonizing Post-Colonial Studies and Paradigms of Political-Economy: Transmodernity, Decolonial Thinking, and Global Coloniality." *TRANSMODERNITY: Journal of Peripheral Cultural Production of the Luso-Hispanic World* 1(1): 1–36.

Grosfoguel, R., 2012a. "Decolonizing Western Uni-versalisms: Decolonial Pluri-versalism from Aimé Césaire to the Zapatistas." *TRANSMODERNITY: Journal of Peripheral Cultural Production of the Luso-Hispanic World* 1(3): 88–104.

Grosfoguel, R., 2012b. "The Dilemmas of Ethnic Studies in the United States: Between Liberal Multiculturalism, Identity Politics, Disciplinary Colonization, and Decolonial Epistemologies." *Human Architecture: Journal of the Sociology of Self-Knowledge* 10(1): 81–9.

Grosfoguel, R., 2013. "The Structure of Knowledge in Westernized Universities: Epistemic Racism/Sexism and the Four Genocides/Epistemicides of the Long 16th Century." *Human Architecture: Journal of the Sociology of Self-Knowledge* 11(1): 73–90.

Grosfoguel, R., 2016. "What Is Racism?" *Journal of World-Systems Research* 22(1): 9–15. https://doi.org/10.5195/jwsr.2016.609.

Grosfoguel, R., and G. Martín-Muñoz, 2010. "Introduction: Debating Islamophobia." *Human Architecture: Journal of the Sociology of Self-Knowledge* 8(2): 1–3.

Grosfoguel, R., and E. Mielants, 2006. "The Long-Durée Entanglement between Islamophobia and Racism in the Modern/Colonial Capitalist/Patriarchal World-System: An Introduction." *Human Architecture: Journal of the Sociology of Self-Knowledge* 5(1): 1–12.

Grosfoguel, R., L. Oso, and A. Christou, 2015. "'Racism,' Intersectionality and Migration Studies: Framing Some Theoretical Reflections." *Identities* 22(6): 635–52. https://doi.org/10.1080/1070289X.2014.950974.

Gupta, T. D., 2006. "Racism/Anti-racism, Precarious Employment, and Unions." In L. F. Vosko (ed.), *Precarious employment: Understanding labour market insecurity in Canada*, 333–49. Montreal, Québec, Canada: McGill–Queen's University Press.

Gupta, T. D., 2008. *Racism and Paid Work*. Toronto: University of Toronto Press.

Habib, M. S., and W. K. madey al-kindy, 2014. "Al-Sayyed Mohammad Hussein Fadlallah His Life and Attitudes of the Lebanese Issue." *Journal of Babylon Center for Humanities Studies* 4(3): 155–204.

Haddad, R., 1999. "A Modern-Day 'Slave Trade': Sri Lankan Workers in Lebanon." *Middle East Report* 211: 39–41. https://doi.org/10.2307/3013337.

Haddad, S., 2002. "The Political Transformation of the Maronites of Lebanon: From Dominance to Accommodation." *Nationalism and Ethnic Politics* 8(2): 27–50. https://doi.org/10.1080/13537110208428660.

Haddad, S., 2010. "Fatah al-Islam in Lebanon: Anatomy of a Terrorist Organization." *Studies in Conflict & Terrorism* 33(6): 548–69. https://doi.org/10.1080/10576101003754677.

Haddad, Y. Y., 2007. "The Post-9/11 'Hijab' as Icon." *Sociology of Religion* 68(3): 253–67.

Haddad, Y. Y., and T. Golson, 2007. "Overhauling Islam: Representation, Construction, and Co-option of 'Moderate Islam' in Western Europe." *Journal of Church and State* 49(3): 487–515.

Hajjar, S. G., 2009. "The Convoluted and Diminished Lebanese Democracy." *Democracy and Security* 5(3): 261–76. https://doi.org/10.1080/17419160903304864.

Hakim, C., 2013. *The Origins of the Lebanese National Idea*, 1st ed. Berkeley: University of California Press.

Hamdan, A. N., 2013. "Where's the State?" Practicing the Past in Beirut, Lebanon (MA). University of California, Los Angeles.

Hammersley, M., and P. Atkinson, 1983. *Ethnography: Principles in Practice*. London: Tavistock.

Hamzeh, A. N., and R. H. Dekmejian, 1996. "A Sufi Response to Political Islamism: Al-Aḥbāsh of Lebanon." *International Journal of Middle East Studies* 28(2): 217–29. https://doi.org/10.1017/S0020743800063145.

Hanafi, S., 2014. *Palestinian Refugees*, 1st ed. London: Routledge.

Hanafi, S., 2019. "'We Speak the Truth!': Knowledge and Politics in Friday's Sermons in Lebanon." *CAA* 12(2): 53–80. https://doi.org/10.1525/caa.2019.122003.

Hanafi, S., J. Chaaban, and K. Seyfert, 2012. "Social Exclusion of Palestinian Refugees in Lebanon: Reflections on the Mechanisms That Cement Their Persistent Poverty." *Refugee Survey Quarterly* 31(1): 34–53. https://doi.org/10.1093/rsq/hdr018.

Hancock, C., 2015. "'The Republic Is Lived with an Uncovered Face' (and a Skirt): (Un)dressing French Citizens." *Gender, Place & Culture* 22(7): 1023–40. https://doi.org/10.1080/0966369X.2014.958061.

Handcock, M. S., and K. J. Gile, 2011. "On the Concept of Snowball Sampling." *Gender, Place & Culture* 22(7): 1023–40.

Harb, M., and L. Deeb, 2013. "Contesting Urban Modernity: Moral Leisure in South Beirut." *European Journal of Cultural Studies* 16(6): 725–44. https://doi.org/10.1177/1367549413497694.

Harb, M., A. Kassem, and W. Najdi, 2019. "Entrepreneurial Refugees and the City: Brief Encounters in Beirut." *Journal of Refugee Studies* 32(1): 23–41. https://doi.org/10.1093/jrs/fey003.

Harb, S. G., 2010. Gender Politics, Women's Rights and International Norms in Lebanon (PhD). Florida International University, Florida.

Harris, W., 2012. *Lebanon: A History, 600–2011*. Oxford: Oxford University Press.

Hashem, L., 2017. "Feminist and Women's Struggles in Lebanon's 'Popular Movement': The Intersections of the Public and the Private. Heinrich Boll Foundation Middle East." https://lb.boell.org/en/2017/01/18/feminist-and-womens-struggles-lebanons-popular-movement-intersections-public-and-private.

Hassan, S. H., and H. Harun, 2016. "Factors Influencing Fashion Consciousness in Hijab Fashion Consumption among Hijabistas." *Journal of Islamic Marketing* 7(4): 476–94. https://doi.org/10.1108/JIMA-10-2014-0064.

Hawkins, S., 2011. "Who Wears Hijab with the President: Constructing a Modern Islam in Tunisia." *Journal of Religion in Africa* 41(1): 35–58.

Hazran, Y., 2009a. "Between Authenticity and Alienation: The Druzes and Lebanon's History." *Bulletin of the School of Oriental and African Studies* 72(3): 459–87. https://doi.org/10.1017/S0041977X09990036.

Hazran, Y., 2009b. *The Shiite Community in Lebanon: From Marginalization to Ascendancy*. Crown Center Middle East Studies, Middle East Brief n37. Massachusetts.

Hazran, Y., 2010. "Lebanon's Revolutionary Era: Kamal Junblat, The Druze Community and the Lebanon State, 1949 to 1977." *Muslim World* 100(1): 157–76. https://doi.org/10.1111/j.1478-1913.2009.01311.x.

Heit, H., 2006. "Western Identity, Barbarians and the Inheritance of Greek Universalism." *European Legacy* 10(7): 725–39. https://doi.org/10.1080/10848770500335800.

Helou, M., 2001. "Lebanese Women and Politics: A Comparison between Two Field Studies." *Al-Raida Journal* 18(92): 33–40.

Hermez, S., 2015. "When the State Is (N)Ever Present: On Cynicism and Political Mobilization in Lebanon." *Journal of the Royal Anthropological Institute* 21(3): 507–23. https://doi.org/10.1111/1467-9655.12249.

Ho, C., 2007. "Muslim Women's New Defenders: Women's Rights, Nationalism and Islamophobia in Contemporary Australia." *Women's Studies International Forum* 30(4): 290–8. https://doi.org/10.1016/j.wsif.2007.05.002.

Hogan, J., 2009. *Gender, Race and National Identity: Nations of Flesh and Blood*. New York: Routledge.

Hogan, S., 2012. "Ways in Which Photographic and Other Images Are Used in Research: An Introductory Overview." *International Journal of Art Therapy* 17(2): 54–62. https://doi.org/10.1080/17454832.2012.699533.

Hollywood, A., 2006. "Performativity, Citationality, Ritualization." In E. T. Armour, S. M. St. Ville (eds.), *Bodily Citations: Religion and Judith Butler*. New York: Columbia University Press, pp. 252–75.

Hollywood, A., 2016. *Acute Melancholia and Other Essays: Mysticism, History, and the Study of Religion*. New York: Columbia University Press.

Hopkins, P. E., 2007. "Thinking Critically and Creatively about Focus Groups." *Area* 39(4): 528–35. https://doi.org/10.1111/j.1475-4762.2007.00766.x.

Hourani, N., 2010. "Transnational Pathways and Politico-economic Power: Globalisation and the Lebanese Civil War." *Geopolitics* 15(2): 290–311. https://doi.org/10.1080/14650040903486934.

Hourani, N., 2015. "Capitalists in Conflict: The Lebanese Civil War Reconsidered." *Middle East Critique* 24(2): 137–60. https://doi.org/10.1080/19436149.2015.1012842.

Houston, C., 2016. "The Brewing of Islamist Modernity: Tea Gardens and Public Space in Istanbul." *Theory, Culture & Society* 18(6): 77–97. https://doi.org/10.1177/02632760122052057.

Howe, M., 2005. "Palestinians in Lebanon." *Middle East Policy* 12(4): 145–55. https://doi.org/10.1111/j.1475-4967.2005.00231.x.

Iddrisu, M. S., 2019. Unveiling Veiled Voices: Understanding the Experiences of Muslim Women Who Wear the Hijab in Public Spaces (MA). University of Texas at El Paso, Texas.

Ideland, M., 2018. "Science, Coloniality, and 'the Great Rationality Divide.'" *Science & Education* 27(7): 783–803. https://doi.org/10.1007/s11191-018-0006-8.

Iftkhar, S., 2009. Contested Citizenship: The 2003–2004 Media Debate over the Muslim Headscarf in France (PhD). University of Wisconsin, Wisconsin.

Imad, A. G., 2006. *Al-Harakat Al-Islamiya Fi loubnan*. Beirut: Dar Altaliaa.

Indarti, Peng, L. H., 2016. Modern Hijab Style in Indonesia as an Expression of Cultural Identity and Communication, In 2016 International Conference on Applied System Innovation (ICASI), pp. 1–4. https://doi.org/10.1109/ICASI.2016.7539878.

Itani, A., A. Q. Ali, and M. Manaa, 2009. *Al-Jamaah Al-Islamiya fi Loubnan: mounzou Al-nashaa hata 1975*. Al Manhal.

Itani, B., 2016. "Veiling at the American University of Beirut: Religious Values, Social Norms and Integration of Veiled Students." *Contemporary Arab Affairs* 9(4): 536–51. https://doi.org/10.1080/17550912.2016.1245386.

Itaoui, R., 2016. "The Geography of Islamophobia in Sydney: Mapping the Spatial Imaginaries of Young Muslims." *Australian Geographer* 47(3): 261–79. https://doi.org/10.1080/00049182.2016.1191133.

Jacobsen, C. M., 2011. "Troublesome Threesome: Feminism, Anthropology and Muslim Women's Piety." *Feminist Review* 98(1): 65–82.

James Carr. 2015. *Experiences of Islamophobia: Living with Racism in the Neoliberal Era*. Taylor and Francis.

Jasser, G., 2006. "Voile qui dévoile intégrisme, sexisme et racisme." *Nouvelles Questions Féministes* 25(3): 76–93.

Jiménez-Lucena, I., 2006. "Gender and Coloniality: The 'Moroccan Woman' and the 'Spanish Woman' in Spain's Sanitary Policies in Morocco." *História, Ciências, Saúde: Manguinhos* 13(2): 325–47. https://doi.org/10.1590/S0104-59702006000200008.

Johnson, M., 1986. *Class and Client in Beirut: The Sunni Muslim Community and the Lebanese State, 1840–1985*. London: Ithaca Press.

Jouili, J. S., and S. AmirMoazami, 2006. "Knowledge, Empowerment and Religious Authority among Pious Muslim Women in France and Germany." *Muslim World* 96(4): 617–42. https://doi.org/10.1111/j.1478-1913.2006.00150.x.

Jouni, M. H., 2012. How Are Islamic Banks Operating in Lebanon? (MA) American University of Beirut.

Jureidini, R., and N. Moukarbel, 2004. "Female Sri Lankan Domestic Workers in Lebanon: A Case of 'Contract Slavery'?" *Journal of Ethnic and Migration Studies* 30(4): 581–607. https://doi.org/10.1080/13691830410001699478.

Kaedbey, D. E., 2014. Building Theory across Struggles: Queer Feminist Thought from Lebanon (PhD). The Ohio State University, Ohio.

Kahf, M., 2008. "From Her Royal Body the Robe Was Removed: The Blessings of the Veil and the Trauma of Forced Unveilings in the Middle East." In J. Heath (ed.), *The Veil: Women Writers on Its History, Lore, and Politics*. Berkeley: University of California Press, pp. 27–43.

Kanana, A. N., 2011. *Taathor binaa Aldawla fi Loubnan*. Beirut: Al-rihab Publisher Est.

Kandiyoti, D., 1991. *Women, Islam, and the State*. Philadelphia, Pennsylvania: Temple University Press.

Kapur, R., 2018. *Gender, Alterity and Human Rights: Freedom in a Fishbowl*. Northampton, MA: Edward Elgar.

Karimi, H., 2018. "The Hijab and Work: Female Entrepreneurship in Response to Islamophobia." *International Journal of Politics, Culture, and Society* 31(4): 421–35. https://doi.org/10.1007/s10767-018-9290-1.

Kasaba, R., 2010. "Turkey from the Rise of Atatürk." In F. Robinson (ed.), *The New Cambridge History of Islam: Volume 5: The Islamic World in the Age of Western Dominance, The New Cambridge History of Islam*. Cambridge: Cambridge University Press, pp. 299–335. https://doi.org/10.1017/CHOL9780521838269.013.

Kassem, A., 2020. "Moving beyond the Nation-State: Addressing Religious Freedoms in Lebanon." *Rowaq Arabi* 25(2): 53–66.

Kassem, A. 2022a. "Belated Arabo-Islamic Difference in Excess: Racialised Religious Practice under Modernity/coloniality in Lebanon." *Journal of Contemporary Religion* 37(2): 223–42.

Kassem, Ali. 2022b. "Islamic Visibility in Lebanon, the Banking Sector and Eurocentric Modernity: Erasure, Development, and the Post-Colonial Nation-State." *Globalizations*: 1–17.

Kassem, R., 2013. *Almoujabat wal Mouassasat Alelamiya fi Loubnan*. Beirut: Beirut Observer.

Kaufman, A., 2001. "Phoenicianism: The Formation of an Identity in Lebanon in 1920." *Middle Eastern Studies* 37(1): 173–94.

Kaufman, A., 2004. *Reviving Phoenicia: The Search for Identity in Lebanon*. London: I.B. Tauris.

Kaya, I., 2000. "Modernity and Veiled Women." *European Journal of Social Theory* 3(2): 195–214. https://doi.org/10.1177/13684310022224769.

Keddie, N. R., 2012. *Women in the Middle East: Past and Present*. Princeton, NJ: Princeton University Press.

Kenway, J., and J. McLeod, 2004. "Bourdieu's Reflexive Sociology and 'Spaces of Points of View': Whose Reflexivity, Which Perspective?" *British Journal of Sociology of Education* 25(4): 525–44. https://doi.org/10.1080/0142569042000236998.

Khalaf, S., 2004. *Civil and Uncivil Violence in Lebanon: A History of the Internationalization of Communal Conflict*. New York: Columbia University Press.

Khalidi, W., 1979. *Conflict and Violence in Lebanon: Confrontation in the Middle East.* Cambridge, MA: Harvard University Center for International Affairs.

Khandaker, L., 2017. "Politicizing Muslims: Constructing a 'Moderate' Islam." Global Islamic Studies Honors Papers, Connecticut College.

Khatib, L., 2008. "Gender, Citizenship and Political Agency in Lebanon." *British Journal of Middle Eastern Studies* 35(3): 437–51. https://doi.org/10.1080/13530190802525189.

Khattab, N., and S. Hussein, 2017. "Can Religious Affiliation Explain the Disadvantage of Muslim Women in the British Labour Market?" *Work, Employment and Society* 32(6): 1011–28. https://doi.org/10.1177/0950017017711099.

Khiabany, G., and M. Williamson, 2008. "Veiled bodies—Naked Racism: Culture, Politics and Race in the Sun." *Race & Class* 50(2): 69–88. https://doi.org/10.1177/0306396808096394.

Kikoski, C. K., 2000. "Feminism in the Middle East." *Journal of Feminist Family Therapy* 11(4): 131–46. https://doi.org/10.1300/J086v11n04_10.

Kluttz, C. H., 2009. Toward al-haqiqa: An Analysis of Lebanon's "Cedar Revolution" (MA). The American University of Paris, France.

Knio, K., 2005. "Lebanon: Cedar Revolution or Neo-sectarian Partition?" *Mediterranean Politics* 10(2): 225–31. https://doi.org/10.1080/13629390500124259.

Knudsen, A., 2005. "Islamism in the Diaspora: Palestinian Refugees in Lebanon." *Journal of Refugee Studies* 18(2): 216–34. https://doi.org/10.1093/refuge/fei022.

Knudsen, A., 2009. "Widening the Protection Gap: The 'Politics of Citizenship' for Palestinian Refugees in Lebanon, 1948–2008." *Journal of Refugee Studies* 22(1): 51–73. https://doi.org/10.1093/jrs/fen047.

Kosba, M., 2018. "Paradoxical Islamophobia and Post-Colonial Cultural Nationalism in Post-Revolutionary Egypt." In E. Bayrakli and F. Hafez (eds.), *Islamophobia in Muslim Majority Societies*. Routledge, pp. 107–24.

Koura, F., 2018. "Navigating Islam: The Hijab and the American Workplace." *Societies* 8(4): 125. https://doi.org/10.3390/soc8040125.

Krueger, R. A., 2014. *Focus Groups: A Practical Guide for Applied Research*. Thousand Oaks, CA: Sage.

Kumar, Deepa. 2021. *Islamophobia and the Politics of Empire: 20 Years after 9/11*. La Vergne: Verso. Print.

Ladson-Billings, G., 2003. "Racialized Discourses and Ethnic Epistemologies." In N. K. Denzin and Y. S. Lincoln (eds.), *The Landscape of Qualitative Research: Theories and Issues*. Thousand Oaks, CA: Sage, pp. 252–77.

Lagasi, A., 2013. The Geographies of Second-Generation Muslim Women: Identity Formation and Everyday Experiences in Public Space (MA). University of Ottawa, Canada.

Lazaridis, G., and K. Wadia, 2015. *The Securitisation of Migration in the EU: Debates since 9/11*. London: Palgrave Macmillan.

Le Gall, J., 2003. "Le rapport à l'islam des musulmanes shi'ites libanaises à Montréal." *Anthropologie et Sociologie* 27(1): 131–48. https://doi.org/10.7202/007005ar.

Le Thomas, C., 2012. *Les écoles chiites au Liban: Construction communautaire et mobilisation politique.* Paris: KARTHALA Editions.

Lean, Nathan Chapman, and John L. Esposito. 2012. *The Islamophobia Industry: How the Right Manufactures Fear of Muslims/Nathan Lean*; Foreword by John L. Esposito. London: Pluto Press.

Lee, J., 2008. Globalization and Its Islamic Discontents: Postcolonialism, Women's Rights, and the Discourse of the Veil (MA). University of Calgary, Canada.

Leenders, R. (ed.), 2012. "Corruption." In Reinoud Leenders (ed.), *Spoils of Truce: Corruption and State-Building in Postwar Lebanon.* Ithaca, NY: Cornell University Press, pp. 1–17.

Lefebvre, H., 2000. *Everyday Life in the Modern World*, 2nd revised ed. New York: Athlone Press.

Lefèvre, R., 2014. *Tackling Sunni Radicalization in Lebanon.* Carnegie Middle East Centre.

Lefèvre, R., 2015. *Lebanon's Dar al-Fatwa and the Search for Moderation.* Carnegie Middle East Centre.

Lentin, A., 2011. "What Happens to Anti-Racism When We Are Post Race?" *Feminist Legal Studies* 19(2): 159–68. https://doi.org/10.1007/s10691-011-9174-5.

Lindholm, C., 2013. "Cultural Collision: The Branded Abaya." *Fashion, Style & Popular Culture* 1(1): 45–55. https://doi.org/info:doi/10.1386/fspc.1.1.45_1.

Longrigg, S. H., 1958. *Syria and Lebanon under French Mandate.* Oxford: Oxford University Press.

Lugones, M., 2007. "Heterosexualism and the Colonial/Modern Gender System." *Hypatia* 22(1): 186–209.

Lugones, M., 2010. "Toward a Decolonial Feminism." *Hypatia* 25(4): 742–59.

Lynch, N., 2018. "Aníbal Quijano: The Intellectual Par Excellence." *Global Dialogue* 9(1): 27–8.

Maasri, Z., 2016. "Troubled Geography: Imagining Lebanon in 1960s Tourist Promotion." In F. Kjetil and L.-M. Grace (eds.), *Designing Worlds: National Design Histories in the Age of Globalization.* Oxford: Berghahn Books, pp. 125–40.

Macdonald, M., 2006. "Muslim Women and the Veil." *Feminist Media Studies* 6(1): 7–23. https://doi.org/10.1080/14680770500471004.

MacLeod, A. E., 1992. "Hegemonic Relations and Gender Resistance: The New Veiling as Accommodating Protest in Cairo." *Signs* 17(3): 533–57.

Macmaster, N., 2009. *Burning the Veil: The Algerian War and the Emancipation of Muslim Women, 1954–62.* Manchester: Manchester University Press.

Magearu, A., 2018. "A Phenomenological Reading of Gendered Racialization in Arab Muslim American Women's Cultural Productions." *The Comparatist* 42: 135–57. http://dx.doi.org/10.1353/com.2018.0007.

Mahmood, S., 2001a. "Feminist Theory, Embodiment, and the Docile Agent: Some Reflections on the Egyptian Islamic Revival." *Cultural Anthropology* 16(2): 202–36.

Mahmood, S., 2001b. "Rehearsed Spontaneity and the Conventionality of Ritual: Disciplines of Şalat." *American Ethnologist* 28(4): 827–53. https://doi.org/10.1525/ae.2001.28.4.827.

Mahmood, S., 2003. "Ethical Formation and Politics of Individual Autonomy in Contemporary Egypt." *Social Research* 70(3): 837–66.

Mahmood, S., 2009. "Religious Reason and Secular Affect: An Incommensurable Divide?" *Critical Inquiry* 35(4): 836–62. https://doi.org/10.1086/599592.

Mahmood, S., 2012a. *Politics of Piety: The Islamic Revival and the Feminist Subject*. Princeton, NJ: Princeton University Press.

Mahmood, S., 2012b. "Sectarian Conflict and Family Law in Contemporary Egypt." *American Ethnologist* 39(1): 54–62.

Mahmood, S., 2015. *Religious Difference in a Secular Age: A Minority Report*. Princeton, NJ: Princeton University Press.

Mahmud, Y., and V. Swami, 2010. "The Influence of the Hijab (Islamic Head-Cover) on Perceptions of Women's Attractiveness and Intelligence." *Body Image* 7(1): 90–93. https://doi.org/10.1016/j.bodyim.2009.09.003.

Maira, S., 2009. "'Good' and 'Bad' Muslim Citizens: Feminists, Terrorists, and U. S. Orientalisms." *Feminist Studies* 35(3): 631–56.

Makdisi, U., 2000. *The Culture of Sectarianism: Community, History, and Violence in Nineteenth-Century Ottoman Lebanon*. Berkeley: University of California Press.

Maldonado-Torres, N., 2007. "On the Coloniality of Being." *Cultural Studies* 21(2–3): 240–70. https://doi.org/10.1080/09502380601162548.

Maldonado-Torres, N., 2008. "Secularism and Religion in the Modern/Colonial World-System: From Secular Postcoloniality to Postsecular Transmodernity." In M. Morana, E. Dussel, and C. A. Jáuregui (eds.), *Coloniality at Large: Latin America and the Postcolonial Debate*. Durham, NC: Duke University Press, pp. 361–84.

Maldonado-Torres, N., 2010. "The Time and Space of Race: Reflections on David Theo Goldberg's Interrelational and Comparative Methodology." *Patterns of Prejudice* 44(1): 77–88. https://doi.org/10.1080/00313220903507644.

Maldonado-Torres, N., 2011. "Thinking through the Decolonial Turn: Post-continental Interventions in Theory, Philosophy, and Critique—An Introduction." *TRANSMODERNITY: Journal of Peripheral Cultural Production of the Luso-Hispanic World* 1(2): 1–15.

Maldonado-Torres, N., 2014a. "AAR Centennial Roundtable: Religion, Conquest, and Race in the Foundations of the Modern/Colonial World." *Journal of the American Academy of Religion* 82(3): 636–65. https://doi.org/10.1093/jaarel/lfu054.

Maldonado-Torres, N., 2014b. "Race, Religion, and Ethics in the Modern/Colonial World." *Journal of Religious Ethics* 42(4): 691–711. https://doi.org/10.1111/jore.12078.

Maldonado-Torres, N., 2017. "On the Coloniality of Human Rights." *Revista Crítica de Ciências Sociais* 114: 117–36. https://doi.org/10.4000/rccs.6793.

Mamdani, M., 2004. *Good Muslim, Bad Muslim: America, the Cold War, and the Roots of Terror*. New York: UNISA Press.

Mancini, S., 2012. "Patriarchy as the Exclusive Domain of the Other: The Veil Controversy, False Projection and Cultural Racism." *International Journal of Constitutional Law* 10(2): 411–28. https://doi.org/10.1093/icon/mor061.

Mango, O., 2008. "Arab American Women: Identities of a Silent/Silenced Minority" PhD. Arizona State University, Arizona.

Marcos, S., 2006. *Taken from the Lips: Gender and Eros in Mesoamerican Religions*, 1st ed. Boston: Brill.

Martín-Muñoz, G., 2010. "Unconscious Islamophobia." *Human Architecture: Journal of the Sociology of Self-Knowledge* 8(2): 21–8.

Mason-Bish, H., and I. Zempi, 2019. "Misogyny, Racism, and Islamophobia: Street Harassment at the Intersections." *Feminist Criminology* 14(5): 540–59.

Massad, J. A., 2015. *Islam in Liberalism*. Chicago: University of Chicago Press.

Massoumi, N., T. Mills, and D. Miller, 2017. *What Is Islamophobia?: Racism, Social Movements and the State*. London: Pluto Press.

Mayblin, L. 2017. *Asylum after Empire: Colonial Legacies in the Politics of Asylum Seeking*. London: Rowman and Littlefield.

Mawla, S., 2016. *Alsalafiya wal Salafiyoun Aljodod: min Afghanistan ila Loubnan*. Beirut: Sā'ir al-Mashriq.

Mayer, T. (ed.), 1999. *Gender Ironies of Nationalism: Sexing the Nation*, 1st ed. London: Routledge.

Mazzei, J., and E. E. O'Brien, 2009. "You Got It, So When Do You Flaunt It?: Building Rapport, Intersectionality, and the Strategic Deployment of Gender in the Field." *Journal of Contemporary Ethnography* 38(3): 358–83. https://doi.org/10.1177/0891241608330456.

Mbembe, A., 2016. "Africa in the New Century." *Massachusetts Review* 57(1): 91–104. https://doi.org/10.1353/mar.2016.0031.

Mcclintock, A., 1995. *Imperial Leather: Race, Gender, and Sexuality in the Colonial Contest*. London: Taylor & Francis Group.

Medina, J., 2014. "This Battlefield Called My Body: Warring over the Muslim Female." *Religions* 5(3): 876–85. https://doi.org/10.3390/rel5030876.

Meer, Nasar. 2022. *The Cruel Optimism of Racial Justice*. 1st ed. Bristol: Policy Press.

Megahed, N., and S. Lack, 2011. "Colonial Legacy, Women's Rights and Gender-Educational Inequality in the Arab World with Particular Reference to Egypt and Tunisia." *International Review of Education* 57(3): 397–418. https://doi.org/10.1007/s11159-011-9215-y.

Mehra, B., 2002. "Bias in Qualitative Research: Voices from an Online Classroom." *Qualitative Report* 7(1): 1–19.

Memmi, A., 2016. *The Colonizer and the Colonized*, main ed. London: Souvenir Press.

Mendoza, B., 2016. "Coloniality of Gender and Power: From Postcoloniality to Decoloniality." In M. Hawkesworth and L. Disch (eds.), *The Oxford Handbook of Feminist Theory*. 1st ed. New York: Oxford University Press, pp. 100–21.

Mercier, O. R., 2013. "Indigenous Knowledge and Science: A New Representation of the Interface between Indigenous and Eurocentric Ways of Knowing." *He Pukenga Korero: A Journal of Māori Studies* 8(2): 20–8.

Mereeb, N., 2017. *Almouhajjaba Mamnouaa min Altawzif fi Loubnan*. Janoubiya. http://janoubia.com/2017/07/11 (accessed September 1, 2018).

Michael, M., 2004. "On Making Data Social: Heterogeneity in Sociological Practice." *Qualitative Research* 4(1): 5–23. https://doi.org/10.1177/1468794104041105.

Mignolo, W. D., 2002. "The Geopolitics of Knowledge and the Colonial Difference." *South Atlantic Quarterly* 101(1): 57–96. https://doi.org/10.1215/00382876-101-1-57.

Mignolo, W. D., 2005. *The Idea of Latin America*, 1st ed. Malden, MA: Blackwell.

Mignolo, W. D., 2007. "Introduction: Coloniality of Power and De-colonial Thinking." *Cultural Studies* 21(2–3): 155–67. https://doi.org/10.1080/09502380601162498.

Mignolo, W. D., 2009a. "Epistemic Disobedience, Independent Thought and Decolonial Freedom." *Theory, Culture & Society* 26(7–8): 159–81. https://doi.org/10.1177/0263276409349275.

Mignolo, W. D., 2009b. "Who Speaks for the 'Human' in Human Rights?" *Hispanic Issues Series* 5(1): 7–24.

Mignolo, W. D., 2009c. "Dispensable and Bare Lives: Coloniality and the Hidden Political/Economic Agenda of Modernity." *Human Architecture: Journal of the Sociology of Self-Knowledge* 7: 69–87.

Mignolo, W. D., 2011a. "Geopolitics of Sensing and Knowing: On (De)coloniality, Border Thinking and Epistemic Disobedience." *Postcolonial Studies* 14(3): 273–83. https://doi.org/10.1080/13688790.2011.613105.

Mignolo, W. D., 2011b. "Modernity and Decoloniality." *Latin American Studies*. Oxford: Oxford University Press, 2011.

Mignolo, W. D., 2011c. *The Darker Side of Western Modernity: Global Futures, Decolonial Options*. Durham, NC: Duke University Press.

Mignolo, W. D., 2011d. "The Global South and World Dis/order." *Journal of Anthropological Research* 67(2): 165–88.

Mignolo, W. D., 2011e. "Epistemic Disobedience and the Decolonial Option: A Manifesto." *TRANSMODERNITY: Journal of Peripheral Cultural Production of the Luso-Hispanic World* 1(2): 44–65.

Mignolo, W. D., 2012. *Local Histories/Global Designs: Coloniality, Subaltern Knowledges, and Border Thinking*. Princeton, NJ: Princeton University Press.

Mignolo, W. D., 2013. "Delinking: The Rhetoric of Modernity, The logic of Coloniality and the Grammar Of de-Coloniality." In W. D. Mignolo and A. Escobar (eds.), *Globalization and the Decolonial Option*, 1st ed. London: Routledge, pp. 303–68.

Mignolo, W. D., 2018. "Decoloniality and Phenomenology: The Geopolitics of Knowing and Epistemic/Ontological Colonial Differences." *Journal of Speculative Philosophy* 32(3): 360–87.

Mignolo, W. D., and A. Escobar (eds.), 2009. *Globalization and the Decolonial Option*, 1st ed. London: Routledge.

Mignolo, W. D., and M. Tlostanova, 2008. "The Logic of Coloniality and the Limits of Postcoloniality." In R. Krishnaswamy and J. C. Hawley (eds.), *The Postcolonial and the Global*. Minneapolis: University of Minnesota Press, pp. 109–23.

Mignolo, W. D., and R. Vázquez, 2013. *Colonial Wounds/Decolonial Healings*. Social Text Online Periscope, Decolonial Aesthesis.

Mignolo, W. D., and C. E. Walsh, 2018. *On Decoloniality: Concepts, Analytics, Praxis*. Durham, NC: Duke University Press.

Mikdashi, M., 2014. "Sex and Sectarianism: The Legal Architecture of Lebanese Citizenship." *Comparative Studies of South Asia, Africa and the Middle East* 34(2): 279–93.

Miller, R. E., and R. Wilford (eds.), 1998. *Women, Ethnicity and Nationalism: The Politics of Transition*. London: Routledge.

Moaddel, M., 2013. *The Birthplace of the Arab Spring: Values and Perceptions of Tunisians and a Comparative Assessment of Egyptian, Iraqi, Lebanese, Pakistani, Saudi, Tunisian, and Turkish Publics*. College Park, MD: University of Maryland.

Mondon, A., and A. Winter, 2017. "Articulations of Islamophobia: From the Extreme to the Mainstream?" *Ethnic and Racial Studies* 40(13): 2151–79. https://doi.org/10.1080/01419870.2017.1312008.

Moors, A., 2007. "Fashionable Muslims: Notions of Self, Religion, and Society in Sanà." *Fashion Theory* 11(2–3): 319–46. https://doi.org/10.2752/136270407X202853.

Moors, A., 2012. "The Affective Power of the Face Veil: Between Disgust and Fascination." In D. Houtman and B. Meyer (eds.), *Things: Religion and the Question of Materiality*. New York: Fordham University Press, pp. 282–95.

Moosavi, L., 2015. "The Racialization of Muslim Converts in Britain and Their Experiences of Islamophobia." *Critical Sociology* 41(1): 41–56. https://doi.org/10.1177/0896920513504601.

Moran-Ellis, J., V. D. Alexander, A. Cronin, M. Dickinson, J. Fielding, J. Sleney, and H. Thomas, 2006. "Triangulation and Integration: Processes, Claims and Implications." *Qualitative Research* 6(1): 45–59. https://doi.org/10.1177/1468794106058870.

Moruzzi, N. C., 1994. "A Problem with Headscarves: Contemporary Complexities of Political and Social Identity." *Political Theory* 22(4): 653–72.

Mottahedeh, N., 2008. *Displaced Allegories: Post-Revolutionary Iranian Cinema*. Durham, NC: Duke University Press.

Moukarbel, N., 2007. Sri Lankan Housemaids in Lebanon: A Case of "Symbolic Violence" and "Everyday Forms of Resistance." PhD, Brighton: University of Sussex.

Mouser, A. E., 2007. "Defining 'Modern' Malay Womanhood and the Coexistent Messages of the Veil." *Religion* 37(2): 164–74. https://doi.org/10.1016/j.religion.2007.06.006.

Moussa, K., 2014. *Dar Alfatwa sawt alitidal wa marjaiyaoh*. Beirut: Al-Mustakbal.
Nair, P., 2013. "Beirut." *Wasafiri* 28(1): 10–12. https://doi.org/10.1080/02690055.2013.744791.
Nammour, J., 2007. "Les identités au Liban, entre complexité et perplexité." *Cites* 29(1): 49–58.
Narayan, U., and S. G. Harding (eds.), 2000. *Decentering the Center: Philosophy for a Multicultural, Postcolonial, and Feminist World, a Hypatia Book*. Bloomington: Indiana University Press.
Nash, J. C., 2008. "Re-thinking Intersectionality." *Feminist Review* 89: 1–15.
Nathan, E., and A. Topolski, 2016. *Is There a Judeo-Christian Tradition? A European Perspective*. Boston: De Gruyter. https://doi.org/10.1515/9783110416596.
Navarro, L., 2010. "Islamophobia and Sexism: Muslim Women in the Western Mass Media." *Human Architecture: Journal of the Sociology of Self-Knowledge* 8(2): 95–114.
Ndlovu-Gatsheni, S. J., 2015. *Empire, Global Coloniality and African Subjectivity*, 1st ed. New York: Berghahn Books.
Nir, O., 2014. "The Sunni–Shi'i Balance in Lebanon in Light of the War in Syria and Regional Changes." *Middle East Review of International Affairs (Online); Herzliya* 18(1): 54–75.
O'Bagy, E., 2012. *Middle East Security Report 6: Jihad in Syria*. Washington, DC: Institute for the Study of War.
Okin, S. M., 1999. *Is Multiculturalism Bad for Women?* Princeton, NJ: Princeton University Press.
O'Neill, B., E. Gidengil, C. Côté, and L. Young, 2015. "Freedom of Religion, Women's Agency and Banning the Face Veil: The Role of Feminist Beliefs in Shaping Women's Opinion." *Ethnic and Racial Studies* 38(11): 1886–1901. https://doi.org/10.1080/01419870.2014.887744.
Osamu, N., 2006. "Anthropos and Humanitas: Two Western Concepts of 'Human Being.'" In N. Sakai and J. Solomon (eds.), *Translation, Biopolitics, Colonial Difference*. Hong Kong: Hong Kong University Press.
Owen, E. R. J., 1976. "The Political Economy of Grand Liban 1920–1970." In E. R. J. Owen (ed.), *Essays on the Crisis in Lebanon*. London: Ithaca Press, pp. 23–33.
Oyewumi, O., 1997. *Invention of Women: Making an African Sense of Western Gender Discourses*, 1st ed. Minneapolis: University of Minnesota Press.
Oyewumi, O., 2011. *Gender Epistemologies in Africa: Gendering Traditions, Spaces, Social Institutions, and Identities*, 2011 ed. New York: Palgrave.
Pande, A., 2012. "From 'Balcony Talk' and 'Practical Prayers' to Illegal Collectives: Migrant Domestic Workers and Meso-Level Resistances in Lebanon." *Gender and Society* 26(3): 382–405.
Pande, A., 2013. "'The Paper That You Have in Your Hand Is My Freedom': Migrant Domestic Work and the Sponsorship (Kafala) System in Lebanon." *International Migration Review* 47(2): 414–41.

Partridge, D. J., 2012. *Hypersexuality and Headscarves: Race, Sex, and Citizenship in the New Germany*. Bloomington: Indiana University Press.

Parvez, Z. F., 2011a. "Debating the Burqa in France: The Antipolitics of Islamic Revival." *Qualitative Sociology* 34(2): 287–312. https://doi.org/10.1007/s11133-011-9192-2.

Parvez, Z. F., 2011b. Politicizing Islam: State, Gender, Class, and Piety in France and India (PhD). University of California, Berkeley.

Patel, T. G., 2017. "It's Not about Security, It's about Racism: Counter-Terror Strategies, Civilizing Processes and the Post-race Fiction." *Palgrave Commons* 3(1): 1–8. https://doi.org/10.1057/palcomms.2017.31.

Peri, R. D., 2014. "Re-defining the Balance of Power in Lebanon: Sunni and Shiites Communities Transformations, the Regional Context and the Arab Uprisings." *Oriente Moderno* 94(2): 335–56. https://doi.org/10.1163/22138617-12340064.

Possamai, Adam, James T. Richardson, and Bryan S. Turner. *The Sociology of Shari'a: Case Studies from Around the World*. Springer, 2014.

Povinelli, E. A., 2002. *The Cunning of Recognition: Indigenous Alterities and the Making of Australian Multiculturalism*. Durham, NC: Duke University Press.

Punch, K., 2014. *Introduction to Social Research: Quantitative and Qualitative Approaches*, 3rd ed. Los Angeles: Sage.

Puwar, N., 1997. "Reflections on Interviewing Women MPs." *Sociological Research Online* 2(1): 1–10.

Quijano, A., 2000. "Coloniality of Power and Eurocentrism in Latin America." *International Sociology* 15(2): 215–32. https://doi.org/10.1177/0268580900015002005.

Quijano, A., 2007. "Coloniality and Modernity/Rationality," *Cultural Studies*, 21(2): 168–78.

Rabil, R. G., 2013. "Fathi Yakan the Pioneer of Islamic Activism in Lebanon." *Levantine Review* 2(1): 54–65.

Rabil, R. G. (ed.), 2014. "Salafism, the Divided House, and the Syrian Rebellion: Jihad in the Path of Allah." In Robert G. Rabil (ed.), *Salafism in Lebanon, from Apoliticism to Transnational Jihadism*. Washington, DC: Georgetown University Press, pp. 213–36.

Rajaee, F., 2007. *Islamism and Modernism: The Changing Discourse in Iran*. Austin: University of Texas Press.

Ramírez, Á., 2015. "Control over Female 'Muslim' Bodies: Culture, Politics and Dress Code Laws in some Muslim and Non-Muslim Countries." *Identities* 22(6): 671–86. https://doi.org/10.1080/1070289X.2014.950972.

Read, J. G., and J. P. Bartkowski, 2000. "To Veil or Not to Veil? A Case Study of Identity Negotiation among Muslim Women in Austin, Texas." *Gender and Society* 14(3): 395–417.

Richards, L., 2014. *Handling Qualitative Data: A Practical Guide*, 3rd ed. Los Angeles: Sage.

Rizk, M., 2016. *Inaya Ezzeddine: Star Lhoukouma wa Moufajatiha*. Beirut: Al-Akhbar.

Robinson, R. S., 2015. "Sexuality, Difference, and American Hijabi Bloggers." *Hawwa* 13(3): 383–400. https://doi.org/10.1163/15692086-12341289.

Rootham, E., 2015. "Embodying Islam and Laïcité: Young French Muslim Women at Work." *Gender, Place & Culture* 22(7): 971–86. https://doi.org/10.1080/0966369X.2014.939150.

Rossi, A., S. Rynne, and A. Nelson, 2013. "Doing Whitefella Research in Blackfella Communities in Australia: Decolonizing Method in Sports Related Research." *Quest* 65(1): 116–31. https://doi.org/10.1080/00336297.2012.749799.

Rozario, S., 2006. "The New Burqa in Bangladesh: Empowerment or Violation of Women's Rights?" *Women's Studies International Forum, Islam, Gender and Human Rights* 29(4): 368–80. https://doi.org/10.1016/j.wsif.2006.05.006.

Saab, B., 2014. "Reflections on the Plight of Syrian Refugees in Lebanon." *British Journal of General Practice* 64(619): 94. https://doi.org/10.3399/bjgp14X677220.

Saadawi, N., 1997. *The Nawal El Saadawi Reader*. London: Zed Books.

Saeed, Tania. 2016. *Islamophobia and Securitization Religion, Ethnicity and the Female Voice*. Cham: Springer International Publishing.

Said, E. W., 2003. *Orientalism*, 25th Anniversary ed. with 1995 Afterword ed. London: Penguin Books.

Saktanber, A., and G. Çorbacioğlu, 2008. "Veiling and Headscarf-Skepticism in Turkey." *Social Politics: International Studies in Gender, State & Society* 15(4): 514–38.

Salameh, F., 2010. *Language, Memory, and Identity in the Middle East: The Case for Lebanon*. Plymouth: Lexington Books.

Salamey, I., and P. Tabar, 2008. "Consociational Democracy and Urban Sustainability: Transforming the Confessional Divides in Beirut." *Ethnopolitics* 7(2-3): 239–63. https://doi.org/10.1080/17449050802243350.

Saleh, Y., 2010. Confinements and Liberations: The Many Faces of the Veil (PhD). Rutgers, the State University of New Jersey, New Brunswick.

Salem, P. E., 1994. "The Wounded Republic: Lebanon's Struggle for Recovery." *Arab Studies Quarterly* 16(4): 47–63.

Saliba, G., 2007. *Islamic Science and the Making of the European Renaissance*. Cambridge, MA: MIT Press.

Salibi, K., 1998. *A House of Many Mansions*. London: I.B. Tauris.

Salibi, K. S., 1976. *Cross Roads to Civil War: Lebanon 1958-1976*. London: Ithaca Press.

Salloukh, B. F., 2017. "The Syrian War: Spillover Effects on Lebanon." *Middle East Policy* 24(1): 62–78. https://doi.org/10.1111/mepo.12252.

Sandikci, O., and G. Ger, 2001. "Fundamental Fashions: The Cultural Politics of the Turban and the Levi's." *ACR North American Advances* 28: 146–50.

Sankari, J., 2008. *Masirat Kaed Shii: Alsayed Mohammad Hussein Fadlallah*. Beirut: Dar al Saqi.

Sayyid, S., 2014. *Recalling the Caliphate: Decolonisation and World Order*, 1st ed. London: Hurst.

Schmitz, M., 2010. "The Current Spectacle of Integration in Germany: Spatiality, Gender, and the Boundaries of the National Gaze." In Ulrike, Maren Möhring, Mark Stein, and Silke Stroh (eds.) *Hybrid Cultures – Nervous States: Britain and Germany in a (Post)Colonial World. Lindner*, 1st ed. Amsterdam: Brill.

Scott, J. W., 2007. *The Politics of the Veil*. Princeton, NJ: Princeton University Press.

Sedghi, H., 2007. *Women and Politics in Iran: Veiling, Unveiling, and Reveiling*. Cambridge: Cambridge University Press.

Semaan, N. M., 1999. "Judicial Review of Legislation: A Comparative Study between USA, France and Lebanon." MA. Beirut: American University of Beirut.

Shaaban, B., 1995. "The Muted Voices of Women Interpreters." In M. Afkhami (ed.), *Faith and Freedom: Women's Human Rights in the Muslim World*. Syracruse, NY: Syracruse University Press, pp. 61–77.

Shaery-Eisenlohr, R., 2008. *Shi'ite Lebanon: Transnational Religion and the Making of National Identities*. New York: Columbia University Press.

Shaheed, A. lee fox, 2008. "Dress Codes and Modes: How Islamic Is the Veil?" In J. Heath (ed.), *The Veil: Women Writers on Its History, Lore, and Politics*. Berkeley: University of California Press, pp. 290–306.

Shahrokni, N., 2013. State and the Paradox of Gender Segregation in Iran (PhD). University of California, Berkeley.

Shariati, A., 1980. *Marxism and Other Western Fallacies: An Islamic Critique*. Berkeley: Mizan Pr.

Shariati, A., 1986. *What Is to Be Done: The Enlightened Thinkers and an Islamic Renaissance*. Houston: Institute for Research and Islamic Studies.

Shariati, A., 2005. *Man and Islam*. North Haledon, NJ: Islamic Publications International.

Shariati, A., 2006. *Civilization and Modernization What's the Difference*. Malaysia: Citizens International.

Shariati, A., 2011. *Retour à soi*. Beyrouth: Editions Albouraq.

Shawish, H., 2010. Campaign to Save the Arabic Language in Lebanon. BBC News. https://www.bbc.com/news/10316914.

Shehadeh, L. R. 2004. "Coverture in Lebanon." *Feminist Review* 76(1): 83–99. https://doi.org/10.1057/palgrave.fr.9400133.

Shields, V. E., 2008. "Political Reform in Lebanon: Has the Cedar Revolution Failed?" *Journal of Legislative Studies* 14(4): 474–87. https://doi.org/10.1080/13572330802442881.

Shively, K., 2005. "Religious Bodies and the Secular State: The Merve Kavakci Affair." *Journal of Middle East Women's Studies* 1(3): 46–72.

Shohat, E., and R. Stam, 1994. *Unthinking Eurocentrism: Multiculturalism and the Media*, 1st ed. London: Routledge.

Silva, E. B., 2016. "Unity and Fragmentation of the Habitus." *Sociological Review* 64(1): 166–83. https://doi.org/10.1111/1467-954X.12346.

Silverman, D., 2013. *Doing Qualitative Research: A Practical Handbook*, 4th ed. London: Sage.
Singh, H., 2007. "Confronting Colonialism and Racism: Fanon and Gandhi." *Human Architecture* 5(3): 341–52.
Sirriyeh, H., 1999. "The Breakdown of the State in Lebanon." *Civil Wars* 2(4): 138–40. https://doi.org/10.1080/13698249908402425.
Skovgaard-Petersen, J., 1996. "Religious Heads or Civil Servants? Druze and Sunni Religious Leadership in Post-war Lebanon." *Mediterranean Politics* 1(3): 337–52. https://doi.org/10.1080/13629399608414592.
Skovgaard-Petersen, J., 1998. "The Sunni Religious Scene in Beirut." *Mediterranean Politics* 3(1): 69–80. https://doi.org/10.1080/13629399808414641.
Smith, L. T., 1999. *Decolonizing Methodologies: Research and Indigenous Peoples*, 2nd ed. London: Zed Books.
Smith-Hefner, N. J., 2007. "Javanese Women and the Veil in Post-Soeharto Indonesia." *Journal of Asian Studies* 66(2): 389–420. https://doi.org/10.1017/S002191180 7000575.
Sobh, R., R. Belk, and J. Gressel, 2014. "Mimicry and Modernity in the Middle East: Fashion Invisibility and Young Women of the Arab Gulf." *Consumption Markets & Culture* 17(4): 392–412. https://doi.org/10.1080/10253866.2013.865166.
Sogge, E. L., 2014. The Local Politics of Global Jihad: A Study on the Evolution of Militant Islamism in the Palestinian Refugee Camp of Ain al-Hilwe (MA). University of Oslo, Oslo.
Sonn, T., 2001. "Modernity, Islam, and the West." In J. L. Esposito and Z. I. Ansari (eds.), *Muslims and the West: Encounter and Dialogue*. Islamabad: Islamic Research Institute Press, pp. 216–31.
Soukarieh, M., 2009. "Speaking Palestinian: An Interview with Rosemary Sayigh." *Journal of Palestine Studies* 38(4): 12–28. https://doi.org/10.1525/jps.2009.38.4.12.
Soyer, M., 2013. "Off the Corner and into the Kitchen: Entering a Male-Dominated Research Setting as a Woman." *Qualitative Research*, 14(4): 459–72. https://doi.org/10.1177/1468794113488130.
Spagnolo, J. P., 1971. "Mount Lebanon, France and Dâûd Pasha: A Study of Some Aspects of Political Habituation." *International Journal of Middle East Studies* 2(2): 148–67. https://doi.org/10.1017/S002074380000101X.
Spielhaus, R., and F. Ast, 2012. "Tackling Double Victimization of Muslim Women in Europe: The Intersectional Response." *Mediterranean Journal of Human Rights* 16(2): 357–82.
Stanley, C. A., and P. Slattery, 2003. "Who Reveals What to Whom? Critical Reflections on Conducting Qualitative Inquiry as an Interdisciplinary, Biracial, Male/Female Research Team." *Qualitative Inquiry* 9(5): 705–28. https://doi.org/10.1177/10778 00403253004.
Steger, A.-K., 2017. *Islamic Feminism' in Lebanon: Portraying a Counter-Discourse*. Beirut: Heinrich Boell Foundation, Middle East.

Steinberg, G., J.-P. Hartung, and A. Blauhut, 2010. "Islamist Groups and Movements." In Werner Ende and Steinbach Udo (eds.), *Islam in the World Today, A Handbook of Politics, Religion, Culture, and Society*. Ithaca, NY: Cornell University Press, pp. 682–96.

Stephan, R., 2012. "Women's Rights Activism in Lebanon." In Pernille Arenfeldt and Nawar Al-Hassan Golley, *Mapping Arab Women's Movements: A Century of Transformations from Within*. Cairo: American University in Cairo Press.

Stephan, R., 2014. Four Waves of Lebanese Feminism. E-International Relations. https://www.e-ir.info/2014/11/07/four-waves-of-lebanese-feminism/ (accessed March 1, 2019).

Stone, Christopher Reed. *Popular Culture and Nationalism in Lebanon: The Fairouz and Rahbani Nation*. London: Routledge, 2007.

Strabac, Z., T. Aalberg, A. T. Jenssen, and M. Valenta, 2016. "Wearing the Veil: Hijab, Islam and Job Qualifications as Determinants of Social Attitudes towards Immigrant Women in Norway." *Ethnic and Racial Studies* 39(15): 2665–82. http://dx.doi.org/10.1080/01419870.2016.1164878.

Suleiman, J., 2006. "Marginalised Community: The Case of Palestinian Refugees in Lebanon." In Development Research Centre on Migration, Globalisation and Poverty. University of Sussex.

Suleiman, Y., 2003. *The Arabic Language and National Identity: A Study in Ideology*. Edinburgh: Edinburgh University Press.

Tabar, P., 2014. "The Maronite Church in Lebanon: From Nation-Building to a Diasporan/Transnational Institution." In F. de Bel-Air (ed.), *Migration et Politique Au Moyen-Orient, Contemporain Publications*. Beyrouth: Presses de l'Ifpo, pp. 185–201.

Talachian, M., 2004. The Veil and the State: Debating the Unveiling and Re-veiling of Women in Twentieth-Century Iran (MA). Florida Atlantic University, United States.

Tang, K. C., and A. Davis, 1995. "Critical Factors in the Determination of Focus Group Size." *Fam Pract* 12(4): 474–5. https://doi.org/10.1093/fampra/12.4.474.

Taylor, S., 2006. "Narrative as Construction and Discursive Resource." *Narrative Inquiry* 16(1): 94–102.

Tegho, J., 2011. On the Other Side of the Coin: The Political Credibility of Hezbollah and Its Impact on Domestic and Regional Politics (MA). Georgetown University, United States.

Tejirian, E. H., and R. S. Simon, 2012. *Conflict, Conquest, and Conversion: Two Thousand Years of Christian Missions in the Middle East*. New York: Columbia University Press. https://doi.org/10.7312/teji13864.

Terray, E., 2004. "L'hystérie politique." In C. Nordmann (ed.), *Le foulard islamique en questions*. Paris: Amsterdam, pp. 103–17.

Thompson, E., 2000. *Colonial Citizens: Republican Rights, Paternal Privilege, and Gender in French Syria and Lebanon*. New York: Columbia University Press.

Thorleifsson, C., 2016. "The Limits of Hospitality: Coping Strategies among Displaced Syrians in Lebanon." *Third World Quarterly* 37(6): 1071–82. https://doi.org/10.1080/01436597.2016.1138843.

Tinker, C., and N. Armstron, 2008. "From the Outside Looking In: How an Awareness of Difference Can Benefit the Qualitative Research Process." *Qualitative Report* 13(1): 53–60.

Tlostanova, M., 2014. "How 'Caucasians' Became Black? Imperial Difference and the Symbolization of Race." *Personality. Culture. Society* 16(3–4): 96–115.

Tlostanova, M., 2015. "Between the Russian/Soviet Dependencies, Neoliberal Delusions, Dewesternizing Options, and Decolonial Drives." *Cultural Dynamics* 27(2): 267–83.

Tlostanova, M.V., and W. D. Mignolo, 2012. *Learning to Unlearn: Decolonial Reflections from Eurasia and the Americas*. Columbus: Ohio State University Press.

Topal, S., 2017. "Female Muslim Subjectivity in the Secular Public Sphere: Hijab and Ritual Prayer as 'Technologies of the Self.'" *Social Compass* 64(4): 582–96. https://doi.org/10.1177/0037768617727485.

Toulmin, S. E., 1992. *Cosmopolis: The Hidden Agenda of Modernity*. Chicago: University of Chicago Press.

Traboulsi, F., 2007. *A History of Modern Lebanon*. London: Pluto Press.

Trad, S., and G. Frangieh, 2007. "Iraqi Refugees in Lebanon: Continuous Lack of Protection." *Forced Migration Review Iraq* 35–6.

Trainer, S., 2017. "Piety, Glamour, and Protest: Performing Social Status and Affiliation in the United Arab Emirates." *Journal of Contemporary Ethnography* 46(3): 361–86. https://doi.org/10.1177/0891241615611728.

Treacher, A., 2005. "On Postcolonial Subjectivity." *Group Analysis* 38(1): 43–57. https://doi.org/10.1177/0533316405049365.

Troianovski, A., 2016. "World News: Merkel Urges Ban on Full Facial Veil." *Wall Street Journal*: A.10.

Truong, N., 2016. Elisabeth Badinter appelle au boycott des marques qui se lancent dans la mode islamique. Le Monde.fr. https://www.lemonde.fr/idees/article/2016/04/02/elisabeth-badinter-une-partie-de-la-gauche-a-baisse-la-garde-devant-le-communautarisme_4894360_3232.html.

Turkmen, B., 2012. "Islamic Visibilities, Intimacies, and Counter Publics in the Secular Public Sphere." In A. Cinar, S. Roy and Mahayudin Haji Yahaya (eds.), *Visualizing Secularism and Religion Egypt, Lebanon, Turkey, India*. Ann Arbor: University of Michigan Press, pp. 47–69.

Tyrer, D., 2013. *Politics of Islamophobia: Race, Power and Fantasy*. London: Pluto Press.

Usta, J., A. R. Masterson, and J. M. Farver, 2019. "Violence against Displaced Syrian Women in Lebanon." *Journal of Interpersonal Violence* 34(18): 3767–79. https://doi.org/10.1177/0886260516670881.

Vakulenko, A., 2007. "'Islamic Headscarves' and the European Convention on Human Rights: An Intersectional Perspective." *Social & Legal Studies* 16(2): 183–99.

Van Es, M. A., 2019. "Muslim Women as 'Ambassadors' of Islam: Breaking Stereotypes in Everyday Life." *Identities* 26(4): 375–92. https://doi.org/10.1080/10702 89X.2017.1346985.

Van Sommer, A., and S. M. Zwemmer, 2008. *Our Moslem Sisters: A Cry of Need from Lands of Darkness Interpreted by Those Who Heard It*. Whitefish: Kessinger.

Vázquez, R., 2009. "Modernity Coloniality and Visibility: The Politics of Time." *Sociological Research Online* 14(4): 1–7. https://doi.org/10.5153/sro.1990.

Vázquez, R., 2011. "Translation as Erasure: Thoughts on Modernity's Epistemic Violence." *Journal of Historical Sociology* 24(1): 27–44.

Vázquez, R., 2012. "Towards a Decolonial Critique of Modernity: Buen Vivir, Relationality and the Task of Listening." In R. Fornet-Betancourt (ed.), *Capital, Poverty, Development, Denktraditionen Im Dialog: Studien Zur Befreiung Und Interkulturalität 33. Wissenschaftsverlag??*, Mainz: Aachen, pp. 241–52.

Verdeil, C., 2006. "Between Rome and France, Intransigent and Anti-Protestant Jesuits in the Orient: The Beginning of the Jesuits' Mission of Syria, 1831–1864." In Martin Tamcke and Michael Martin (eds.), *Christian Witness between Continuity and New Beginnings: Modern Historical Missions in the Middle East*. Berlin: Lit Verlag, pp. 23–32.

Vloeberghs, W., 2012. "The Hariri Political Dynasty after the Arab Spring." *Mediterranean Politics* 17(2): 241–8. https://doi.org/10.1080/13629395.2012.694046.

Vogels, C., 2019. "A Feminist and 'Outsider' in the Field: Negotiating the Challenges of Researching Young Men." *International Journal of Qualitative Methods* 18. https://doi.org/10.1177/1609406919855907.

Wacquant, L. J. D., 2008. *Urban Outcasts: A Comparative Sociology of Advanced Marginality*. Cambridge: Polity.

Wagner, W., R. Sen, R. Permanadeli, and C. S. Howarth, 2012. "The Veil and Muslim Women's Identity: Cultural Pressures and Resistance to Stereotyping." *Culture & Psychology* 18(4): 521–41. https://doi.org/10.1177/1354067X12456713.

Walker, M., 2005. "Feminist Methodologies." In B. Somekh and C. Lewin (eds.), *Research Methods in the Social Sciences*. Thousand Oaks, CA: Sage, pp. 66–73.

Walsh, C., 2016. "On Gender and Its 'Otherwise.'" In W. Harcourt (ed.), *The Palgrave Handbook of Gender and Development*. London: Palgrave Macmillan, pp. 34–47.

Wawzonek, J. J., 2017. "Sodomitical Butterflies: Male Homosexual Desire in Colonial Latin America." *Mount Royal Undergraduate Humanities Review (MRUHR)* 4: 98–114.

Welborne, B. C., 2011. Between the Veil and the Vote: Exploring Incentives to Politically Incorporate Women in the Arab World (PhD). University of Colorado at Boulder, Colorado.

Williams, R. H., and G. Vashi, 2007. "'Hijab' and American Muslim Women: Creating the Space for Autonomous Selves." *Sociology of Religion* 68(3): 269–87.

Williamson, M., and G. Khiabany, 2010. "UK: The Veil and the Politics of Racism." *Race & Class* 52(2): 85–96. https://doi.org/10.1177/0306396810377003.

Wilson, J. A., 2015. "Ramadan Reflections." *The Marketeers* 115–18.
Winkel, H., 2018. "Global Historical Sociology and Connected Gender Sociologies: On the Re-nationalization and Coloniality of Gender." *InterDisciplines. Journal of History and Sociology* 9(2): 89–134. https://doi.org/10.4119/indi-1073.
Winter, S., 2010. *The Shiites of Lebanon under Ottoman Rule, 1516–1788*. Cambridge: Cambridge University Press.
Wolfreys, J. 2018. *Republic of Islamophobia: The Rise of Respectable Racism in France*. London: Hurst.
Womack, D. F., 2012. "Lubnani, Libanais, Lebanese: Missionary Education, Language Policy and Identity Formation in Modern Lebanon." *Studies in World Christianity* 18(1): 4–20. https://doi.org/10.3366/swc.2012.0003.
Wright, R., 2011. "The Pink Hijab." *Wilson Quarterly* 35(3): 47–51.
Yasmine, R., and C. Moughalian, 2016. "Systemic Violence against Syrian Refugee Women and the Myth of Effective Intrapersonal Interventions." *Reproductive Health Matters* 24(47): 27–35.
Yeganeh, N., 1993. "Women, Nationalism, and Islam in Contemporary Political Discourse in Iran." *Feminist Review* 44: 3–18.
Yeğenoğlu, M., 2011. "Clash of Secularity and Religiosity: The Staging of Secularism and Islam through the Icons of Atatürk and the Veil in Turkey." In A. Possamai, B. Turner, and J. Barbalet (eds.), *Religion and the State: A Comparative Sociology*. London: Anthem Press, pp. 225–44. https://doi.org/10.7135/UPO9780857288073.011.
Yel, A. M., and A. Nas, 2014. "Insight Islamophobia: Governing the Public Visibility of Islamic Lifestyle in Turkey." *European Journal of Cultural Studies* 17(5): 567–84. https://doi.org/10.1177/1367549413515258.
Yountae, A., 2017. "Secularism Meets Coloniality: Mariategui's Andean Political Theology." *Political Theology* 18(8): 677–92. https://doi.org/10.1080/1462317X.2017.1325991.
Zahedi, Ashraf, 2007. "Contested Meaning of the Veil and Political Ideologies of Iranian Regimes." *Journal of Middle East Women's Studies* 3(3): 75–98.
Zantout, M. R., 2011. *Women, Mothers, and Children: Colonization and Islamic Law in the Lebanese State* (PhD). McGill University, Canada.
Zempi, I., 2016. "'It's a Part of Me, I Feel Naked without It': Choice, Agency and Identity for Muslim Women Who Wear the Niqab." *Ethnic and Racial Studies* 39(10): 1738–54. https://doi.org/10.1080/01419870.2016.1159710.
Zempi, I., and N. Chakraborti, 2014. *Islamophobia, Victimisation and the Veil*. London: Palgrave Macmillan.
Zempi, I., and N. Chakraborti, 2015. "'They Make Us Feel Like We're a Virus': The Multiple Impacts of Islamophobic Hostility towards Veiled Muslim Women." *International Journal for Crime, Justice and Social Democracy* 4(3): 44–56. https://doi.org/10.5204/ijcjsd.v4i3.236.

Zima, P. V., 2015. *Subjectivity and Identity: Between Modernity and Postmodernity*. London: Bloomsbury.
Zogheib, P., 2014. Lebanese Christian Nationalism: A Theoretical Analyses of a National Movement (MA). Northeastern University, Massachusetts.

Index

abaya, 49, 58, 87, 99–101, 135–6, 140
absencing, 10, 71, 74
   epistemic absencing, 83–4, 114–15, 121, 142–3 *see also* epistemicide
   material absencing 61, 74, 78, 142–3 *see also* invisibilizing
agency, 137, 148
ahistorical, 129
Ahl lbayt, 138–41
Al-Hariri, Bahia, 25–6
Al-Hariri, Rafic, 25, 32
Algeria, 27
alienation, 93, 103, 147
Amal Movement, 26
American University of Cairo, 153
anti-colonial, 107, 155
anti-patriarchy, 125–7
Arab, 38, 39, 44
   arabo-Muslim, 39, 42, 45, 65, 89, 96
   arab nationalism, 21
Arabic Language, 24, 38, 44
Asad, Talal, 124, 129
Ashrafieh, 38, 40, 58–9
assimilation, 106, 107, 116
Aung San Suu Kyi, 156
autocratic, 21

backwardness, 43, 153, *see also* Civility
banks, 68–74
Bayrakli, Enes, 12, 55, 104
Beirut, 19, 21–4, 36
benevolence, 53
Bhabha, Homi, 43
Bhambra, Gurminder, 9, 10, 17, 43, 87
biological, 107
biopolitics, 56
bordering, 20, 77
borderland, 143, 149
borders, 43, 142
Brayson, Kim, 82, 128, 156
burkini, 57

Canada, 96, 156
Cape Town, 157
capitalism, 11, 21, 59, 77, *see also* neoliberalism
China, 156
Christianity, 12, 44, 114, 115, 121
   Christian missions, 18
   Maronites, 17–20
citizenry, 28, 32, 39, 146
   heterogenous citizenry, 20, 60, 83
civility, 35, 42, 115
civilized, 32, 37, 42, 43, 44, 52, 116, 150, 153
   civilising mission, 24
class, 13, 48, 54, 60, 100
clientelism, 20
colonial difference, 43, 46, 49, 67, 106, 154
colonial matrix of power, 9–13
   coloniality, 3, 5, 10–15, 44, 96, 98, 100, 105, 106, 109, 116–17, 120–4, 128, 135, 141–58, *see also* modernity/coloniality
   coloniality of being, 71, 74
   coloniality of knowledge, 83, 112–29, 135, *see also* epistemicide
   colonized subjects, 105
colonialism, 10, 20, 44, 61, 70, 98
   colonial legacies, 32, 152, *see also* coloniality
   french colonialism, 19–21, 27, 36
commercial, 69
commercialization, 111, 124
community, 19, 37, 41, 48, 52, 60–1, 64, 69, 101, 102, 104, 112, 125, 131, 140, 150, 151, 155
consent, 94
conservatism, 72, 79, 80
consumerism, 97
   consumer culture, 97
   global consumer capital, 71
corruption, 25, 82, 151
cosmopolitanism, 24, 60, 93

co-create, 93
culture, 5, 12, 23–4, 34–9, 42, 91, 93, 97–8, 100, 112, 114, 137, 142
    Arab culture, 37, 124
    European culture, 93
    Lebanese culture, 25
    monoculture, 10
    Muslim culture, 35
    Native cultures, 98
    Western(ized) culture, 37, 97, 121
cultured, 42, 45, 150

Dahieh, 69, 81
debt, 81
decolonial, 1, 6–7, 8–10, 18, 141, 150–2, 155
    decolonial listening, 7–9
Deeb, Lara, 22, 49, 69, 141
deficiency, 34, 55 *see also* lack
dehumanization, 45, 47, 80, *see also* objectification
delinking, 137, 141, 142, 151
dependence, 157
depoliticizing, 118–21
devaluing, 75, 83
    devaluing labour 67
Difa', 112, 116, 123
difference in excess, 15, 33
dilution, 97, 99, 102, 108
    emptying, 97–9
    hollowing, 97, 146
disavowal, 10, 15, 24, 34, 50, 116, 124, 128, 153
discipline, 55–6, 61, 74, 83, 137, 148
discourse, 37, 49–50, 112, 123, 128–30, 137
dispensability, 43, 103 *see also* Precarity
distaste, 54
distinction, 97
diversity, 69
double-consciousness, 105, 135, 143, 148

Egypt, 31, 153
elite, 21
embodimend, 38, 48, 130, 139, 154
empathy, 7–9, 157
enforced Muslim authenticity, 100–1, 147
Enlightenement, 19
enslavement, 10–11

entanglement, 1, 12, 92, 100, 124, 149, 154
enunciation, 11, 25, 74, 121, 128
    locus of enunciation, 5, 43
    unenunciable, 143
epistemic territory, 15, 120
epistemicide, 10, 83, 84, 142, 143
epistemologies, 5, 10, 116, 117
erasure, 2, 3, 6, 10, 14, 31, 50, 53, 55, 59, 60, 61, 64, 71, 74, 76, 78, 82, 84, 96, 98, 102, 106, 117, 129, 131, 141, 142, 145, 146, 147, 148, 153, 154, 155, 156, 157, 158
    anti-erasure, 118–29
    anti-Muslim erasure, 15, 21, 76, 148
    Islamophobic erasure, 142, 146
    process of erasure, 95, 117, 146
    self-erasure, 101
    structures of Erasure, 157
    techniques of Erasure, 14
essentialism, 3, 5–7, 85, 93, 129
ethical self, 133
ethnicity, 12, 36–9
ethos, 28, 52, 97
eurocentric, 5, 2, 9–12, 15, 26, 32, 36, 37, 38, 39, 40, 42, 43, 44, 46, 49, 50, 62, 63, 64, 82, 92, 93, 95, 96, 98, 108, 109, 114, 116, 121, 123, 128, 129, 132, 135, 141, 142, 143, 145, 146, 148, 149, 151, 152, 153, 154, 155, 157
    eurocentric modernity, 9–13 *see also* coloniality
    eurocentrism, 10–13, 119
Europe, 5, 43
excess, 36, 39
    difference in excess, 42
    Muslim excess, 34–5
Ezzeddine, Inaya, 26, 103–5

family, 52-2
Fanon, Frantz, 14, 27, 44, 48, 62, 93, 94, 95, 97, 98, 100, 106, 107, 115, 121, 145, 157, 158
fashion, 86, 104
    fashion hijab, 90, 102, 107, 153
    fashioning, 89, 108
Federici, Silvia, 12
First world, 63
forgery, 157
France, 64, 76, 107, 119, 155

frigidity, 44
futurity, 49, 128, 141 *see also* Past, *see also* Time

gender, 7, 12, 150
genocide, 10, 156
geography, 58
good Muslim/bad Muslim, 104–5, 150
government, 28, 47, 88, 103, 156
Granada, 9
Greek, 113–16
   Greek demos, 116
Grosfoguel, 10, 11, 12, 13, 46, 55, 97, 100, 116
guilty, 77, 82, 121
Gulf Countries, 65–6, 153
Gupta, 67

habits, 31, 44, 46, 93, 98, 137
habitus
   Aristotelian habitus, 132
   Muslim habitus, 137, 148
   wounded habitus, 46, 48, 50, 60, 94, 143
Hafez Farid, 12, 55, 104
harassment, 20, 75, 79, 87, 104
Harb, Mona, 22, 69
hegemonic, 4, 5, 8, 14, 15, 26, 42, 44, 47, 50, 54, 64, 76, 108, 116, 125, 128, 129, 142, 145, 152
Hezbollah, 69, 81, 152
hierarchy, 11, 19, 34, 46, 60, 66, 92, 93, 107
   hierarchical Othering, 43
   hierarchization, 12, 24, 55
   hierarchy of humanity, 13, 14, 50, 96
hijab, 3, 25, 38
   modern hijab, 88, 105, 153
   non-modern hijab, 99, 103
   turban, 87
human, 11, 13, 45
Hungary, 156
hygiene, 40–2, 62

independence, 18–20, 30
India, 156
individualizing, 147
inequality, 1, 20, 67
insider/Outsider, 8
internalized racism, 55
International Monetary Fund, 151
interpellated, 48
intersectionality, 28, 61, 145, 150, 154
invisibilizing, 61, 74–78
Iran, 28, 57
Islam, 5, 129
   light Islam, 95
   muslimness, 34, 106
Islamophobia, 1, 12, 39, 47, 49, 56, 97, 104, 124, 150, 156

lack, 42–6
language, 24
Laïcité, 18, 64, *see also* secularism
Lebanon, 17–19, 23–4, 39, 47, 59, 66, 76, 117, 149
   Greater Lebanon, 19
   Lebanese civil war, 21–2
   Lebanese independence, 18–20
   Lebanese nationalism, 22–3
   Lebanese national imaginary, 20, 40, 46–9, 152
   Lebanon's golden age, 151–2
Lebanese University, 47, 76, 104
legal system, 20, 76, 80–2, 155
lived experiences, 1–3, 71, 81, 87, 108
local-global, 4, 18, 20, 25, 70–1, 34–5, 157
localized, 18, 30

Maasri, Zeina, 23
Mahmood, Saba, 92, 129, 132–3, 140
Malaka, 137, *see also* Habitus
Maldonado-Torres, Nelson, 7, 12, 43–4, 71, 92, 121
Mamdani, Mahmood, 105
mandate, 19–21, 36
manufactured inequalities, 67, 132, 151–4
marginalization, 21, 39, 57, 60, 80, 117, 151
marker, 12, 24, 59, 83, 100, 116, 151, 154
Maronitism 21–2, *see also* Lebanese nationalism
Materialism, 97
media, 25, 93, 102
micro-aggressions, 83, 146
Mignolo, Walter, 7, 10, 11, 12, 13, 44, 121, 124
migration regimes, 59, 95
misogyny, 156, *see also* patrairachy, *see also* sexism

mobility, 62, 91–2
mobilization, 57, 151, 157
modern, 9–10, 41
  modern time, 20, 66, 179
  modernity, 9–10, 11, 43, 157–8
  modernity/coloniality, 11, 15, 82, 86, 111, 116, 124, 143, 155
  modernizing discourse, 29
  modern science, 122
moral panic, 156
morality, 113, 132
  moral subjects, 143, 148
  Muslim moral person 132
mosques, 118, 129, 156–157
mummification, 97, 98
municipal, 57–60
Muslim, 5
  Muslim ancestrality, 138
  Muslim dress, 26
  Muslim subject, 4, 36, 49, 73, 97–9, 129–38, 142
Myannmar, 156

nationalism, 156
nation-state, 39, 80, 82, 156
neoliberalism, 22, *see also* Capitalism
  neoliberal logic, 83, 103
  neoliberal market, 70, 77
  neoliberal modernization, 23
negation, 10, 44, 131
negotiation, 141
neurosis, 95, 107
niqab, 3, 63–4, 72–4, 101, 153
non-governmental organisations, 42, 72, 111
  Islamic non-governmental organisations, 73
nuns, 72, 114

objectification, 27, 58, 62, 128 *see also* dehumanization
October Revolution, 151
oligarchic, 151
ontological, 11, 43, 121
oriental, 25
orientalist, 28
Organisation Internationale de la Francophonie, 24
othering, 45, 143

otherness, 39, 45, 96
Ottoman Sultanate, 17, 27

parochial Secularism, 117
parochial universalism, 112, 116
past, 139 *see also* time
pathologized, 101
patriarchy, 12, 14, 27, 30, 39, 41, 54, 73, 77, 100, 125, 126, 127, 131, 141, 142, 145, 147, 155, *see also* misogyny, sexism
perceived conservatism, 58, 62, 106
performativity, 129, 134, 136, 138
phenotype, 37–9, 151, 154
pluralistic, 86
plurality, 27, 118, 120, 142
pluriversality, 10
positionality, 9
postcolonial, 5, 8, 14, 27, 31, 39
  postcolonial modernization, 32, 152
post-racism, 106
poverty, 49
Povinelli, Elizabeth, 100
power relations, 13
precarity, 78, 81, 152, 157
presentable, 68, 74–5, 103, 107
privatizing, 31, 52, 77, 118–21, 146–7, 153
  de-privatization, 29
problem, 34, 40, 104
  deproblematization, 118, 126
  problematization, 37, 119
public debt, 151

Qatar, 66–7
Quijano, Anibal, 13

race, 7, 11–13, 67, 93, 156
racialization, 12, 37, 38, 46, 47, 49, 50, 60, 64, 65, 74, 92, 93, 99, 103, 121, 152, 153
racism, 11–13, 46, 121
rapport, 7–8
rationalism, 12, 19, 119, 147
recognition, 100, 116, 150
Reconquista, 11
refugees, 150, 151, 154
  Syrian refugees, 48, 58
refusal, 35, 149, 158
relationality, 141, 148

religious law, 20
research legitimacy, 7
resistance, 111, 137, 141
responsibility, 53–4, 101, 125
rhetoric, 56, 156
rhetorical Narrative, 10
rights, 155

Said, Edward, 9
Saida, 63
Saudi Arabia, 22
Sayyid, Salman, 36, 73
scars, 95, 157
sectarianism, 55, 149
secular, 91, 92, 93
   secularism, 12, 104, 118, 120, 121
   secularization, 77
   secularized, 12, 77, 91, 150
self-dilution, 101
self-erasure, 101
self formation, 130–42
self-hate, 55, 149, 154, 157
self-orientalism, 12, 55, 149, 154, *see also* Self-hate
semiotic ideology, 142
service sector, 70
sexism, 12, 150, *see also* patriarchy, *see also* misogyny
Shaikha, 99–100
shame, 40, 74, 76
Shariati, Ali, 36, 98, 116
Shias, 18–22
slavery, 67
social media, 96, 43
social movement, 57
spatialization, 57, 60, 61, 67, 73, 80
   mental maps of exclusion, 60
spectrum, 62, 70, 87–8
   kaleidoscopic spectrum, 87–8, 92, 108
speech act, 132
stares, 41, 62–3
state, 78, 80–2, 88
   state apparatus, 80–1
   state-building, 27, 32, 145, 152
   state-centrism, 81
stigma, 28, 31, 49, 50, 59, 66, 73

Sunnis, 18–22
symbolism, 142

Taif Accord, 22
techniques, 6, 10, 14, 27, 78, 83
Tehran, 28–9
telos, 129–38, 142–3
terrorism, 63, 104
Third world, 63
threat, 28, 34, 38, 49, 63–4, 72, 81, 115, 156
time, 114, *see also* past
   linear time, 41, 141
Tlostanova, Madina, 7, 12, 121
tolerance, 36, 45, 61, 76, 105, 147, 153
tourism, 24, 70
Trabousli, Fawwaz, 17–21
Tripoli, 44, 61, 79, 82
Tunisia, 30
Turkey, 27, 39, 57, 105, 111

unequal, 19, 60, 104
   unequal development, 62–4
   unequal citizenship, 60
United Kingdom, 47, 63, 69
United States of America, 21, 93, 96
universalism, 19, 112–17, 147
unlawfulness, 62
unveiling, 27–31
Uyghur Muslims, 156

Vázquez, Rolando, 141
Violence, 10, 30, 50, 72, 101, 152, 157
vulnerabilizing, 83

warlords, 151
westernization, 4, 21, 55, 60, 83, 91, 93, 149, 150, 152
   westernized elite, 35, 151, 149
   western(ized) university, 8, 58
West Asia, 26–32, 152–5
whiteness, 93, 95, 96, 107
World Bank, 151
world-system, 10–11
wounding, 92, 103, 105, 143, 148

zone of nonbeing, 13, 55, 83, 100, 107

www.ingramcontent.com/pod-product-compliance
Lightning Source LLC
Chambersburg PA
CBHW061827300426
44115CB00013B/2275